JESUS IN HISTORY

An Approach to the Study of the Gospels

SECOND EDITION

Howard Clark Kee
Bryn Mawr College

HARCOURT BRACE JOVANOVICH, INC.
New York   San Diego   Chicago   San Francisco   Atlanta

In memory of
Henry Joel Cadbury
and
Rudolf Bultmann

ISBN: 0-15-547382-4

Library of Congress Catalog Card Number: 77-75349

Printed in the United States of America

Preface

The second edition of *Jesus in History* has as its primary aim to make explicit what seems to me essential to the understanding of ancient texts in general and the gospels in particular: the social and cultural assumptions of the writers and their respective communities. Although New Testament interpreters in this century have spoken freely of the *Sitz im Leben* of New Testament traditions, they have, in fact, been more interested in dealing with theological ideas abstractly or in assigning labels, such as "Palestinian" or "Hellenistic," as though Palestine itself were not thoroughly Hellenized in the centuries following the triumph of Alexander in the East. The approach of this text is, I think, consonant with a methodology developing among biblical scholars in the present day, of which Martin Hengel's masterful *Judaism and Hellenism* is a prime example. Wayne Meeks of Yale has been working along similar lines. During a sabbatical leave in 1974–75, I participated in the Biblical-Sociological Seminar in Berkeley, chaired by Professor Norman Gottwald, which was of great assistance in heightening my own consciousness of early Christian sociocultural forces and in helping me refine my methods.

The methodological assumptions of this text are detailed in the Introduction. The remainder of the work retains the structure of the first edition. The first chapter begins by tracing the main features of what has been called the "quest for the historical Jesus," with the aim of showing how positive results were mixed with further complications of the problem. Chapters 2 and 8 offer analyses of the material relating to Jesus from non–New Testament sources, secular and religious. The core of the book (chapters 3 through 7) shows the range of ways in which the communities that passed on the gospel tradition perceived Jesus' place in history.

I am grateful to colleagues who have offered constructive suggestions about this book, especially Professors Gerard Sloyan of Temple University, James Charlesworth of Duke University, and J. Paul Sampley of Indiana University. Everett M. Sims, of Harcourt Brace Jovanovich, encouraged me to undertake the revision, and his editorial staff has been of great help in preparing the copy for the press.

HOWARD CLARK KEE

Contents

raised from the dead, he replied, "Why, I was talking to him not a half hour ago!"

But the problem is more complex. It cannot be resolved by a simple "Yes" or "No" decision concerning the historicity of the gospel reports about Jesus. A prior question must be faced: What do we mean when we use the term "historical"? To phrase it in terms directly related to our historical inquiry about Jesus, if the answer to "What can be known about Jesus in history?" is, "We must determine what really happened in his life," the issue remains, "What do we mean by 'real'?" In interpreting any experience or any document—but especially in trying to understand material from a time and culture widely removed from our own—the outcome of our inquiry is likely to be determined by what *we* assume about reality. The documentary evidence is the same for the skeptic Celsus as for the believing Christians of the early centuries; for Billy Sunday as it was for the incredulous reporters. What divides these antagonists is the specifics of their framework of assumptions about the world and its possibilities. If the structure of the "real" excludes from the outset the possibility of events such as instantaneous healings and the raising of the dead, then the miracles reported in the gospels will be judged not to have taken place. If there are no such things as demons, then the gospel accounts of exorcisms will have to be accounted for historically on some other grounds than the literal reports offered in the gospel tradition. On the other hand, if heaven is a place beyond the stars, then the voice from heaven that addressed Jesus at his baptism (Mark 1:11) and the visible descent of the Spirit (Matt. 3:16) in bodily form (Luke 3:22) can be given credence as a description of what really occurred. What is involved is not simply an arbitrary decision to believe the New Testament or not to; rather, that decision is shaped by the structure of reality that believers or skeptics bring with them when they look at the evidence.

Is there any way to avoid this dilemma? Some interpreters of the gospels have tried to avoid what they regard as the twin pitfalls of skepticism and naive credulity by treating the gospel narratives as mythical or metaphorical statements of universal religious truths whose value lies in their meaning rather than in their facticity. Modern impetus for this approach was provided by David Friedrich Strauss, whose work is briefly reviewed in Chapter 1. Interpreting the myth—or "demythologizing," as it has come to be called—has enjoyed a revival in recent decades, chiefly through the writings of Rudolf Bultmann. His proposal for dealing with what he calls the "mythological" element in the gospels —by which he means the accounts of heaven as above and hell as below, of angels and demons, of miracles as supernatural manifestations—is to transform them into metaphors of the religious experience of individuals who share the faith.[1] He sees the essence of faith to lie in man's being called to decision: in deciding for the will of God and against the demands that the world makes, the individual "dies" to the old structures of life and is "raised up" to a new life in a new order of existence. Other approaches to the mythical element in the gospels propose to treat them in terms of certain psychological understandings of human existence, such as the archetypal images of Jungian psychology, by which interpreters seek to discern universal symbolic significance in biblical and other religious traditions. But whether the criterion for discovering the significance of the gospels is depth psychology or existentialist philosophy, the bracketing out of the social and historical dimensions of life in favor of private, experiential considerations leaves unaddressed the question, "How are we to understand Jesus historically?"

The attempts to evade the historical question in favor of internalized meaning are reminiscent of the passage in Lewis Carroll's *Through the Lookinglass*, in which Alice encounters the Cheshire Cat. After giving Alice directions, the grinning cat fades from sight until only the grin remains. Alice observes, "I've often seen a cat without a grin, but a grin without a cat is the most curious thing I've ever seen!" The demythologizers seem to be well content with the meaningful grin without the historical cat.

Scholars have a perfect right to limit their investigations to a circumscribed area of human existence or to decide to accept only that kind of evidence which is compatible with their own

---

[1] Rudolf Bultmann, *Jesus Christ and Mythology* (New York: Scribner's, 1958).

focus on specific thinkers and issues that illustrate how the historical questions about Jesus were posed by these pioneering writers, and how, as a result, they are posed for us.

FAITH CHALLENGED BY REASON: MIRACLES AND THE DOCTRINE OF EXCLUSIVE REVELATION

John Locke (1632–1704) and his contemporaries were the first to raise such questions about the Bible as, Can we believe in accounts of miracles? and Can we accept the New Testament as the exclusive revelation of God? So long as the Bible as a whole and the gospels in particular were believed to be sacred books containing revealed truth, it was possible to treat any seeming discrepancy as only an apparent difficulty and any report that strained the credulity of the reader as a summons to faith rather than as an occasion for doubt. If John's gospel reports that Jesus cleansed the Temple at the beginning of his ministry but the other gospels say he did so at the end, the explanation is that he did it twice, or that John wrote a spiritual gospel[2] that has no interest in chronological sequence. The first serious challenge to the truth of the gospels came with the resurgence of the originally Stoic belief in natural law in the seventeenth and early eighteenth centuries. Miracles were regarded as violations of natural law. How could a man whose reason led him to discern the truth of universal natural laws assert the truth of documents that purported to be revealed but that, especially in the accounts of mira-

---

& World, 1960). A masterful study of the development of a critical approach to the New Testament is that of W. G. Kümmel, *The New Testament: The History of the Investigation of Its Problems*, trans. S. M. Gilmour and H. C. Kee (Nashville: Abingdon, 1972). This volume includes excerpts from critical scholars, evaluative descriptions of their theories, bibliography, and brief biographical sketches of the scholars.

[2] A term used by Clement of Alexandria with reference to the gospel of John. Reported by Eusebius in his *Ecclesiastical History* 6. 14. 7, Loeb edition, vol. 2, trans. J. F. L. Oulton (Cambridge, Mass.: Harvard University Press, 1953).

cles, were in direct conflict with natural law? In a little book called *The Reasonableness of Christianity as Delivered in the Scriptures* (1695), Locke appealed to his readers to meet on the common ground provided by reason and to work together for interpretations of Scripture and religious traditions that, he believed, when properly understood contained nothing that was in conflict with reason. The implications of his book for orthodox faith were thought to be so radical that Locke published it anonymously, but his identity as its author soon became known, and he was subjected to bitter personal attack.

Locke sought to demonstrate the reasonableness of Christianity in two main ways: (1) by showing that certain passages in the gospels, though outwardly puzzling, actually related wise actions by Jesus or at least sensible precautions; and (2) by maintaining that belief in the possibility of knowledge of God through natural law and belief in a special revelation of God through Christ were not incompatible. Specifically, Locke dealt at length with the fact that in the gospels Jesus seems to want to conceal his messiahship, even though, as Locke acknowledges, the confession of Jesus as Messiah is essential to man's salvation. The explanation is that if Jesus had publicly announced that he was the Messiah or had allowed his disciples to do so, the Jewish people would have assumed—wrongly—that he was putting himself forward as a king in the political, nationalistic sense, and the universal outreach of the gospel, which, Locke believed, characterized Jesus' message, would have been obscured. Jesus showed wisdom in selecting as disciples men who were not intellectually aggressive, since otherwise they might have propagandized too effectively for the initial stage of what was only later to become a universal faith. When the time arrived for launching the world mission, God had ready the brilliant Paul for that demanding task.

In attempting to demonstrate the compatibility of belief in revelation and in reason, Locke stated that the truth of natural law had been attained by others than Christians, and that much of Judaism as well as of the thought of Plato was compatible with Christianity as reasonable men understood it. What was the need, then, for God's special revelation in Christ? According to Locke, records of Jesus. On the contrary, rationalistic interpretations of the miracle stories seemed to transform the gospel accounts from Good News into gross misunderstanding.

The problem posed by the New Testament's limitation of revelation to a specific time (the first several decades A.D.) and a single place (Palestine) has never been resolved, but in the nineteenth century it failed to hold a place of importance equivalent to that of the problem of historical knowledge of Jesus and faith in miracles. There are several reasons for this. For the orthodox, special revelation was no problem at all, since their belief in divine sovereignty enabled them to place this question in the category of an inscrutable mystery, known only to God, and many critical thinkers, on the other hand, discovered that Jesus could be regarded in universal terms. Some philosophically inclined historians considered Jesus to be a manifestation of the divine spirit, so that while he was historically unique, he was only the highest and best instance of a process of divine self-disclosure that was going on through other channels and in other cultures. The critics who concentrated on the teachings of Jesus found their principle of universality in his ethics, which were aimed at achieving the highest good for the whole of humanity, but which were compatible with the best of ethical ideals the world around. The philosophies of Immanuel Kant (1724–1804) and Georg Wilhelm Friedrich Hegel (1770–1831) fostered these interpretations of Jesus as the ideal god-man and as the teacher of man's loftiest moral ideal.

THE RECONCILIATION OF FAITH
AND REASON IN MYTH

By the early part of the nineteenth century, the search for universal principles opened up a new way of attacking the problem of faith and history in the gospel narratives. The new method held out the hope that the gospels could be analyzed in a rational way. The emergent scholarly attention to the literatures and cultures of other peoples in the late eighteenth century had created an awareness that other peoples in other cultural settings thought about and reacted to the world around them in ways quite different from those that prevailed in the Europe of 1800. At the same time, men assumed, as they had in the past, that external features may differ, but the underlying humanity is one; a kernel of universal truth awaits discovery behind and beneath the merely accidental cultural differences. Thus it was considered important to seek the universal meaning in the words of ancient and alien literatures and to probe the writer's intent in order to discern the underlying truth, of which he may have been only dimly aware if at all.

Applied to the study of the gospels, this attitude opened the way for a fresh look at the history of Jesus and especially at the miracle stories. The concept that made possible a gospel analysis that avoided both the credulousness of the supernaturalistic approach and the extreme rationalism of the historical approach was that of *myth*. The man who first employed the mythical approach to the gospels with thoroughness and consistency was David Friedrich Strauss (1808–74), a German scholar. As a young instructor in the theological faculty at the University of Tübingen, he published a massive two-volume work, *Das Leben Jesu* [The life of Jesus] (1835–36), simultaneously achieving enduring renown and ruining his chances for a professorial post by reason of the radical conclusions he reached as to the historical reliability of the gospel accounts.

Strauss did not regard myth as fraudulent fiction, invented by a writer consciously bent on deception.[5] Rather, he understood myth to be "the representation of an event or an idea in a form which is historical, but which is determined by sensual, phantasy-laden modes of thought and speech from antiquity."[6] The stress

---

[5] *Das Leben Jesu*, vol. 1 (Tübingen: C. F. Osiander, 1835–36), p. 69. An English translation of the third edition by George Eliot has recently been published, with an introduction by Peter C. Hodgson: *The Life of Jesus Critically Examined* (Philadelphia: Fortress, 1975); in which, see pp. 52, 81–82.

[6] Strauss, *Das Leben Jesu*, vol. 1, pp. 38–41, 67–68 (*The Life of Jesus Critically Examined*, pp. 53–54).

> contemporaries and upon the following generations; the ideal part, or if it be wished, the philosophical part, is that the Messiah was expected to resemble Moses and Elijah, and as a consequence, the illumination of his face is a mythical motif based on the Old Testament narratives, themselves partly mythical and partly historical.[8]

Thus for Strauss it was the faith discerned by reason behind the biblical record that was to be affirmed, not the outward form of the revelatory writings.

REACTIONS AGAINST MYTHICAL INTERPRETATION OF THE GOSPELS

The reaction provoked by Strauss's mythical life of Jesus was violent in his own time, and its effects continue to be evident in studies of the historical Jesus today, both among orthodox writers, who in some cases show little firsthand knowledge of Strauss, and among those who are as skeptical as Strauss about the possibility of knowledge of Jesus but who propose a theological reconstruction of the meaning of Jesus that is different from Strauss's. Although interpreters since Strauss continue to be interested in the mythopoetic interpretation of the gospels, the more powerful impact of his work is evident in the ongoing effort of scholars to achieve a historical reconstruction of the life of Jesus by critical methods.

Attempts at Historical Reconstruction of the Life of Jesus

There are two men who, more than any others, represent the attempt to develop a purely historical approach to the question of the history of Jesus: Ferdinand Christian Baur (1792–1860) and Heinrich Julius Holtzmann (1832–1910). Their work may be

---

[8] *Ibid.*, pp. 75–76.

said to mark, respectively, the beginning and the culmination of the consistently historical view of the New Testament. Both these men sought to answer the question, What can be known historically about the origins of Christianity in general and about the life of Jesus in particular?

Baur's great contribution was to develop a thoroughly historical method for assessing the evidence. His chief concern was to show the importance of investigating the rise of Christianity from the same standpoint as any secular event. Under the influence of the German philosopher Hegel, who depicted history as moving through conflict between opposing forces (thesis and antithesis) to higher levels of spiritual achievement (synthesis), Baur found in the conflict between the Jewish and Gentile parties in the first-century Jerusalem church not only the clue to the dynamics of the church's subsequent growth but also the seeds of the theological tendencies represented by the various books of the New Testament. Using this as the beginning point of his historical reconstruction, Baur set about bringing into a coherent whole the scattered details of biblical evidence in order to construct from them a comprehensive picture of Christian beginnings. His entire procedure was based on the conviction that history is a network of cause and effect and that the task of the historian is to rediscover the links that form the network, thereby demonstrating the factors that caused the past to develop as it did. To achieve his goal of a unified approach to the history of Christian beginnings, he adopted what he believed to be a position of pure objectivity:

> My standpoint is in one word the purely historical one; namely, that the one thing to be aimed at is to place before ourselves the materials given in the history [of the New Testament] as they are objectively, and not otherwise, so far as that is possible. How far I have succeeded in this is not for me to say; but I am not conscious of having followed any other aim.[9]

[9] *The Church History of the First Three Centuries*, 3rd ed., vol. 1, trans. Allan Menzies (London: Williams & Norgate, 1878), p. x. (An appreciative, thorough, and illuminating study of Baur is by P. C. Hodgson, *The Formation of Historical Theology: A Study of Ferdinand Christian Baur* [New York: Harper & Row, 1966]. Hodgson shows how important for Baur's christology was the historical reality of Jesus [pp. 100–41].)

it was increasingly acknowledged that Mark was the first of the first three gospels and that John represented a quite independent tradition. Holtzmann noted, for example, that where Mark and Matthew report the same incident, it is told in a shorter form by Matthew than by Mark, even though Matthew is a longer work than Mark by far. The same is true of parallel accounts of miracle stories in Mark and Luke. A clear instance of this is the story of the Healing of the Daughter of Jairus (Mark 5:21–43; Matt. 9:18–26; Luke 8:40–56). What is told by Matthew in nine verses and by Luke in seventeen takes twenty-three in Mark. And the relative crudity of Mark's language shows that he is not expanding either of the more polished versions found in Matthew and Luke.

Building on the work that had demonstrated Mark to be the earliest of the synoptics,[18] Holtzmann went on to show that Matthew and Luke had used a common sayings source in their gospels but had relied on Mark for the basic framework and major narrative content. The large body of material reporting the teachings of Jesus in Matthew and Luke—of which the Sermon on the Mount is an obvious example—has no parallel in Mark, and yet in many extended passages Matthew and Luke exhibit such close verbal similarity that their use of a common sayings source seems to be the obvious explanation. That Mark is the oldest of the gospels and that Matthew and Luke have used a common sayings source are still almost universally accepted as best accounting for the similarities and differences in basic structure and content among the gospels. The theory that Matthew and Luke each had a written source of his own has not gained wide acceptance; the fact that the gospel tradition was for many decades transmitted orally rather than in written form accounts for discrepancies between the two gospels. Although the rise of other analytical methods has lessened the importance of purely literary source analysis of the gospels, Holtzmann's arguments for the priority of Mark and identification of the common sayings

---

[18] C. H. Weisse, *Die evangelische Geschichte kritisch und philosophisch bearbeitet* [The gospel history critically and philosophically examined], 2 vols. (Leipzig: Breitkopf & Härtel, 1838).

source for Matthew and Luke are lasting contributions. Interest in locating literary sources continued fruitfully in the English-speaking world even after the focus of critical work in Germany had shifted elsewhere.[19] But subsequent developments in critical studies of the gospel were not to invalidate the results of literary criticism.

In his effort at historical reconstruction, Holtzmann came to one conclusion, however, that has been challenged and largely discredited. He assumed that by establishing the priority of Mark, he could logically conclude that the order of events in the life of Jesus as reported in Mark was historically trustworthy. He further believed that he could show successive stages in the development of Jesus' messianic consciousness, beginning with the coming of the Spirit at his baptism and culminating in his tragic death. But Holtzmann's conclusions rested on a false assumption and an undemonstrable hypothesis: the assumption that a more ancient historical source was of necessity more accurate historically and the hypothesis that the sequence of events reported in the gospels corresponded to the actual course of Jesus' life, so that one could draw cause-and-effect conclusions from the order of the narrative. In fact, all that can be inferred from Mark's ordering of the gospel material is that that is how Mark thought it ought to be arranged. There is no evidence that there was a known sequence that Mark could have utilized if he had wanted to; all the evidence points to the possibility that the gospel tradition circulated as isolated sayings and narrative units, so that Mark had complete freedom in arranging them in the order that best suited his purposes. Unfortunately, it is not only Holtzmann's valid conclusions about the priority of Mark that survive; his unwarranted assumptions about the order of events in Mark continue to be the basis for many attempts to write lives of Jesus.

---

[19] A thorough analysis of the synoptics from the standpoint of literary dependence is that of J. C. Hawkins, *Horae synopticae* (Oxford: Clarendon, 1909). B. H. Streeter, in *The Four Gospels* (New York: Macmillan, 1925), builds on the work of Hawkins and others, but he investigates the various types of gospel text tradition as represented by groups of ancient manuscripts and seeks to assign both the gospels and the types of manuscript tradition in which the gospels are preserved to specific centers of the early church.

and therefore subjected to comparison with other writings of their time. Accordingly, the Jewish documents of the first century B.C., as well as the rabbinic interpretations originating around the time of Jesus (and included in the talmudic and other rabbinic writings in subsequent centuries), were studied to see how much Jesus conformed to or differed from the teachings of the rabbis of his time. In addition to the interpretations of Jewish Law made by those who stood in the mainstream of Judaism, writings that came from the period after the books included in the Hebrew canon were written proved to be especially illuminating: They showed the meaning of terms used in the gospels but never defined there, such as Kingdom of God and Son of Man.

Very popular during the first century B.C. were *apocalyptic* writings, with their descriptions in symbolic language of the imminent irruption of divine power that would overwhelm the satanic forces and vindicate God's faithful people. These works of late Judaism varied considerably in detail, especially as to the forms in which divine deliverance was expected—from revealers of heavenly wisdom to quasi-military figures whose coming would bring about the defeat of the demonic hosts. The Christians partly adopted, partly adapted apocalyptic ideas from Jewish writings. When Pharisaic Judaism became dominant following the disastrous revolts of A.D. 66–70 and 130–135, Jewish expectations of Messiah and the Kingdom of God were recast, and the apocalypses were excluded from the Jewish canon, except for Daniel.

Originally working independently of each other, Johannes Weiss (1827–1918) and Albert Schweitzer (1875–1965) reached the conclusion that apocalypticism was the primary source for understanding the ministry and teaching of Jesus. Jesus had taken over not only its terminology and concepts but its sense of imminent fulfillment, which was the basis of the urgency that characterized his life and work. Schweitzer's reconstruction of the ministry of Jesus was seriously flawed by his acceptance of the order of events in Matthew as historical, but this should not obscure the fact that his stress on the centrality of Jesus' apocalypticism was historically sound. Only in recent decades has apocalypticism in the gospel tradition come to be taken with the seriousness it deserves. The distasteful conclusions Schweitzer reached concerning Jesus' understanding of himself—that Jesus was a fanatic who thought he could force the hand of God and bring in the Kingdom, but whose confrontation with the Jerusalem authorities brought about his own death—discouraged students of the gospels from recognizing what was valid in Schweitzer's proposal: that apocalyptic Judaism provided the framework for the message and ministry of Jesus.

Other lines of research at the turn of the present century stressed the parallels between Jesus and redemptive figures from the Hellenistic religions, especially the mystery religions with their divine saviors who offered the secret knowledge and sacraments by which a mortal could participate in immortality. Some scholars went so far as to propose that the Jesus of the gospel narratives never existed but was a mythical figure invented by religious propagandists. But the very great benefit from this kind of comparison of Christian with late Hellenistic and early Roman literature and religious documents was that it shed a great deal of light on the language and literary forms in which religious propagandizing was carried on in the early Roman world. Archeological discoveries brought to light private letters and business records that showed in astonishing detail how people lived and how they expressed themselves in unpretentious forms of communication. With very few exceptions, the early Christian writings cannot be compared meaningfully with writings of real literary merit of the first century A.D., but when studied in parallel with nonliterary material of that period, the New Testament books can be understood with greater clarity as products of their own time.[25]

Form Criticism: The Tradition-Historical Method

In the nineteenth century, Old Testament scholars exploring the literary and historical origins of the so-called five books of Moses (Genesis through Deuteronomy) believed they could discern several literary strands woven into the present books. They reached

[25] Adolf Deissmann, *Light from the Ancient East*, trans. L. R. M. Strachan (New York: Harper & Row, n.d.). On the features which distinguish early Christian literature from that of the Hellenistic world, see A. N. Wilder, *The Language of the Gospel* (New York: Harper & Row, 1964).

an impasse, however, when they were forced to conclude that these literary components had been edited relatively late in Israel's history (6th–5th centuries B.C.), so that by literary means scholars could not gain access to the earlier stages of Israel's history. By his recognition that these literary strands incorporated what had originally been *oral* tradition—stories, legends, poems, legal formulations—Hermann Gunkel pioneered in developing a method of biblical scholarship. Through analysis and classification of those oral forms he was able to show how the tradition had evolved from the oldest recoverable (oral) forms to the stage where they are presently embedded in the written tradition.[26]

Sensing that there was an analogy between this enterprise and the need to get back to older layers of tradition incorporated in the gospels, New Testament scholars sought to move behind the literary stage (e.g., Q, and the sources supposedly used by Matthew and Luke and John; see Chapter 3) by analyzing, classifying, and reconstructing the history of the originally oral forms or units in which the gospel tradition was handed down prior to being incorporated into the written gospels. As was the case with the oral units in the Old Testament, the scholars assumed that not only could the units be recovered as to form and content, but also that the functions they had served in the life of the early Christian community could be determined. This method of analysis was called *Formgeschichte*, literally "form-history," but more appropriately *tradition history*. Unfortunately, the method was early called "form criticism," by analogy with "literary criticism," and the label has stuck. The functional setting of the tradition was designated the *Sitz im Leben*, or "setting in life." The *Sitz* could shift, however: The original setting of a unit of tradition might have been the situation of Jesus' career, but then the tradition would have been modified when it was preserved by and in the interests of a particular Christian community. And it might have undergone further change when it came to be incorporated in a gospel.

[26] Hermann Gunkel, *The Legends of Genesis: The Biblical Saga and History* (New York: Schocken, 1964).

This approach to the recovery of the historical setting of the gospel tradition was undertaken independently by three scholars whose methods turned out to be quite similar and whose publications appeared within the space of three years. Karl Ludwig Schmidt of Basel (1891–1956) published in 1919 a seminal essay in which he showed (1) that the gospels had been compiled from units of tradition preserved by a church in the service of its specific needs, and (2) that as a literary genre the gospel had no real parallel in the literature of the period.[27] Martin Dibelius (1883–1947) of Heidelberg in 1919 traced the similarities between the gospel tradition (the oral units) and various forms of folk literature, centering attention on the two chief functions of the tradition in the life of the church: preaching and moral instruction.[28] In 1921, Rudolf Bultmann (1884–1976) published his monumental *History of the Synoptic Tradition*.[29] It consisted of an exhaustive analysis of the gospel tradition, classifying it by type, showing how it was modified in the process of transmission, and how the evangelists brought it together in order to make it serve their own special aims.

Both Dibelius and Bultmann remarked on the sociocultural setting in which the oral tradition had been preserved and in the interests of which its written form was produced.[30] Neither one, however, proceeded to define the social setting in anything more than vague, general terms. Thus Bultmann differentiates the "primitive Palestinian" from "Hellenistic" Christianity.[31] Dibelius considers the sayings[32] and the paradigms[33] (succinct narratives that end in a saying of Jesus) to have their "setting in

[27] *Der Rahmen der Geschichte Jesu* [The framework of the story of Jesus] (Berlin: Trowitsch & Sohn, 1919).
[28] *Die Formgeschichte der Evangelien* [Form criticism of the gospels] (Tübingen: Siebeck, 1919; 3rd ed., 1959, edited by Günther Bornkamm and with a supplement by Gerhard Iber); English translation by B. L. Woolf, based on the second German edition, *From Tradition to Gospel* (New York: Scribner's, n.d.).
[29] Third German edition trans. John Marsh (New York: Harper & Row, 1963).
[30] Dibelius, *Tradition*, p. 7; Bultmann, *History*, p. 5.
[31] Bultmann, *History*, pp. 5, 240–41.
[32] Dibelius, *Tradition*, p. 13.
[33] Dibelius, *Tradition*, pp. 65, 69.

life" in early Christian preaching, while the *Novellen* (longer narratives with more detail) represent varied "secular" interests, such as the depiction of Jesus' divine nature or simply his miracle technique.[34] By neither of these form critics, however, are we offered clues about the life-world of the evangelist or a specific sociocultural setting out of which these traditions may have come down to us. Studies in recent decades—both literary and archeological—of the impact of Hellenistic culture on Palestine and the Middle East from the time of Alexander the Great on have shown how deeply Jewish life and thought in Syria and Palestine was penetrated by Hellenization, even among those who were consciously resistant to the attempts of Hellenistic rulers to force their culture on the Jews.[35] Remains of ancient synagogues with Greek inscriptions, representational art (theoretically forbidden by the Mosaic law against graven images), including portraits of the deity and the signs of the zodiac, show how thoroughly imbued with Hellenistic culture were the most pious Jews. The distinction between "Palestinian" and "Hellenistic" is useless, so that the question remains, What was the sociocultural setting for the oral tradition and for the gospels, wherever they may have been written geographically?

Classification of the oral tradition along purely formal lines has not been possible. The formal nomenclature employed by Dibelius does not match with that of Bultmann, and the two systems cannot be neatly harmonized. The categories themselves are not watertight: Bultmann's first category of *sayings* is actually a brief *narrative* that culminates in a saying, as in the story of the man with the withered hand (Mark 3:1–6). This same formal category is called by Dibelius a "narrative type." The passion narrative (Mark 14–15) has no distinguishing formal characteristics, but is identified solely on the basis of its content. It lacks parallel in either secular or religious literature, Jewish or Greek, and under close scrutiny shows strong evidence of having been composed by Mark on the basis of his reading of the Jewish

[34] Dibelius, *Tradition*, pp. 97, 103.
[35] Martin Hengel, *Judaism and Hellenism*. 2 vols. (Philadelphia: Fortress, 1974).

scriptures—in a Greek translation![36] Accordingly, the classic form-critical studies are unable to account for the form, content, genre, or function of the passion narrative. The fault lies in the arbitrary categories of form and function (preaching/instruction) as well as in the superficial cultural distinctions that have been imposed on the gospel tradition. The fundamental questions go unanswered: What kind of community would have transmitted such a tradition? What models then available influenced the form in which the tradition has come down to us? What function did the tradition serve in the community within and for which it was written?

The Gospel Writers as Creative Interpreters of Jesus

A more recent development of the tradition-historical method—though, as noted earlier, it is present in seminal form in the work of Bultmann—is the study of the individual gospel writers to see how, through their selection, arrangement, and modification of the gospel tradition, each has presented Jesus in such a way as to convey his own distinctive understanding of him. There was not in the early church *one* image of Jesus that served as a model, with variations, for all the various New Testament writers. Rather, there was a dynamic tradition, which the gospel writers felt free to adapt and to shape in serving their communities' own respective purposes.

Among the first to recognize the shaping of the tradition by the evangelists was William Wrede (1859–1906), whose pioneering work on Mark was published in 1901,[37] the same year that Schweitzer's basic work on the life of Jesus appeared and nearly two decades before Bultmann's book on form criticism. Wrede sought to show that the idea in Mark that Jesus had kept his

---

[36] H. C. Kee, "The Function of Scriptural Quotations and Allusions in Mk 11–16," in *Jesus und Paulus*, ed. E. E. Ellis and E. Grässer (Göttingen: Vandenhoeck & Ruprecht, 1975), p. 175.

[37] *Das Messiasgeheimnis in den Evangelien* (Göttingen: Vandenhoek & Ruprecht, 1901); English translation by J. C. G. Grieg, *The Messianic Secret* (Greenwood, S.C.: Attic Press, 1971).

sciousness. But the most serious objection to the efforts to reconstruct the historical Jesus is that critics suppose that if they can
just get behind the church tradition, behind the picture of Jesus
offered by the New Testament, there they will find the real Jesus
as he actually and bodily lived. The critic will ferret him out and
exhibit him in all his old relationships, all of which will appear
as desirable and delightful. But that charming person, Kähler
insists, is not the real Christ:

> The real, that is the actual Christ, who strides through the his-
> tory of his people, with whom millions have had communion in
> childlike faith, with whom the great witnesses of faith have
> communed as they struggled, accepted, conquered and sur-
> rendered—the real Christ is the preached Christ.[42]

The attempt to look behind the biblical record at "what
really happened" is not only unwarranted by the nature of evidence but idle:

> Is there any real loss if the origin of the picture remains dark
> for us? No one saw the loaves prepared and grow, but in re-
> sponse to Jesus' word of thanks they satisfied thousands. The
> loaves were simply there and they were quite genuine bread. So
> it is with all the wonder-working of our God: what we see and
> possess belongs to this world; but its origin we do not know at
> all; all that we can detect is that it comes from beyond.[43]

Kähler's harshest words are reserved for those historical critics
who assume that faith is somehow dependent on the outcome of
their work. In rebuttal to such a claim, he asserts that faith is not
dependent on an understanding of the relationship of the human

[42] *Der sogenannte historische Jesus und der geschichtliche biblische Christus*
[The so-called historical Jesus and the historic, biblical Christ] (1892), p. 44
(p. 66). The first and second editions were edited and published in combined form by E. Wolf under the original title (Munich: Kaiser Verlag,
1953). Page numbers given here refer to Wolf's edition; those in parentheses
refer to the English edition, trans. and ed. C. E. Braaten (Philadelphia:
Fortress, 1964).
[43] *Ibid.*, p. 74 (p. 91).

and divine natures of Jesus as conceived in "a head schooled in philosophy."[44] Faith dare not make itself dependent on the uncertain results of a picture that is only ostensibly reliable—a picture of Jesus that has been tortuously carved out by means of a method of historical research that arose only relatively recently and that is as devoid of prospects for achieving results as is any shadow picture sketched by dogma and formed out of simple concepts:

> In relation to Christ, whom we should trust and whom we dare to trust, the learned theologian must be no better off and no worse off than the simplest Christian: no better off, since he comes no closer to the living Saviour than anyone else; no worse off, since he too must overcome the obstacles to faith. To overcome these, there is only a single royal way: Repent and believe the Good News, Jesus Christ died for our sins according to the scriptures, and was buried and was raised on the third day according to the scriptures.[45]

The sharp distinction between the church's preaching of Jesus as the Christ and the historian's analysis of the gospel traditions has been maintained by leading twentieth-century theologians, such as Paul Tillich[46] (1886–1965) and Rudolf Bultmann, the most influential New Testament scholar of our time. Tillich has a more positive attitude toward the work of biblical critics than did Kähler, his teacher, but the critics' contribution is more a demonstration of the courage of a faith that will subject to critical scrutiny the biblical picture of Jesus as the Christ than a direct link between their historical findings and the theologians' assertions about Jesus.

The Message of the Cross

Bultmann not only was an admirer of historical criticism, but was himself a critic of the first rank as well as a theologian. For him,

---

[44] *Ibid.*, p. 49 (p. 72).
[45] *Ibid.*, pp. 49–50 (p. 73).
[46] *Systematic Theology*, vol. 2 (Chicago: University of Chicago Press, 1957), pp. 113–18.

scendent meaning in the one whom they now called Lord and Christ had its point of historical origin in someone whom they or their immediate predecessors in the Christian faith had known, seen, and heard (see 1 John 1:1; Luke 1:2)—a man known as Jesus of Nazareth. Is it possible that this man, to whom such great deeds and such exalted meaning were attributed, never existed?

SUGGESTIONS FOR FURTHER READING

For an excellent presentation of the factors and thinkers that contributed to the rise of religious skepticism, with its resultant effects on the question of our historical knowledge of Jesus, see Franklin Baumer, *Religion and the Rise of Scepticism* (New York: Harcourt Brace Jovanovich, 1960). A set of selections from the primary sources useful in the application of critical historical method to the life of Jesus is Hugh Anderson's *Jesus** (New York: Oxford, 1964). The classic study of the development of the historical Jesus question down to the opening of the present century is Albert Schweitzer, *The Quest of the Historical Jesus** (New York: Macmillan, 1910).

The most forceful and enduringly influential essay rejecting the historical quest is Martin Kähler, *The So-called Historical Jesus and the Historic Biblical Christ,** ed. Carl Braaten (Philadelphia: Fortress, 1964). A historian's classic attempt to recover the historical Jesus is Adolf von Harnack, *What Is Christianity?** (New York: Harper & Row, 1957).

A new method that enabled scholarship to move behind the written sources to the oral tradition was initiated by Rudolf Bultmann, in *History of the Synoptic Tradition* (New York: Harper & Row, 1963), and Martin Dibelius, in *From Tradition to Gospel* (New York: Scribner's, 1935). The positive results of form-critical analysis of the gospels may be seen in Rudolf Bultmann, *Jesus*

* *Available in a paperback edition.*

*and the Word** (New York: Scribner's, 1934). For cautiously appreciative studies of form criticism, see Vincent Taylor, *The Formation of the Gospel Tradition* (New York: St. Martin's, 1935), and Bruce Vawter, *The Four Gospels: An Introduction* (New York: Doubleday, 1967). A fine statement on form criticism (like Vawter's, from the Roman Catholic viewpoint) is in *Sacramentum Mundi*, a theological encyclopedia edited by Karl Rahner (New York: Herder & Herder, 1968). Useful surveys of changing methods and theological insights in the historical quest may be found in J. M. Robinson, *A New Quest of the Historical Jesus** (Naperville, Ill.: Allenson, 1959), and Heinz Zahrnt, *The Historical Jesus* (New York: Harper & Row, 1963).

Excellent introductions to critical methods for the study of the gospels are Edgar V. McKnight, *What is Form Criticism?* and Norman Perrin, *What Is Redaction Criticism?* (both published in 1969 by Fortress Press, Philadelphia). A comprehensive study of redaction-critical work on the gospels is Joachim Rohde, *Rediscovering the Teaching of the Evangelists* (Philadelphia: Westminster, 1969), which exemplifies the emphasis on theological features as contrasted with sociocultural dimensions with which we are concerned in the present study.

* *Available in a paperback edition.*

2 Jesus in Extrabiblical Sources

Is it possible that Jesus never existed? A half-century ago doubts about the historical existence of Jesus were earnestly voiced by certain historians and theologians,[1] most notably by Arthur Drews (1865–1935)[2] in Germany and by his disciple, William Benjamin Smith (1850–1934),[3] in America. These men claimed that Jesus was a mythical figure invented by propagandists for the developing Christian faith, who built on the strand in the Jewish tradition (especially after the time of the Maccabees) that sought to bring the Gentiles as proselytes into the community of Israel. According to Smith, the effort to achieve universal salvation was the essence of nascent Christianity, but the Old Testament prophecies and conceptions were not sufficiently concrete to appeal as widely as was necessary to accomplish Gentile conversion:

> There was one and only one device that could meet the demand
> of the situation and at the same time lay close at hand: and
> that was to follow the precedent of Isaiah, so native and fa-

[1] See the discussion in Maurice Goguel, *Jésus de Nazareth: mythe ou histoire?* [Jesus of Nazareth: Myth or history?] (Paris: Payot, 1925).
[2] *Die Christusmythe* [The Christ myth], 2 vols. (Jena: Diederichs, 1909–11).
[3] *The Birth of the Gospel: A Study of the Origin and Purport of the Primitive Allegory of the Jews* (New York: 1927; reprinted, New York: Philosophical Library, 1957).

miliar to the Hebrew mind, so appealing to the oriental fancy, and to present the Righteous Servant, the Torch-Bearer, the Light for the Gentiles, as a Man, a suffering son of the earth, "tempted in all points in our likeness without sin."[4]

The process of creating the gospels began with the story of the passion, to which were added the accounts of the ministry and later of the prehistory of Jesus. Smith reported,

> The final product, the symbolic quasi-biography which the world knows as the Gospels, we have found was the literary precipitate of a long-continued pictorial teaching that stretched all round the Mediterranean. These writings become self-luminous when and only when we *abandon the baseless assumption* of historical documents. . . . The story of Jesus is, therefore, an idealization of the destiny of the nation Israel in its universal inclusiveness.[5]

Smith's contemporaries did not dismiss his work as nonsense, nor should we today. He had far too many accurate insights and far too firm a grasp of historical facts about Christian origins to be labeled a crank. His intuition that some of the gospel narratives were created or at least modified in order to demonstrate the fulfillment of the Old Testament was propounded by David Friedrich Strauss in the nineteenth century in *Das Leben Jesu* [The life of Jesus], a book that has continued to cast its sober influence over gospel studies down to the present day. Smith's awareness of the Hebrew practice of depicting a group under the figure of an individual, a corporate personality, is an insight that, developed by others, has been of fundamental importance for Old Testament studies in recent decades.[6]

---

[4] *Ibid.*, p. 651.
[5] *Ibid.*, pp. 141–42 (Smith's italics).
[6] The classic study of corporate personality is by H. W. Robinson, *Corporate Personality in Ancient Israel* (Philadelphia: Fortress, 1964); see also his *Inspiration and Revelation in the Old Testament* (New York: Oxford University Press, 1946), pp. 69–74. See also the discussions in Johannes Pedersen, *Israel: Its Life and Culture*, 4 vols. (New York: Oxford University Press, 1926, 1940; Vols. 1 and 2 reprinted, 1964; Vols. 3 and 4 reprinted with additions, 1959).

Jesus' divinity. But if the emphasis falls on the "surprising feats" mentioned in the next sentence, then the inappropriateness of calling Jesus merely a man may have meant, not that Jesus was divine, but that he was a magician under demonic control. As we shall see, this was precisely the charge most commonly leveled against Jesus in the rabbinic sources. If we assume that in making explicit statements about Jesus as Messiah and about the resurrection Josephus is merely conveying what Jesus' followers claimed in his behalf, then there would be no reason to deny that he wrote them nearly as they stand.[10] It seems very unlikely that the passage in its entirety is a Christian interpolation; thus it can serve as evidence outside Christian writing for the existence of Jesus.

Even if we assume that the passage has come down to us almost as Josephus wrote it, however, it still provides us only limited information about Jesus. It presupposes that he lived and attests that he conducted a ministry that attracted considerable attention, even among those who thought him to be a wizard, that the Romans condemned him—presumably as a threat to the peace and therefore probably as an insurrectionist—and that the belief in his resurrection developed soon after his death. The information from Josephus confirms the main points in the gospel account, but it in no way supplements it, since even in the gospels Jesus' opponents accuse him of performing his exorcisms by being in league with the prince of demons (Mark 3:22). It is also obvious that, although Josephus thought mention of Jesus worthwhile, he gave it no more place in his narrative than his accounts of other conflicts between the Jews and their Roman overlords, and far less space than his spicy story of the goings-on in the temple of Isis in Rome.[11]

The second of Josephus' references to Jesus[12] occurs in a

---

[10] See the discussion of the authenticity of this passage in Vol. 9 of L. H. Feldman's translation of Josephus' *Antiquities*, pp. 48–51 and notes on pp. 48 and 49. Feldman reproduces and evaluates an attempt by Robert Eisler to restore the passage to its original form. See also the essay on this material by Paul Winter in E. Schürer and G. Vermes, *History of the Jewish People in the Time of Jesus Christ* (Edinburgh: T. & T. Clark, 1973), pp. 428–41.
[11] *Ibid.*, 18. 65–80.
[12] *Ibid.*, 20. 200.

section dealing with the struggles for power that characterized life in Judea in the years prior to the Jewish Revolt of A.D. 66. Jesus' brother, James, had succeeded to the leadership of the church in Jerusalem and was apparently highly regarded by the majority of the Jewish community as well. No information whatsoever about Jesus is provided by this passage in Josephus, but it does confirm the general picture presented in the gospels that Jesus was a well-known figure in first-century Judaism, who could be identified in a passing reference as the Jesus who was called the Messiah by his followers. There is no hint here of a Christian interpolation, which adds more weight to this as an important historical allusion and renders untenable the allegation that Jesus was a fictional figure invented by the Christians. Since mention of Jesus at this point in his narrative serves only to identify James and contributes nothing substantial to his account, Josephus certainly leaves his readers with the impression that Jesus is a historical person like any other of whom he writes.

The Roman Historians: Pliny, Suetonius, and Tacitus

Among Roman writers, the oldest reference to Jesus that has survived is found in one of the letters that Pliny the Younger (A.D. 62–113) wrote to Emperor Trajan. Around A.D. 110, writing from the seat of his governorship in Bithynia, a Roman province on the Black Sea coast in Asia Minor, Pliny asked for guidance in dealing with Christians, whose numbers and influence seem to have been on the rise in the area at this time. So greatly had the impact of the Christian faith been felt throughout the Black Sea provinces that the temples of the officially sanctioned gods were nearly deserted.[13] Christ was worshipped "as a god" and both the Eucharist and the love feast, the joyous fellowship meal that preceded it, were being celebrated by adherents of the new faith. Pliny's evidence shows us, therefore, that Christianity had a strong foothold on the Black Sea coast about eighty years after the cru-

[13] Pliny *Letters* 10. 94. The full text in English, with ample commentary, is in A. N. Sherwin-White, *Fifty Letters of Pliny* (New York: Oxford University Press, 1967).

cifixion, although his description of Christian practices adds nothing to our knowledge of the life of Jesus.

The Roman historian Suetonius, a contemporary of Pliny, mentions in his *Lives of the Twelve Caesars* that under the reign of Claudius (A.D. 41–54), there was a disturbance among the Jews that reached such a peak of intensity that they had to be expelled from the city. The instigator of this internal struggle was someone named Chrestos. Suetonius reports, "Since the Jews constantly made disturbances at the instigation of Chrestos, he [Claudius] expelled them from Rome."[14]

It is generally acknowledged that Chrestos, a common name, was used by Suetonius instead of Christos, which would not have been at all familiar to most Latin-speaking people. Perhaps the cause of the disturbance among the Jewish community in Rome was the coming, not of Christos, but of Christian preachers with their message that Jesus was the Christ(os). Although it is possible that Suetonius had his date confused and that the disturbance actually occurred during the reign of Tiberius (A.D. 14–37), it is more likely that the expulsion of the Jews from Rome was the occasion for the migration from Rome to Corinth of Priscilla and Aquila, the Christian couple who aided Paul in founding and building up the Corinthian church (Acts 18:2–26; Rom. 16:3; 1 Cor. 16:19). As in the case of the evidence from Pliny, all that we learn from Suetonius is that there was a Christian community in Rome as early as A.D. 49–50.[15]

In his *Annals*, Tacitus (A.D. 55?–117?), a third Roman writing early in the second century, describes in vivid detail the fire that destroyed much of Rome during the reign of Nero (A.D. 54–68). In order to divert suspicion from himself as the one who had ordered the city set afire, Nero placed the blame on the Christians, of whom a "multitude" were convicted.

[14] Suetonius *Lives of the Twelve Caesars* 25. 4, trans. Joseph Gavorse (New York: Modern Library, 1931; reprinted, 1959), p. 226. "Chrestos" would be the Greek form, "Chrestus" the Latinized form.

[15] A discussion of the date of Claudius' decree concerning the Jewish disturbance is given in F. J. Foakes-Jackson and Kirsopp Lake, *The Beginnings of Christianity*, Vol. 5 (New York: Macmillan, 1933), pp. 459–60. For a different interpretation of the evidence, see John Knox, *Chapters in a Life of Paul* (Nashville: Abingdon, 1950), pp. 81–83.

Neither human help, nor imperial munificence, nor all the modes of placating heaven, could stifle scandal or dispel the belief that the fire had taken place by order, *i.e.*, of Nero. Therefore, to scotch the rumor, Nero substituted as culprits and punished with the utmost refinements of cruelty, a class of men, loathed for their vices, whom the crowd styled Christians. Christus, the founder of the name, had undergone the death penalty in the reign of Tiberius, by sentence of the procurator Pontius Pilate, and the pernicious superstition was checked for a moment, only to break out once more, not merely in Judea, the home of the disease, but in the capital itself, where all things horrible or shameful in the world collect and find a vogue. First, then, the confessed members of the sect were arrested; next, on their disclosures, vast numbers were convicted, not so much on the count of arson as for the hatred of the human race. And derision accompanied their end: they were covered with wild beasts' skins and torn to death by dogs; or they were fastened on crosses, and when daylight failed were burned to serve as lamps by night. Nero had offered his gardens for the spectacle, and gave an exhibition in his Circus, mixing with the crowd in the habit of a charioteer, or mounted on his car.[16]

Allowing for exaggeration, we can still infer that the Christian community was at least large enough in Rome to attract public notice and aggressive enough to invite the hatred of the masses. In identifying the Christians among the many religious sects he scorned, Tacitus mentions that "Christus" was executed during the reign of Tiberius, probably about 29, having been sentenced by the procurator Pontius Pilate. Tacitus' account is the most precise and extensive information that the pagan authors provide about Jesus. Although his details match exactly what is known from Christian accounts, Tacitus, like Pliny and Suetonius, provides us with nothing that supplements what we know of Jesus from the gospels. The writings of the Roman historians are, however, important evidence for Jesus' existence as a historical person: They show that non-Christian historical writers, and by

---

[16] Tacitus *Annals* 15. 44, Loeb edition, vol. 4, trans. J. Jackson (Cambridge, Mass.: Harvard University Press, 1931).

inference their audiences, believed Jesus to have existed, and that they considered his death and his continuing influence after death to be significant enough to rate a few brief references.

EVIDENCE IN JEWISH RELIGIOUS SOURCES

The Hebrew sources in which Jesus is mentioned or alluded to have been thoroughly analyzed by both Jewish and Christian scholars.[17] The main sources are the oral interpretations and exposition of the Law given by the authoritative rabbis of the first two centuries A.D., which were codified as the Mishnah in the third century and, with additional commentary, as the Talmud in Jerusalem in the fourth century and in Babylon in the fifth. The interpretations attributed to the rabbis of the third to the fifth centuries are also included in the Talmud, and this rabbinic material, which was written down later, may incorporate older, possibly reliable material; but only the interpretations of the Tannaim, the rabbis of the first two centuries A.D., which are included in the Mishnah, are of primary value for a Jewish historical perspective on Jesus. Even the tannaitic sources are suspect, however, since there is a clear tendency in the development of the talmudic traditions to lend weight to a polemical view by assigning it to one of the early (tannaitic) teachers.[18]

Interpretations of the Tannaim

Chief among the tannaitic scholars who provide information about Jesus is Rabbi Eliezer, whose teacher, Rabbi Johanan ben Zakkai, was a contemporary of Jesus and may well have heard

[17] For a succinct summary, see Klausner, *Jesus of Nazareth*, pp. 17–54. See also R. T. Herford, *Christianity in Talmud and Midrash* (London, 1903; reprinted, Clifton, N.J.: Reference Book Publishers, 1966). The entire book is devoted to a sifting of late Jewish sources relating both to Jesus and to early Christianity.

[18] Important methodological considerations about the trustworthiness of rabbinic sources are offered in Jacob Neusner, *From Politics to Piety: The Emergence of Pharisaic Judaism* (Englewood Cliffs: Prentice-Hall, 1973), pp. 81–96.

him. However, for a figure who assumes for Christians an over-whelmingly significant place in the history of the first century, surprisingly little attention is paid to Jesus by Jewish writers in general, and most references are of a polemical or at least deroga-tory nature. Such references as there are are obscured by the fact that in the Talmud Jesus is not mentioned by name. In some texts he is referred to as "a certain person"; in others he is called "Balaam." (In the Old Testament, Balaam was a non-Israelite prophet whose services were available on a fee basis and who was so obstinate that God on one occasion rebuked him through the mouth of his faithful jackass [Num. 22:21–35].) In still other early talmudic passages, Jesus is called "Ben Stada" or "Ben Pandira" (a variant is "Panthera"); in each case "Ben" means "son of," and the clear implication is that Jesus was an illegiti-mate child. According to one passage from the Talmud (partly from Rabbi Eliezer and partly from the later Rabbi Hisda):

> It is tradition that Rabbi Eliezer said to the wise, "Did not Ben Stada bring spells from Egypt in a cut which was upon his flesh?" They said to him, "He was a fool, and they do bring a proof from a fool." [Ben Stada is Ben Pandira.] Rabbi Hisda said, "The husband was Stada, the paramour was Pandira." The husband was Pappos ben Jehudah, the father was Stada. The mother was Miriam the dresser of women's hair; as we say in Pumbeditha [a center of rabbinical learning in Babylon], "Such a one has been false to her husband."[19]

It is not known what is implied by the cut in the flesh, except that it has to do with magical practices. The tactic of the rab-binic tradition was not to deny Jesus' existence, but to discredit both him and his mother as unworthy to be considered as par-ticipants in a divine purpose.

By contrast, Rabbi Eliezer appears in another passage to have been attracted by Christianity to such an extent that he was seized by the Roman governor on suspicion of being a Christian, perhaps during a pogrom under Emperor Trajan aimed at de-stroying the leadership of the early church (about A.D. 110):

[19] b Shabbath 104[b]. Quoted from Herford, *Christianity in Talmud and Midrash*, p. 35.

Rabbi Eliezer . . . was arrested for Minuth [holding Christian beliefs], and they brought him to the tribunal for judgment. The governor said to him, "Doth an old man like thee occupy himself with such things?" He said to him, "Faithful is the judge concerning me." The governor supposed that he only said this of him, but he was not thinking of any but his Father who is in heaven. [The governor] said to him, "Since I am trusted concerning thyself, thus also will I be. I said, perhaps these societies [the Christian churches] err concerning these things. *Dimissus*, Behold thou art released." And when he had been released from the tribunal, he was troubled because he had been arrested for Minuth. His disciples came to him to console him, but he would not take comfort. Rabbi Aqiba [early second century] came in and said to him, "Rabbi, shall I say to thee why thou art grieving?" He said to him, "Say on." He said to him, "Perhaps one of the Minim [Christians] has said to thee a word of Minuth and it has pleased thee." He said, "By heaven, thou hast reminded me! Once I was walking along the streets of Sepphoris, and I met Jacob of Chephar Sichnin, and he said to me a word of Minuth in the name of Jesus Ben Pantiri, and it pleased me. And I was arrested for words of Minuth because I transgressed the words of Torah, "Keep thy way far from her, and come not nigh the door of her house, for she hath cast down many wounded [Prov. 5:8]."[20]

The significance of this rabbinical tradition is that it shows how seriously both Roman and rabbinical authorities regarded the teachings of Jesus and how eager they were to suppress the movement that his followers carried on in his name. Although there is no direct historical evidence about Jesus in these traditions, it is noteworthy that the passage above attacks Christianity by classifying it as a heresy to be shunned, not by denying the existence of its founder or declaring it to be a fraud perpetrated by the disciples. The passage also implies that Christianity is a highly visible movement in Sepphoris, the chief city of central Galilee, only a few miles from Nazareth, Jesus' home town. Personal non-Christian recollections of him could well have survived in this region. In any case, the rabbinic sources presuppose Jesus' actual existence, but they offer little historical information about him. Rather, they are a polemic directed against the people who were wandering about the land spreading the message of Jesus and against the memory of Jesus, a man of dubious family connections, who led the itinerant preachers and teachers of error. The Talmud contains many statements that are wholly polemical —for example, that Jesus was the illegitimate son of an adulteress by a Roman soldier named Pandira or Panthera and that for forty days before his execution a herald went about announcing what was to happen and pleading in vain for someone to rise to Jesus' defense.[21]

In this way Joseph Klausner summarizes the extent of the objective historical information about Jesus that can be drawn from the tannaitic strata of the Talmud:

> There are reliable statements to the effect that his name was Yeshu'a of Nazareth; that he "practiced sorcery" (i.e. performed miracles, as was usual in those days) and beguiled and led Israel astray; that he mocked at the words of the Wise [the officially sanctioned interpreters of the Law]; that he expounded scripture in the same manner as the Pharisees; that he had five disciples; that he said he was not come to take aught away from the Law or to add to it; that he was hanged (crucified) as a false teacher and beguiler on the eve of the Passover which happened on a sabbath; and that his disciples healed the sick in his name.[22]

[21] Klausner, *Jesus of Nazareth*, p. 46.

[22] *Ibid.* Apart from obviously polemical traditions, the only early information about Jesus that is in direct conflict with the gospel narrative concerns his disciples. Although the tradition is not explicit, it implies that Jesus had only five disciples and that all were executed. Only the first of the disciples named, Matthai, has a name closely resembling that of any of Jesus' followers in the gospel tradition. There is no trace in early Christian tradition of the martyrdom of five of Jesus' followers at the hands of Jews. Two explanations offered by Herford (*Christianity in Talmud and Midrash*, pp. 90–95) are plausible: (1) that three of the names are merely puns on epithets for Jesus: Naqi = "the innocent one," Netzer = "the root" (from Isa. 11), Buni = "my son," and (2) that the names are actually those of early Christians, but the event referred to occurred at a later time, perhaps during the brief period of Jewish persecution of Christians under Bar Kochbah in the third decade of the second century A.D. Whatever the basis and credibility of this talmudic tradition, it would add little to our knowledge or understanding of Jesus.

Later Interpretations from the Talmud and the Midrash

If the range of inquiry about Jesus in the Talmud and the Midrash (rabbinic commentary on the Scriptures) is extended down to the fourth century, the information is somewhat more extensive but at the same time so late and so obviously polemical as to be valueless as historical evidence. It is summarized by R. T. Herford as follows:

Jesus, called a Notzri [the Nazarene], Ben Stada, or Ben Pandira, was born out of wedlock. His mother was called Miriam, and was a dresser of women's hair. Her husband was Pappos ben Jehudah. Her paramour was Pandira. She is also said to have descended from princes and rulers, and to have played the harlot with a carpenter.

Jesus had been in Egypt and brought magic thence. He was a magician, and led astray and deceived Israel. He sinned and caused the multitude to sin. He mocked at the words of the wise and was excommunicated. He was tainted with heresy.

He called himself God, also the son of man and said that he would go up to heaven. He made himself to live by the name of God.

He was tried in Lud as a deceiver and as a teacher of apostasy. [Lud is Lydda, which lies inland from modern Tel Aviv.] Witnesses were concealed so as to hear his statements, and a lamp was lighted over him, that his face might be seen. He was brought to the Beth Din [literally, the House of Justice; that is, the Jewish court].

He was tried in Lud on the eve of Pesah [that is, the Passover], which was also the eve of the Sabbath. He was stoned and hung, or crucified. . . . Under the name of Balaam, he was put to death by Pinḥas the robber (Pontius Pilate) and at the time of his death was thirty-three years old. He was punished in Gehinnom [the valley of Hinnom, which runs southwest of Jerusalem and was used as a place for dumping refuse in ancient times] by means of boiling filth.

He was a revolutionary. He was near to the kingdom. He had five disciples. Under the name of Balaam [a notorious hireling

> prophet who caused the death of many in Israel; Josh. 13:22]
> he is excluded from the world to come.[23]

Later on, Jewish polemic went to even greater lengths to discredit Jesus, but it never denied his existence or the basic facts of a ministry of teaching and healing and of his execution.

Later still, probably in the tenth century, there appeared a novelistic work in Hebrew known as Toledoth Yeshua, which recounted the story of Jesus' life, drawing mostly on the gospel accounts but embellishing them with legendary features and casting the whole in a mold shaped by polemics and ridicule. The narrative is filled with racy details, such as the trickery by which the handsome Pandira (or Panthera) seduced the unsuspecting Miriam (Mary), and with such legendary elements as the report of Jesus' having written the Ineffable Name of God on a piece of leather and sewn it to his thigh so that he would not forget it. But it also contains gross errors and anachronisms—for example, Helen of Adiabene (middle of the first century) is confused with Helen the mother of Emperor Constantine (fourth century), and a rabbi who actually lived four centuries later is credited with having found the body of Jesus. Klausner is correct, therefore, when he asserts that the Toledoth Yeshua is "nothing beyond a piece of folklore," woven out of late legends and sayings from the Talmud and Midrash and combining perverted versions of the gospel accounts.[24]

There is probably some historical fact at the basis of several of these calumnies against Jesus, but others seem to represent a confusion of Jesus with some other man of the same name who was sentenced as a criminal. Of the latter type is the repeated statement that he was put to death in Lud, an area that according to the gospels he never visited. On the other hand the identification of the day of his execution as the eve of the Passover, which was also a Sabbath eve, fits with the chronology of the gospel of John, although it conflicts with the chronology of the other three gospels, according to which Jesus celebrated the Pass-

[23] Herford, *Christianity in Talmud and Midrash*, pp. 348–49.
[24] Klausner, *Jesus of Nazareth*, p. 57.

over with his disciples the night before his execution. Designation of the valley of Hinnom as the place of his death may be merely symbolic—that is, his rejection by the nation of Israel is linked with the refuse dump—but it could also recall the historical detail of his having been crucified on a hill that overlooked the upper part of this very valley.

The phrase "near to the kingdom" probably means that Jesus was known by friend and foe as one who announced the coming of the New Age, the eschatological Rule or Kingdom of God. For his enemies to describe him as a revolutionary is not farfetched, since he was actually almost certainly put to death by the Romans on precisely this charge: that he was the leader of an insurrectionist movement whose "kingdom" was a threat to Roman rule. Mention of boiling filth is, of course, no more than an indication of the hostility evoked by the very name of Jesus among those opposed to the Christian movement.

Other elements in the charges brought against Jesus among the talmudic traditions are clearly reflections of the gospel accounts, and as such they lack independent historical value. Of this type are the declarations that he called himself God and that he said he would go up to heaven. The report that he was brought to the Jewish court of justice may be either an independent tradition of Jewish origin or an allusion to the gospel reports of his hearing before the Sanhedrin, the local Jewish legislative and judicial assembly.

THE BEARING OF THE DEAD SEA SCROLLS ON UNDERSTANDING JESUS

In 1947 (or possibly as early as 1945), Bedouin living in the Judean desert of Jordan near the northwest shore of the Dead Sea found the first of a number of ancient scrolls hidden in caves in the cliffs just west of the marl terrace that overlooks the sea. Excavations by archeologists in the early 1950s and explorations of caves in the vicinity brought to light thousands of fragments of manuscripts, most of which have since been published for scholarly investigation and translated into several languages for interested laymen. Some of the recovered documents are commentaries —some complete and some preserved only in fragments—on books of the Hebrew Bible; some claim to be revelations of coming events in the history of the Jewish people; some are books of regulations for the life of the community that produced or preserved the writings. This community had its headquarters in a monastic settlement nearby; the ruins of this settlement, uncovered by archeologists beginning in 1955, were known locally as Khirbet Qumran.[25]

Since as early as the second century A.D. there have been reports of occasional finds of ancient scrolls in caves near the Dead Sea, but until the most recent discoveries were made, there was no way to piece together the contents of these writings. In several well-known ancient sources, however, there are accounts of a communal settlement on the shores of the Dead Sea, whose members were called Essenes. A comparison between the picture of the community that can be drawn from the scrolls and the descriptions of the Jewish sect offered by Josephus, Pliny, and Philo of Alexandria leaves little doubt that it was the Essenes who produced the documents we now know as the Dead Sea, or Qumran, Scrolls.

Nearly fifty years earlier, at the turn of the present century, another piece in the puzzle was discovered, although its significance was not immediately recognized. Some sectarian Jewish documents were found in a storeroom of an old synagogue in Cairo. At the time of their publication it was not clear whether they were of medieval or more ancient origin. A link with the Essenes was conjectured, but the evidence was insufficient to draw a firm conclusion. The fact that copies of the same writings —otherwise unknown—have since been found at Qumran shows that they originated with the same Jewish sect. In all likelihood, the scrolls discovered in Cairo were written by the community at

---

[25] A brief account of the excavations at the community center in Qumran is given by J. T. Milik in *Ten Years of Discovery in the Wilderness of Judaea*, trans. John Strugnell (Naperville, Ill.: Allenson, 1959).

Qumran and taken in the ninth century to Egypt by Jewish sectaries.[26]

In the eighteenth century it was proposed that Jesus had been an Essene and that his call to the renunciation of riches and to a life of devotion to the will of God was based on Essene ethics. Also noted was the similarity between the pooling of resources called for in Acts 4:32–37 and the communal life of the Essenes. In the nineteenth century Ernest Renan called Jesus a "brother" of the Essenes and spoke of Christianity as an Essenism that largely succeeded, but he stopped short of making Jesus out to have been a member of the sect. The discovery of the Dead Sea Scrolls and the clear evidence of their link with the Essenes have revived the theory of an Essene origin of Christianity. With the added details from the Dead Sea Scrolls, the hypothesis has now been made more precise.

Some journalists, noting certain possible connections between the Qumran documents and early Christianity, have leaped to the conclusion that the Dead Sea Scrolls show that the Christian account of Jesus is almost wholly fictional, that he was in fact an Essene from Qumran, whose followers invented the stories about him that we have in the gospels.[27] The pattern used by these allegedly pious fictionalizers was that of the founder of the Qumran community, the Teacher of Righteousness, who, it is asserted, was crucified and reportedly rose from the dead. The Christian account of Jesus' death and resurrection was an effort to top the Essene stories.

Scholars have long recognized that there are similarities in the organization, practices, and beliefs of the Essenes and the early Christian community.[28] The Dead Sea Scrolls have provided

---

[26] Paul Kahle, in *The Cairo Genizah* (Oxford: Blackwell, 1957), pp. 1–28, gives a full description of the probable series of circumstances that brought the scrolls from Qumran to Cairo.

[27] Hugh Schonfield, in *The Secrets of the Dead Sea Scrolls* (Cranbury, N.J.: A. S. Barnes, 1957), hints broadly at a link between the later phase of the Qumran "new covenant" community and the Christian portrait of Jesus.

[28] An older discussion, which is still valuable, is found in an appendix to J. B. Lightfoot, *Commentary on St. Paul's Epistle to the Colossians* (London: Macmillan, 1876). More recent discussions include Sherman E. Johnson,

details of the three principal areas of similarity:[29] the role of the Teacher and of Jesus, the Qumran communal meal and the Eucharist, and the Essene and early Christian radical interpretations of the Law. Although similarities can be shown, the practices and beliefs of the two communities are clearly not congruent, and claims for the direct dependence of Jesus or his followers on the Essenes—for the Christian conception of Jesus' redemptive role, for example—cannot be demonstrated conclusively.

The most telling feature against any simple identification of the Qumran community and early Christianity is the sharp difference in their attitudes toward the world. The Qumran group despaired of official Jewish institutions and of the low level of seriousness about obedience to the Law. Accordingly, they withdrew completely from society in order to live the pure life at their own retreat in the desert. Members of the group who failed to conform to the rigid standards were required to leave. Would-be members had to undergo an extended probationary period in order to demonstrate the discipline that was essential to their full participation in the community life. By contrast, Jesus and his followers were denounced by their contemporaries as friends of "publicans and sinners" (Matt. 11:19; Luke 7:34; cf. Mark 2:15–16; Matt. 15:1; Luke 18:10). Further, Jesus is reported as going outside the limits of Jewish territory in his preaching tours, and his followers spread over the Roman world inviting any who would give heed to become members of his New Covenant community. Sociologically speaking, the Qumran type of sectarianism and the Christian "sect" are categorically different in their stance toward the world, even though their respective claims to have been the recipients of divine secrets and their celebration of their unity and their hopes are similar. There is no basis, therefore, for the claims that have been made that Christianity is an Essenism

---

"The Dead Sea Manual and the Jerusalem Church of Acts," in Krister Stendahl, ed., *The Scrolls and the New Testament* (New York: Harper & Row, 1957), pp. 129–42.

[29] See, for example, H. H. Rowley, "The Qumran Sect and Christian Origins," in *From Moses to Qumran* (New York: Association Press, 1963), pp. 239–79.

and my arm was wrenched from the shoulder.
I could not move my hand,
and my foot was caught in a shackle,
and my knees were dissolved like water.
I could take neither pace nor step;
heaviness replaced my fleetness of foot;
my steps were trammeled.
My tongue was tied and protruded;
I could not lift my voice
in any articulate speech,
to revive the spirit of stumbling,
or encourage the faint with a word.
My lips were dumb altogether.[33]

There is an obvious similarity between this poignant portrayal of suffering and the allusions to the psalms of lament in the gospel accounts of Jesus on the cross, where Jesus' cry "My God, my God . . ." is a free quotation from Psalm 22. One could develop a case for the appropriateness of the anguished lyrical outcry in the Hymns of Thanksgiving for a victim of crucifixion. All that one could conclude, however, is that it is possible to link together these Qumran texts—the historical references to the persecution of the Teacher and the poetry of suffering—and to infer from them that the Teacher was crucified. But even if the Teacher was crucified, his crucifixion would not make him specifically a forerunner of Jesus. We know from the writings of Josephus and from other historical sources that many people considered enemies of the state—or of the religious status quo—were crucified during the first century B.C. Martyrdom had become so widespread that in Judaism a cult of the martyrs arose (Matt. 23:29–31). It was believed that the death of the martyrs had redemptive significance for the faithful,[34] so the death of the Teacher of Righteousness—whether by crucifixion or by another form of execution—could have been understood as the vicarious suffering of one martyr

---

[33] Gaster, *Dead Sea Scriptures*, pp. 169–70.
[34] Edward Lohse, in *Märtyrer und Gottesknecht* [Martyr and servant of God] (Göttingen: Vandenhoek & Ruprecht, 1955), has made a careful study of this theme.

among many rather than as a precise anticipation of the meaning discerned by Christians in the death of Jesus.

Object of faith. Some scholars go beyond the attempt to point out parallels between the death of the Teacher and the death of Jesus to advance the claim that the Qumran community had a doctrine of faith in the Teacher and a belief in his resurrection that directly influenced the rise of these beliefs in Christianity. The text that is usually pointed to in support of this claim is one from the Habakkuk Commentary that applies to faith in the Teacher of Righteousness the familiar phrase "The just shall live by Faith," a concept central for Paul.[35] But in the Qumran context faith means fidelity to his teachings,[36] rather than belief in his redemptive death. Indeed, there is no redemptive role assigned by the Qumran documents to the Teacher of Righteousness or to any other messianic figure. The community is called to obey faithfully the instructions of the Teacher in order to preserve their purity as the true people of God while they await the overthrow of their enemies by direct divine intervention and the establishment of the pure worship of God by the Messiah (or Messiahs) yet to come.

The closest analogy to the Qumran community's view of the Teacher is the view of Jesus in one segment of the early church as primarily a source of divine wisdom. This interpretation of Jesus is represented in the Q document, the hypothetical common source behind the gospels of Matthew and Luke. In Q there is no explicit theological meaning attached to Jesus' suffering and death, as there is in the other gospel traditions. What is significant, however, is not that there is such an analogy between the gospel tradition and a Jewish sectarian view, but that this interpretation of Jesus as the bearer of wisdom did not survive independently in the church. The Q document was combined by Luke and Matthew with the Markan gospel tradition, where the meaning of the suffering and death of Jesus was an important item of

[35] See the interpretation by Dupont-Sommer, *Essene Writings*, p. 263, esp. n. 4.
[36] Habakkuk Commentary 2:4, in Gaster, *Dead Sea Scriptures*, p. 248.

faith. Similarly, in Paul's Letter to the Corinthians Christ is portrayed as the Wisdom of God (1 Cor. 1:18–24), but Paul hastens to explain that it is in the cross of Christ that the divine wisdom is disclosed. For Qumran, however, it was not the death of the Teacher but the wisdom of the divine secrets he disclosed in his teachings that made him an object of veneration.

Dupont-Sommer tries to show that the Teacher of Righteousness was an *eschatological* figure who corresponded to the glorified Christ of the New Testament—a figure whose coming marked the start of God's victory over evil.

> And Thou, O God, hast succoured my soul
> And lifted my horn on high.
> And I will shine with a seven-fold light
> in the Eden which Thou hast made unto Thy glory.
> For Thou art an everlasting light unto me.[37]

But the translation of this passage from the Thanksgiving Hymns that is adopted by most scholars shows that the exaltation has already occurred in God's preservation of the Teacher (or the hymn writer) in the face of fierce opposition. Beginning the quotation several lines earlier brings this out more clearly:

> Thou hast raised high my horn
> over all that reviled me,
> and all who wage battle against me
> are routed without remnant,
> and all that contend with me
> are as chaff before the wind;
> and all impiety bows to my sway.
> For Thou, O my God, hast holpen my soul
> and raised high my horn.
>
> I am lit with a light sevenfold.
> and with that same lustre of glory
> which Thou didst create for Thyself.
> For Thou art unto me as a light eternal
> keeping my feet upon the way.[38]

[37] *Essene Writings*, p. 365.
[38] Gaster, *Dead Sea Scriptures*, p. 165.

From the closing lines it is evident that the light is not a halo of eschatological glory but the eternal illumination by which God guides his people into the path of obedience. The special light the Teacher receives is granted in order that he might guide others in "the way." No hint is really present in this or any other passage that men are to have faith in him as a crucified, resurrected, and exalted redemptive figure. If such details were present in the Dead Sea Scrolls, they would go a long way toward explaining how such theological views came to be associated with Jesus of Nazareth. But it is only after one has familiarized oneself with the New Testament understanding of Jesus that one can go to the Scrolls and read into them these essentially alien ideas. The single link between the death of the Teacher and the death of Jesus is the Jewish cult of the martyrs, which may have influenced the way these deaths were interpreted by the Essene and early Christian communities. No direct influence of the Qumran documents or the Essene ideas on the Christian interpretation of the cross can be shown.

Qumran Rites and Christian Sacraments

Since the discovery of the Qumran documents, scholars have also attempted to establish connections between the practices of the Qumran community and Christian sacraments, specifically Baptism and the Eucharist.

Baptism. Some scholars have theorized that John the Baptist either was an Essene or was under Essene influence; the connection, they find, is indicated particularly by the significance baptism had for him. The argument runs that since many cisterns were found among the ruins at Qumran, and since they had steps for easy ascent and descent, they must have been used as baptisteries. Since John the Baptist was carrying on baptismal activity nearby in the Jordan Valley, it is likely that he was originally associated with the Essenes and shared their understanding of baptism. Furthermore, the argument continues, at Qumran a baptism of fire was expected to cover the earth (as in the Iranian eschatology

It is not yet clear whether the Qumran community awaited only a kingly messiah (the "anointed king" of the text just quoted) or a priestly messiah as well.[52] But it is clear that the scene depicted in the ritual passage just quoted is not that of an ordinary meal; it is the procedure ordained for the End Time, when Belial and the enemies of God will be overthrown and his righteous rule established. It would seem justified, therefore, to conclude that the blessing spoken at the communal meal was an anticipation of the presence of the Messiah (or Messiahs) in the New Age, when God's will would be effected through the anointed king and anointed priest. If this is a correct interpretation of the Qumran documents, then the communal meals at Qumran seem to be related to the fellowship meals that Jesus ate with his disciples and that they continued to celebrate after his death. The disciples were convinced that Jesus would appear once more in their midst in triumph as God's anointed king—the Messiah—or perhaps as king-priest, as the Letter to the Hebrews implies.[53]

Even if a case could not be made for considering the Qumran communal meal an eschatological anticipation, and therefore a forerunner, of the Last Supper,[54] there is other evidence for a close connection between the meaning attached by Jesus to his final meal with his disciples and Jewish eschatological hopes of his day.[55] The crucial passage is Luke 22:15–16,

I have earnestly desired to eat this passover with you before I

[52] See K. G. Kuhn, "The Two Messiahs of Aaron and Israel," in Stendahl, ed., *The Scrolls and the New Testament*, pp. 54–64. A critique of this position can be found in Rowley, *From Moses to Qumran*, pp. 266–68. In the Stendahl volume, Kuhn also discusses the relationship of the Qumran eschatological meal to the early Christian Eucharist in the essay "The Lord's Supper and the Communal Meal at Qumran," pp. 65–93.

[53] The portrayal of Jesus as king and priest in Hebrews 7 has itself been pointed out as showing parallels with Qumran; see Yigael Yadin, "The Dead Sea Scrolls and the Epistle to the Hebrews," in Chaim Rabin and Yigael Yadin, eds., *Aspects of the Dead Sea Scrolls (Scripta Hierosolymitana)*, Vol. 4 (Jerusalem: Hebrew University Press, 1958), pp. 36–55.

[54] Jeremias rejects this interpretation of the Qumran scrolls and denies any link between Qumran and early Christianity on this point. See *Eucharistic Words*, pp. 31–36.

[55] *Ibid.*, pp. 207–11, 256–62.

suffer; for I tell you I shall not eat it until it is fulfilled in the kingdom of God.

Joachim Jeremias has paraphrased Jesus' words in such a way as to bring out their meaning against the background of Jewish liturgical usage of the period:

> I would very much have liked to eat this passover lamb with you before my death. (But I must deny myself this wish.) For I tell you I do not intend to eat of it again until God fulfills (his promises) in the kingdom of God . . . Take (this cup) and divide (it) among you; for I tell you I do not intend from now on to drink of the fruit of the vine until God establishes his kingdom.[56]

Without going into the complex question of the original form and earliest version of the words spoken by Jesus at the Last Supper, we can say that Jesus is here depicted—and probably with historical accuracy—as envisioning a direct link between his final meal with his disciples and the coming of God's Kingdom in the End Time. The great difference between Jesus' practice and that of the Jews of his day is that they ate the Passover meal while he pointedly abstained. Due attention has not always been given to the fact that the Jews seem to have celebrated the Passover not only as a memorial of and renewal of God's covenant with Israel at the time of the deliverance from slavery in Egypt but also as a joyous anticipation of the coming of the Messiah in the last days. Accordingly, the Jews recited antiphonally Psalm 118—a psalm that was a favorite of the early Christians and was understood to predict the coming of Jesus. It was reportedly quoted at the time of his final entry into Jerusalem (Mark 11:9 and parallels) and is quoted in connection with Jesus' parable of the Rejection of the Vineyard-Owner's Son (Mark 12:1–11). As the climax of Matthew's account of Jesus' rejection by the leaders of Judaism, Psalm 118 is explicitly quoted:

> For I tell you, you will not see me again, until you say "Blessed is he who comes in the name of the Lord." (Matt. 23:39)

[56] *Ibid.*, p. 211.

It is obvious, therefore, that the early church, if not Jesus himself, expected him to be vindicated by God at the last day in fulfillment of Psalm 118, which was sung by Jews of this period in connection with the Passover celebration as an expression of their hope in the coming of God's Messiah.

> This is the day which the Lord has made;
> > let us rejoice and be glad in it.
> Save us, we beseech thee, O Lord!
> > O Lord, we beseech thee, give us success!
> Blessed be he who enters in the name of the Lord!
> > We bless you from the house of the Lord.
> The Lord is God,
> > and he has given us light.
> Bind the festal procession with branches,
> > up to the horns of the altar!
>
> Thou art my God, and I will give thanks to thee;
> > thou art my God, I will extol thee.
>
> O give thanks to the Lord, for he is good;
> > for his steadfast love endures forever!
>
> (Ps. 118:24–29)

But the most frequently quoted text among the Christians was verse 22:[57]

> The stone which the builders rejected
> > has become the chief cornerstone.

The rejection of Jesus was therefore understood as the necessary first step toward the fulfillment of Israel's hope of the establishment of the Kingdom of God. Whether Jesus regarded his own death in the light of the prophetic saying in Psalm 118:22 cannot be determined with certainty, but there is no reason to doubt that

---

[57] On the frequency of use of this text and its importance as a theological presupposition in the early church, see C. H. Dodd, *According to the Scriptures: The Sub-Structure of New Testament Theology* (New York: Harper & Row, 1953), pp. 35–36, 99–100, *et passim*; and Barnabas Lindars, *New Testament Apologetic* (Philadelphia: Westminster, 1962), pp. 45–51.

he saw a link between the ministry he had begun and the promised day of triumph to which the Passover celebration pointed. It is not of paramount importance whether the shaping of this thought came from Qumran or from the rabbinic interpretation of the ancient Passover ceremony attested in the Midrash on the Psalms: The earliest Christians were persuaded that the rejection of Jesus, to which Jesus alluded in his word about suffering (Luke 22:15), was the divinely ordained prerequisite to the fulfillment of God's promised Kingdom. The presence of this motif in the meals at Qumran as well as in the ordinary Passover is a clear indication of the fervency of eschatological hope in Jesus' day.

Radical Interpretation of the Law at Qumran and in the Gospel Tradition

Another area of alleged contact between Jesus and Qumran has to do with the interpretation of God's demand in the Jewish Law. Although the strictness of interpretation of the Law among the better-known Jewish sect, the Pharisees, has become proverbial, the Pharisees were in fact seeking to make the Law relevant to daily life and to interpret its precepts in such a way as to take into account the changes that had occurred between Moses' day and their own. It is an unfair caricature to picture the Pharisees as heartless pedants. Indeed, the gospel tradition calls upon the followers of Jesus to surpass the Pharisees in their standards of righteousness (Matt. 5:20).[58] Apparently, the Essenes also thought that the rest of the Jews, including the Pharisees, were not sufficiently strict in preserving legal purity in their observances of the Law. Accordingly, they withdrew to the monastic life of their communal center at Qumran in order to fulfill the Law's demand for holiness. Thus the Essenes and the Christians were in agreement on the general point of radical interpretation of the Law. Specific points of agreement and disagreement are harder to show. We do know, however, that they disagreed on the question of attitude toward one's enemies. Jewish scholars in particular

---

[58] On the distinctive emphases of Matthew's gospel, see Chapter 5 and the works cited there.

have been at pains to point out that there is no passage in the Jewish Scriptures—or in the rabbinic tradition—that summons Israel to hate its enemies (Matt. 5:42). One could infer such an attitude from such utterances as Psalm 137:9 ("Happy shall he be who takes your little ones and dashes them against the rock!") and Psalm 139:21–22,

> Do I not hate them that hate thee, O Lord?
>   And do I not loathe them that rise up against thee?
> I hate them with perfect hatred;
>   I count them my enemies.

A feeling of hatred for one's enemies does not prevail in the Old Testament, however; consider, for example, the exhortations of Proverbs 25:21–22:

> If your enemy is hungry, give him bread to eat;
>   and if he is thirsty, give him water to drink;
> for you will heap coals of fire on his head,
>   and the Lord will reward you.

This compassionate attitude is quoted with approval in the New Testament (Rom. 12:20) and is wholly consonant with the message and response of Jesus to his antagonists. On the contrary, members of the community at Qumran are specifically directed to hate their enemies. Thus, on the question of attitude toward one's enemies the Christian and Qumran communities disagree.

Finally, there are important similarities and differences between Early Christian and Qumranian attitudes toward that central religious institution of Judaism: the Temple. The Essenes were waiting at Qumran until God intervened in their behalf, vindicated them, and enabled them to take over the operation of the temple cultus in what they believed to be the pure and proper manner, in keeping with their interpretation of the legal prescriptions contained in the Law of Moses. By contrast, Jesus' aggressive action in cleansing the temple (Mark 11 and parallels) is matched by his reported prediction of its destruction (Mark 13:2 and par.). The clear implication is that the temple is not an essential feature in worshiping God. That viewpoint is made explicit in the Johannine form of the tradition that true worship of God will not be localized in Jerusalem or any other sacred place (John 4:21–23). The "raising up" of the temple linked in John 2:19 with its announced destruction is directly asserted in John 2:21–22 to mean the raising up of his body—but that is probably a metaphorical reference to the raising up of the church as the real place where the worship of God is to be carried on. Both in the Markan and the Johannine versions of the Jesus tradition, therefore, no place is given to the temple of Jerusalem. On this issue, the Christian and the Qumran traditions are diametrically opposed. The universalistic outreach of the early Christian community is antithetical to the rigid exclusivism of Qumran.

SOME CONCLUSIONS ABOUT THE HISTORICAL VALUE OF THE EXTRABIBLICAL SOURCES

The limitations of the extrabiblical sources for our knowledge of Jesus are obvious. They provide us with no significant information about him that we do not have access to in the gospel accounts. But they are important in two ways. First, the Qumran materials particularly suggest the range of viewpoints among Jews at Jesus' time and the depth of their dissatisfaction with the religious establishment in Jerusalem. Even though there were many differences in detail between the Essenes and the early Christians, the community of vigorous dissenters in the Dead Sea community, who fervently awaited the coming of the New Age in which God would vindicate them, make John the Baptist and Jesus more vividly discernible against the background of contemporary Jewish life and thought. Second, these extrabiblical sources render extremely improbable the claim that Jesus is a pious fiction rather than a historical character. It is scarcely credible that Roman and Jewish writers of the first and second centuries would have perpetuated as historical record stories about an unhistorical figure whom they so patently despised. They treat him as a historical, though regrettable, personage. However much they might have wished him out of existence, they did not and could not deny his historicity.

A pressing question remains: What kind of person was he who evoked such strong and enduring reactions, both favorable and hostile? There is not sufficient evidence to write a biography of Jesus in the modern sense, not even of a segment of his public life. Of his inner psychological motivations, of the personal forces that molded his childhood and therefore shaped his adult life, we know nothing. It would be possible, of course, to extrapolate from what we know of the upbringing of Jewish boys of his epoch, but the fallacy is obvious: No one else grew up to be like him. Recognizing that as historical documents the gospels are biased and incomplete, we must nevertheless turn to them and the traditions preserved in them for detailed knowledge of Jesus.

SUGGESTIONS FOR FURTHER READING

Translations of primary historical materials for studying the background of the New Testament and of Judaism in that period are given in H. C. Kee, *The Origins of Christianity: Sources and Documents* (Englewood Cliffs, N.J.: Prentice-Hall, 1973). The Jewish documents bearing on Jesus and early Christianity are presented and analyzed by R. T. Herford in *Christianity in Talmud and Midrash* (Clifton, N.J.: Reference Library, 1966). Of fundamental value for the Jewish background of Christianity are Flavius Josephus, *Antiquities of the Jews*, especially Vols. 6–8 of the Loeb edition, trans. Ralph Marcus, Allen Wikgren, L. H. Feldman (Cambridge, Mass.: Harvard University Press), and the massive collection of noncanonical Jewish materials, *The Apocrypha and Pseudepigrapha of the Old Testament*, ed. R. H. Charles (Oxford: Clarendon, 1913; reprinted 1963). Two useful collections of translations of the major documents from the Dead Sea community are T. H. Gaster, *The Dead Sea Scriptures** (New York: Doubleday, 1956), and André Dupont-Sommer, *The Essene Writings from Qumran** (Cleveland: Meridian, 1962). Perceptive and learned assessments of the Scrolls are by F. M. Cross, Jr., *The Ancient Library of Qumran,** 2nd ed. (New York: Doubleday, 1958), and Matthew Black, *The Scrolls and Christian Origins* (New York: Scribner's, 1961).

* *Available in a paperback edition.*

Jesus as God's Eschatological Messenger: The Q Document

Probably the first written material concerning Jesus was a collection of his sayings known to modern scholars as Q. Apparently, some unknown Christian or group of Christians brought together traditions attributed to Jesus, consisting mostly of his sayings. The order in which these traditions were arranged was topical rather than chronological, except that the traditions about the baptism came at the beginning and the clearest predictions of the End of the Age came at the end. There was only one narrative account of the miracle story type—a healing—and no mention was made of the passion. Not only are we in the dark about the identity of the author or authors, but we are not even sure about the precise extent of the work, since we do not have a single copy. Some scholars deny that it ever existed.[1] However, the weight of evidence points to the existence of such a writing; this theory accounts most plausibly for the fact that Matthew and Luke have common material, which seems to have been drawn from a single written source, since the common passages are often verbatim, or nearly so, and are frequently presented in the same sequence. Called Q possibly from the German word for

[1] Typical is the essay by Austin Farrer, "On Dispensing with Q," in D. E. Nineham, ed., *Studies in the Gospels* (Naperville, Ill.: Allenson, 1957), pp. 55–88.

"source," *Quelle*,[2] this document, a collection of sayings or perhaps a strand of gospel tradition preserved in a series of short writings, is sufficiently different from Mark and so influential on the content of Matthew and Luke that it deserves to be given detailed treatment as a major factor in preserving traditions about Jesus and in shaping some of the images of him that are found in the New Testament.

THE SAYINGS SOURCE BEHIND MATTHEW AND LUKE

Until Johann Gottfried Eichhorn[3] hypothesized at the beginning of the nineteenth century that Matthew and Luke had utilized a common source, many scholars had assumed that the gospel of Mark was an abridgment of Matthew and that Matthew was the oldest of the gospels. Eichhorn's hypothesis changed their thinking, although his theory that Matthew and Luke used multiple Aramaic sources never gained wide acceptance.[4] Now attempts to prove that Mark and Luke were dependent on Matthew fail to convince any but a handful of scholars.[5] The evidence points

[2] See the discussion of the origin of this term in C. F. D. Moule, *The Birth of the New Testament* (New York: Harper & Row, 1962), p. 84, n. 1.

[3] *Einleitung in das Neue Testament* [Introduction to the New Testament], 3 vols. (Leipzig: Weidmann'sche Buchhandlung, 1810–20).

[4] See the excerpts from (and critique of) Eichhorn in W. G. Kümmel, *The New Testament: The History of the Investigation of Its Problems*, trans. S. M. Gilmour and H. C. Kee (Nashville: Abingdon, 1972), pp. 77–79.

[5] The most recent full-scale discussion of the problem is in W. G. Kümmel, *Introduction to the New Testament*, trans. H. C. Kee (Nashville: Abingdon, 1975), pp. 62–76. W. R. Farmer, in *The Synoptic Problem* (New York: Macmillan, 1964), tries to discredit the theory that Mark is the common element behind the three synoptic gospels by exposing the fallacy in the argument of such scholars as H. J. Holtzmann (see Chapter 1) that Mark's gospel is historically accurate because it was literarily prior. While his criticism of the assumption made by Holtzmann and others is valid, it is not reasonable to deduce from their misuse of the theory of Markan priority that the theory itself is wrong. What Farmer has shown is that any purely literary source theory is inadequate to explain the differences among the first three

rather to the priority of Mark, as a detailed comparison of Mark with Matthew and Luke shows. In many instances Matthew and Luke smooth out the grammar or substitute more felicitous terms for awkward expressions in Mark. Examples are Mark 1:12 = Luke 4:1 and Mark 2:1–12 = Matthew 9:1–8. In the first of these passages Jesus is "led" into the wilderness by the Spirit (Luke) rather than "cast out" or "hurled" there (Mark). In the second passage Mark tells a story, filled with authentic Palestinian local color, about four friends digging through the earthen roof of a village house in order to lower their friend down in front of Jesus. Mark's version is recounted as follows:

> And when he [Jesus] returned to Capernaum after some days, it was reported that he was at home. And many were gathered together, so that there was no longer room for them, not even about the door. . . . And they came, bringing to him a paralytic carried by four men. And when they could not get near him because of the crowd, they removed the roof above him; and when they had made an opening, they let down the pallet on which the paralytic lay. (Mark 2:1–4)

All the details of a small Palestinian village are taken for granted in the narrative: Roofs are made of beaten earth and can be dug through in an emergency; people sleep on pallets, which are as portable and as flexible as quilts; houses have a single entrance and are so small that even a modest gathering in and around the house would make access impossible for four men carrying another on a pallet. Luke, who is unfamiliar with earthen-roofed houses, describes the removal of the roof tiles (5:19). Since he assumes that people sleep only on beds, he reports the awkward process of lowering a bed through an opening made in the tiled roof. Matthew (9:2) omits all the details, relating prosaically that "they" brought a paralytic to Jesus, lying on a "bed."

It is scarcely conceivable that an early Christian writer,

---

gospels. To provide a more nearly adequate explanation, one must use the very methods Farmer avoids: form-critical and redactional studies of the individual gospel writers (see Chapter 1), which are the approaches employed in the present book.

whose aim would be to give his gospel as wide an appeal as possible, would embellish a smooth narrative to make it sound more primitive and Palestinian; on the contrary, he would even out awkward turns of speech and eliminate local references.

Although we may thus assume that Matthew and Luke used Mark as a basic source—between them they reproduce nearly all of Mark, and they almost always follow Mark's sequence[6]—Mark does not account for all the material in Matthew and Luke. There is considerable material that is peculiar to one or the other of the gospels,[7] and more than one-third of Matthew and one-fourth of Luke consist of common material that is not found in Mark. This common material is characterized by a high degree of verbal similarity and by a close correspondence in order, from the baptismal sayings through the Beatitudes to the final eschatological sayings. Remembering that the preliterary language of the tradition would have been Aramaic rather than the Greek of the gospels, we can best account for the verbal similarity by postulating Matthew and Luke's use of a single Greek source. And both the verbal similarity and the similarity in the order of the sayings suggest that the source was written. It seems unlikely that Matthew and Luke would overlap so much or that they would contain so much non-Markan material if, as some scholars maintain, Q were only an oral tradition that served as the main source for all the sayings materials found in Matthew and Luke,[8] or if, as

[6] Most departures from Mark's order are in Matthew, and as we shall see in Chapter 5, pp. 169–71, these shifts result from Matthew's arrangement of his material in alternating blocks of action and discourse. See the chart of this material in W. G. Kümmel, *Introduction*, pp. 65–66. J. B. Tyson concludes from a recent exhaustive study of sequence of material in the gospels that "the study of sequential parallelism will not dictate any one solution to the synoptic problem (*New Testament Studies* 22 [1976]: 276–308, 298). But he acknowledges that either Matthew or Luke supports Mark's sequence in nearly every instance, and that even in Q material there is strict agreement or at least relative agreement on order. Mark's failure to use some thirty pericopes common to Matthew and Luke cannot be explained if Mark used Matthew. The most plausible hypothesis remains: Mark and Q are the primary sources for Matthew and Luke.

[7] See pp. 151–54, for Matthew's special sources; for Luke's, see pp. 173–76.

[8] This is the viewpoint taken by T. R. Rosché, "The Words of Jesus and the Future of the Q Hypothesis," *Journal of Biblical Literature*, Vol. 79 (1960), pp. 210–20.

others propose, Q contained the sayings materials found in Mark as well as in Matthew and Luke.[9]

The Nature and Original Extent of Q

Apart from two brief narrative sections (4:2b–12; 7:2–3, 6–10), Q seems to have consisted almost entirely of sayings of Jesus (and John the Baptist). There is no evidence that it included a narrative of the passion and death of Jesus. That is to say, there are no non-Markan materials common to Matthew and Luke that offer information concerning Jesus' trial and death. Rather, when Matthew or Luke chooses to supplement the Markan account of the passion, each does so independently and then returns to the Markan order and substance. Neither are there any allusions to the passion of Jesus in the Q material; the predictions of the passion in Matthew and Luke are either taken over from Mark or are peculiar to one or the other gospel.

Thus, nothing points to there having been a passion story in Q. But since we know that our oldest gospel, Mark, has a passion narrative as a central feature, is it conceivable that the early church could have had a document from which this element was missing? This question leads directly to another: Are there documents of first-century Judaism or earlier that consisted entirely of sayings, and that might have served as models or as precedents for Q?

The theory has been advanced that there was such a literary type, called by the proponents of the hypothesis Sayings of a Wise Man.[10] But in the extensive wisdom literature of Judaism there is nothing that really resembles the Q material. Analogies have been drawn with such documents from the later Jewish wisdom writings as the Wisdom of Solomon and with Sirach (or Ben Sira; also known as Ecclesiasticus). There are some points of similarity—such as that Wisdom is pictured as seeking lodging (Sir. 24:7) and as demanding discipline from those who follow

---

[9] For example, F. C. Grant, *The Gospels: Their Origin and Growth* (New York: Harper & Row, 1957), pp. 108–09.

[10] J. M. Robinson, "Logoi Sophon: On the Gattung of Q," in *Trajectories through Early Christianity* (Philadelphia: Fortress, 1971), pp. 71–113.

her (Sir. 2:5; 6:20–21)—but the entire outlook of these wisdom books is sharply different from that of Q. From them, wisdom is a matter of obedience to the Law of Moses (Sir. 6:30), and is to be acquired by those who seek out good teachers (Sir. 6:36). Ben Sira focuses on making the most of life, avoiding excess, eschewing pride or dishonesty. Some of the exhortations are as trivial as the contemporary cliché, "Have a good day!" (Sir. 14:14). By contrast, the response to Jesus is determinative of one's eternal destiny. Judgment turns on one's allegiance and fidelity to the words and works that Jesus has commissioned his followers to fulfill. Far from telling them to set their sights low, as Ben Sira does (11:10), or to avoid doing good deeds to strangers or sinners (Sir. 11:29, 34; 12:4), Jesus is quoted in Q as urging his followers to give up every human tie and obligation in devotion to the announcement of the Kingdom (Luke 9:59–61; 12:22–31). And in Luke 7:34 he is described as "a glutton and a drunkard, a friend of tax collectors and sinners"—scarcely an abstemious life-style of the kind enjoined in Sirach. Both Sirach, with its description of the cosmos as constructed from pairs of opposites (42:24), and Wisdom of Solomon, with its depiction of Wisdom as an emanation from God (7:25) in abstract terms drawn from Hellenistic philosophy (7:22–23), move in an atmosphere of abstract ontological speculation that bespeaks an intellectual climate wholly other than that of Q.

It is true that elements of the late Jewish wisdom tradition have influenced Q: that is explicit in Luke 11:49 and 7:35. But wisdom was not the monopoly of a single group in Judaism in the time of Jesus. The close link between wisdom and the role of the prophets in Q is an important indicator that what is being disclosed is not legal or practical wisdom (as in Sirach and Wisdom of Solomon) but eschatological wisdom of an apocalyptic type. Fundamental to all apocalypticism is the self-consciousness of a community that is experiencing rejection and persecution from its contemporaries, but is sustained by its sense of God's favor, both now and in the age to come, when he will act in their behalf to judge the wicked and vindicate them. It is precisely this view of life that is embodied in the Q document. It has its closest approximation in a Jewish setting in the group that lies behind Daniel, Jubilees, and the Enoch literature. But contrary to the point of view expressed in these writings, membership in the community of Q is not restricted to those who obey the Law more rigorously than their Jewish contemporaries, but is open to all—Jews and Gentiles—who recognize in Jesus God's final agent and who discern in his words, in his works, and in the community he has convened the inbreaking of the Rule of God (Luke 11:20, 29–32). They are the ones whose fortunes will be reversed in the Age to Come, and who will share the rule with God's Agent in the New Age (Luke 22:28–30). It is this knowledge of God's purpose, esoteric in essence and yet evangelistic in thrust, that constitutes the wisdom set forth in Q (Luke 10:21–22).

Old Testament scholars have rightly drawn attention to the continuity between the later prophetic tradition (Daniel, Enoch, and Jubilees, for example) and apocalyptic portraits of the End of the Age.[11] Yet Gerhard von Rad is nevertheless accurate in his assertion that the apocalyptic world view is most closely akin to the wisdom tradition. More specifically, Martin Hengel has shown that such apocalyptic features and doctrines as the successive ages of the world, the portrayal of empires as giant statues, the influence of astrology and star speculation, are all akin to Hellenistic thinking. Ironically, apocalypticism gives direct evidence of the impact of Hellenism on Judaism, even though the conscious aim of the apocalyptists was to defend the true People of God against enforced Hellenization.[12] What differentiates the apocalyptic outlook from that of Jewish wisdom in its speculative and legal forms is not that one is influenced by Hellenism and the other is not, but that the apocalyptist has given up on this world and looks beyond present suffering and persecution to vindication in the near future. The main stream of wisdom literature wants to encourage obedience to the Law so that life will be as full and rewarding as possible; beyond that there is expectation either of no survival after death (Sir. 17:27–28) or of the escape from this world of a disembodied soul (Wisd. of Sol. 3:1–4).

[11] So Paul D. Hanson, *The Dawn of Apocalyptic* (Philadelphia: Fortress, 1975).

[12] Martin Hengel, *Judaism and Hellenism*, 2 vols. (Philadelphia: Fortress, 1974), I:180–96.

Imbued with the apocalyptic world view, the members of the community of Q believe they have been summoned and commissioned to carry forward Jesus' ministry (Luke 7:22–23; 10:1–16, 21–22); meanwhile they can expect the same mixed reception accorded him (10:16). Rejection and martyrdom is the fate suffered by God's prophets and emissaries down through history (Luke 13:34–35).

The closest historical analogy we have for the itinerant charismatic preachers pictured in Q (Luke 10:1–20) is that of the prophetic-revolutionary leaders whom Josephus describes as rousing the people in the years just before the Jewish revolt of A.D. 66–70.[13] There are some similarities to the Cynic-Stoic traveling teacher-preachers of the Hellenistic world, as well.[14] Yet Q pictures Jesus as different from either of these groups, in that there is no nationalism in his message and that the charisma he possesses and conveys to his followers does not point to their inner divine nature but to the imminent manifestation of God's judgment of the wicked and vindication of his own people. In the service of the Son of Man and the Kingdom of God, his messengers have abandoned home, family and every human security. That they have done so is an indicator—not of legal or practical wisdom—but of God's revelation of his eschatological purpose.

The Date of Q

The date for Q can no more be fixed precisely than can its extent, but a likely date is about 50. That would be long before Matthew (which is usually dated about 80) and before Mark (probably just before 70), since Q seems to know nothing of the more nearly sequential account of Jesus' career as found in that earliest gospel. Since Q is independent of Mark in both form and content, however, there may be no warrant in proposing relative dates for the two documents. Clearly, however, the gospels of Matthew and Luke were constructed on the basis of Mark as well as Q, and hence were written later than Mark.

[13] Josephus, *Jewish Wars*, Loeb edition, vol. 2, trans. H. St. John Thackeray (New York: Putnam's, 1927), pp. 254–63.
[14] Martin Hengel, *Nachfolge und Charisma* [*Discipleship and Charisma*] (Berlin: Töpelmann, 1968).

A Formal Classification of Q Material

The material included in Q can be classified by form. Assuming that it was preserved originally—or created—in short units (called pericopes by the form critics), Q must have been merely a loosely arranged series of these units. No scheme of classification can be precise, since much of the tradition could be placed under two or more categories; but the following set of formal distinctions may be useful:

Narratives	Na
Parables	Pa
Oracles	Or
Beatitudes	Be
Prophetic Pronouncements	PP
Wisdom Words	WW
Exhortations	Ex

Included under the category of "prophetic pronouncements" are eschatological promises, eschatological correlatives ("as it was . . . so shall it be"),[15] and the formalized pronouncements ("if anyone . . ."; or "whoever does . . .").[16] The remarkable feature of this material is that even those traditions classified as wisdom words and exhortations are strongly eschatological in intention, and bear on the responsibilities of those who take part in the ministry of the kingdom launched by Jesus and about to be culminated. The Q material is permeated by eschatological concerns and outlook, therefore.

Although any reconstruction of Q is hypothetical, the following material appears to have been drawn from a sayings source common to Matthew and Luke (references are to the Lukan version).

[15] Coined by R. A. Edwards to designate the four Q pericopes (Luke 11:30; 17:24, 26, 28–30) where there is an explicit comparison between a situation in the present and the time of eschatological fulfillment.

[16] Called by Ernst Käsemann "Sentences of Holy Law" in an essay translated by W. J. Montague and published in Käsemann, New Testament Questions for Today (Philadelphia: Fortress, 1969), pp. 66–81.

PP	3:7–9, 16b–17	John's Eschatological Preaching
Na	4:2b–12	Jesus' Struggle with Satan
Be	6:20–23	Beatitudes: the Poor, the Hungry, the Hated
WW	6:27–36	Promised Reward for Love and Forgiveness
WW	6:37–42	Rewards of Discipleship
Pa	6:43–46	Parables of Moral Productivity
Pa	6:47–49	Discipleship Must Survive Testing: Parable of the House With and Without Foundation
Na	7:2–3, 6–10	Healing of the Centurion's Slave
PP	7:18–23	Response to John the Baptist's Question
PP	7:24–35	John's Place in God's Plan
PP	9:57–58 (–62?)	Leave Behind Home and Family
PP	10:2–12	Disciples Commissioned to Extend Jesus' Work
Or	10:13–15	Doom on Unrepentant Cities
PP	10:16	Disciples Share in Jesus' Rejection
PP	10:21–22	God's Gift of Wisdom to His Own
Be	10:23–24	Beatitude: Those to Whom Wisdom Is Granted
Ex	11:2–4	Prayer for the Coming of God's Kingdom
WW	11:9–13	God Answers the Prayers of His Own
PP	11:14–20	Jesus' Defeat of Demons as a Sign of the Kingdom
Or	11:24–26	The Return of the Unclean Spirit
PP	11:29b–32	The Sign of Jonah and the One Greater Than Jonah: Jesus as Prophet and Wise Man
Pa	11:33–36	Parabolic Words of Light and Darkness

Or	11:39–40, 42–43	Woes to the Pharisees
Or	11:46–48, 52	Woes to the Lawyers
PP	11:49–51	Wisdom Predicts the Martyrdom of Prophets and Apostles
PP	12:2–3	What Is Hidden Will Be Revealed
Or	12:4–5	Do Not Fear Martyrdom
Pa	12:6–7	Parable of God's Care
PP	12:8–10	Confirmation of Confession/Denial of Son of Man
PP	12:11–12	God's Support of the Persecuted
Pa	12:22–31	Freedom from Anxiety about Earthly Needs
Pa	12:33–34	Freedom from Possessions
Pa	12:39–40	Parable of Preparedness: The Returning Householder
Pa	12:42–46	Parable of the Faithful Steward
PP	12:51–53	Jesus as the Agent of Crises
Pa	12:54–56	Signs of the Impending End of the Age
Pa	12:57–59	Parable of Preparedness for the Judgment
Pa	13:20–21	Parable of the Leaven
WW	13:24	Difficulty in Entering the Kingdom
Pa	13:25–29	Parable of Exclusion from the Kingdom
PP	13:34–35	The Rejection of the Prophets and the Vindication of God's Agent
Pa	14:16–23	Parable of the Eschatological Banquet
PP	14:26–27	Jesus Shatters Domestic Ties, Summons Disciples to Bear the Cross
Pa	15:4–7	The Joyous Shepherd
WW	16:13	Inevitable Choice between Masters
PP	16:16	The End of the Old Era and the New Age Proclaimed

WW	16:17	Confidence in God's Promise
Ex	17:3–4	Forgiveness within the Community
Ex	17:5–6	Faith within the Community
Or	17:23–37	Sudden Judgment to Fall
Pa	19:12–13, 15–26	Parable of the Returning Nobleman and Rewards for Fidelity
PP	22:28–30	The Promise to the Faithful of Sharing in the Rule of God

The Thematic Interests of Q

If we attempt to classify the Q pericopes according to their central interests, rather than their formal characteristics, the results serve only to confirm the picture of the document as thoroughly eschatological. Even material that is hortatory in form is set in the context of eschatological expectation or judgment. There are four main emphases in Q; we shall see how the units of tradition incorporated in the document group themselves under these categories. Again, all references are to Luke.

1   DISCIPLESHIP: ITS PRIVILEGES AND TRIALS

6:20–49	The blessedness and obligations of discipleship
9:57–62	Break with home and family for the sake of the Kingdom
10:2–20	Participation in proclaiming the Kingdom in word and act
10:21–23	God's special revelation of his purpose
11:2–13	God will sustain his people and give them the Kingdom
12:51–53	Jesus the divider of households
14:16–24	Those included and those excluded from the messianic banquet
14:26–27	Discipleship shatters ordinary human relationships
16:13	The demands of discipleship

17:3–6	Forgiveness and faith: essentials for community life

2   THE PROPHET AS GOD'S MESSENGER

3:7–9, 16–17	John the Baptist as forerunner of Jesus and prophet of doom
11:49–51	The fate of the prophet and of his emissaries
12:2–3	The promise of revelation of God's purpose
12:4–10, 11–12, 42–46	God's care for and vindication of his messengers
13:34–35	Jerusalem's rejection and martyrdom of the prophets
16:16–17	John as boundary of the Old Age; God's word is sure

3   REPENTANCE OR JUDGMENT

11:33–36	Warning about darkness and light
11:39–48, 52	Woes against the religious leaders of Judaism
12:54–59 13:14–29	Prepare for the impending judgment
17:23–30, 35, 37	Judgment will be inescapable when it falls
19:12–13, 15–26	Reward for the faithful, but punishment for those lacking ambition, perseverance

4   JESUS AS REVEALER AND AGENT OF GOD'S RULE

4:2b–12	Jesus' successful struggle with the Devil
7:18–35	Jesus as agent of liberation: greater than John
10:24	Jesus as Son, agent of revelation
11:14–22	Jesus as agent of God's Kingdom
13:20–21	Leaven at work now
15:4–7	God's joy at reconciliation of a sinner
22:28–30	God grants the share in the Kingdom to those for whom it has been covenanted and who have endured the trials

It is obvious that one significant element is missing from this list: The passion story plays no role at all. (See above, page 76.) The focus falls instead on Jesus' signs (although only one is actually described); indeed, Q makes even clearer than Mark how the healings and exorcisms are related to the coming of the Kingdom of God. There are no predictions of the suffering of the Son of Man,[17] as there are in Mark; "Son of man" is prominent as a self-designation for Jesus in his earthly ministry (for example, in Luke 9:57–58) and as the title for the One whose coming is awaited at the End of the Age (Luke 17:22–37).

Q'S NARRATIVE MATERIAL

When we organize the Q material according to thematic interests, only the story of the Centurion's Servant fails to fit under any category. If it is regarded as a kind of parable, then the faith of the Gentile and the healing result are a paradigm of the faith of other Gentiles who find in Jesus the liberating, restoring powers of the New Age. That is the main point of this particular healing story: Jesus found in a Gentile faith such as he had not encountered "in Israel" (Matt. 8:5 = Luke 7:9). Similar interest in the Gentiles is expressed in the Q version of the preaching of John the Baptist: John is reported to have rejected the notion that Jews have some special claim to be children of God by virtue of their descent from Abraham, saying God is able to raise up "from these stones [the Gentiles]" a new posterity for Abraham—that is, a true community of the faithful (Matt. 3:9 = Luke 3:8). Still another indication of the special interest of Q in the outreach of Jesus to Gentiles is given in the Parable of the Great Supper, which is preserved in something closer to its original form in Luke's version (14:16–23). This parable suggests that the gospel

[17] The capitalized version of this designation for Jesus is used throughout except in quotations from Scripture, which preserve the RSV lower-case style for "man."

invitation first went out to Israel, which rejected it. Now it is extended to the Gentiles, that is to those "out in the highways and the hedges" (Luke 14:23).

The healing story is the only passage in Q that contains geographical or sequential hints, with the possible exception of two other pericopes. One of these is the pericope of the lament over Jerusalem (Luke 13:34–35 = Matt. 23:37–39), but even in this case Q obviously does not preserve an exact recollection of the time and location of this saying, since Matthew locates it in Jerusalem just prior to the apocalyptic discourse, whereas Luke places it immediately after Jesus' announcement in Galilee of his intention to go to Jerusalem (Luke 13:31–33). The other inference about the locale of Jesus' ministry can be drawn from Luke 10:13–15 (= Matt. 11:21–23), where the cities of Chorazin and Bethsaida, in addition to Capernaum, are mentioned as the scene of Jesus' miracles. Valuable as these place names are, they tell us nothing about the course of Jesus' public ministry.

There seems to be complete justification, therefore, for taking up the Q material by topics rather than trying to impose a logical or chronological sequence upon it. The topical arrangement of Q material implies a quite different understanding of Jesus' place in history from that found in Mark, where the "necessary" sequence of events unfolds according to an apocalyptic scheme. For Q, it is sufficient to contrast the present as the hour of decision concerning Jesus with the future as the hour of God's vindication of Jesus and his people.

Q'S PARENETIC MATERIAL

The saying about serving two masters (Luke 16:13 = Matt. 6:24) belongs to the straight parenetic tradition preserved in Q. The saying turns on the idea of devoted service: Man cannot devote himself wholly to the pursuit of wealth (mammon) and at the same time to the service of God. (An interesting variant of this teaching is found in the gospel of Thomas, where, however, there are two sets of comparisons.) The force of the Q pericope is identical with that of many other sayings of Jesus, with their demand for unconditional devotion to doing God's work. The question of the disciple's eschatological destiny is not even hinted at here, as it is in most Q pericopes.

In Luke 11:34–35 there is a pair of sayings about light, preserved in a longer series of sayings that have in common the image of light (11:33–36). The force of the Q pericope seems to be a warning to the disciple to take care that his eye be sound—that is, that he be able to discern the truth accurately. Otherwise, although he thinks that he "sees" the truth, his whole being ("body") will be filled with darkness. Again, there is only a solemn reminder about the present obligation, rather than any promise or prediction about the future. The same is true for the sayings on forgiveness and faith (Luke 17:3–6) that Luke linked or found linked in the Q source (Matthew distributed them in three different contexts: 18:15; 18:21–22; 17:20). An appeal to be willing to forgive repeatedly is followed by a challenge to have unlimited faith. In Matthew's version great faith can move mountains; in Luke's it can transplant trees into the sea. Both forms of the saying are hyperbole to emphasize that true faith is not limited to what may reasonably be expected to occur. Other variants of this saying on faith are found in Matthew 21:21 and Mark 11:22–23. Here also there is no suggestion of eschatological concern or motivation. In all the other Q material, however, the eschatological dimension is central.

Q'S ESCHATOLOGICAL MATERIAL

In Q, form and function converge on eschatological concerns, as becomes even more evident when the texts are analyzed in some detail. In the following survey, the material is grouped according to subject matter.

Eschatological Warning

The theme of eschatological warning is heard in what was probably the opening passage of Q, the preaching of John the Baptist as reported in the non-Markan version. In contrast to Mark, where the stress falls on the action and appearance of John (1:4–6), Q presents a summary of the content of John's preaching. Its theme is primarily that of judgment. John denounces his hearers as a "brood of vipers," whose eagerness to escape the divine judgment must be matched by a willingness (1) to repent and (2) to demonstrate their repentant attitude by appropriate works. Their prideful boast in Abraham as their progenitor is meaningless, since God is able to create a new covenant people, presumably to replace the disobedient sons of Abraham. There is not a moment to spare, John warns: God's axe is on the point of cutting down all the unfruitful trees. Only those men whose good works reveal a penitent heart will be spared when the wrath of God falls, or to use the figure of Luke 3:16, when the baptism of fire occurs. The useful grain will be gathered, but the chaff will be consumed in the fiery judgment. On this most solemn note, the Q document begins its portrayal of Jesus' ministry, explaining only at a later point (Luke 7:24–35) the relationship between Jesus and John.

The theme of judgment continues in Luke 6:37–42 (= Matt. 7:1–5; 10:24–25; 15:14). The first of the sayings included in this grouping might seem initially to be a general statement advising men not to judge one another: "Judge not, and you will not be judged." But it has been widely recognized by biblical scholars that in late Judaism a verb in the passive voice ("be judged") with no agent expressed conceals an oblique reference to God,[18] so the meaning intended is: "Do not judge others and God will not judge you." What at first glance might seem to be the simple turnabout-is-fair-play principle is actually a major theme of the teaching of Jesus as presented in the gospel tradition: Unless a man is prepared to forgive others, God will not

[18] This construction is discussed in F. W. Blass and Albert Debrunner, *A Greek Grammar of the New Testament and Other Early Christian Literature*, rev. ed., trans. R. W. Funk (Chicago: University of Chicago Press, 1961), paragraphs 130.1, 342.1.

forgive him on the Day of Judgment. The positive side of this view is set forth in Luke 6:38, where the promise is given that those who live generously will be rewarded generously by God in the day of divine reckoning, which is referred to indirectly in the phrase "it will be given to you" (that is, by God).

The saying about the blind leading the blind (Luke 6:39) could be understood as an allusion to man's eschatological fate based on the image of falling into a pit, but the remaining sayings of this group from Q are more general in their moral appeal for humility in the relationship of disciple to teacher and of brother to brother. As is characteristic of the teaching of Jesus in the synoptic tradition, humility is not an abstract quality to be emulated but a concrete way of acting in relation to others. The fact that Q places these sayings in conjunction with the eschatological warning about judgment gives them an urgency that a string of general moral appeals would lack.

A more distinctive emphasis in Q is evident in the pericope announcing judgment on the cities of Galilee that have failed to repent even though Jesus has performed "mighty works" in them (Luke 10:13–15 = Matt. 11:21–23). A contrast is offered between them and Tyre and Sidon, pagan cities from which repentance would surely have come had they been allowed to witness God's mighty acts performed through Jesus. The miracles of Jesus, described here as "powers," are understood to be eschatological signs that attest to the crucial role of Jesus in God's preparing men for the consummation of the present age and the coming of God's Kingdom. The saying in Luke 10:15 addressed to Capernaum, which seems to have served Jesus as a base of operations after his rejection in Nazareth, recalls the oracle in Isaiah 14, in which the doom of Satan is foretold. The title Day Star, Son of Dawn, originally used for a Canaanite deity, is used in Isaiah 14:12 for the king of Babylon, who with the king of Tyre was understood in later Judaism to represent Satan, the Adversary. In this oracle he is reminded that although he aspired to set his throne above that of God and to make himself like the Most High, he will be brought down "to the depths of the Pit" (Isa. 14:15). By implication, the indifference and self-satisfaction that the cities of Galilee showed Jesus are for the Q tradition signs of satanic opposition, not merely of human negligence. The conflict in which Jesus is engaged, therefore, is cosmic and not merely human in origin. God will vindicate Jesus' works on the Judgment Day, when those who refused to be moved by his appeal will be doomed.

The woes on the Pharisees (Luke 11:39-52 = Matt. 23:25-36, with some additions and shifts in order) begin with an attack on the hypocrisy with which the Jewish laws of cleanliness are observed. The reader senses that by the time Q recorded these sayings they were already being interpreted in an allegorical way to refer to the necessity of a clean heart as contrasted with a mere appearance of piety. Equally hypocritical is the Pharisees' preoccupation with the minutiae of religion, such as tithing herbs, which has crowded out concern for such fundamental matters as love and justice. After exposing the discrepancy between the Pharisees' outer show of piety and inner lack of devotion, Jesus attacks directly those who have not only failed to hear God's message through the prophets but also shared in murdering these men sent by God. The two specific murders mentioned in Luke 11:51, those of Abel and Zechariah, are probably intended to encompass the whole span of the history of Israel, from the first murder recorded in the first book of the Hebrew Bible, Genesis, to the last murder in the last book of the canon, 2 Chronicles.[19] That is, the Q tradition affirms that throughout their history those who have called themselves God's people have consistently rejected God's messengers. This is as close as Q comes to an interpretation of the passion of Jesus, which is apparently to be understood as the ultimate rejection of God's final messenger, and therefore as the occasion for the outpouring of God's judgment on his unrepentant people. If we take Matthew's version of this passage to preserve more faithfully the original form of Q, the picture is even clearer:

---

[19] On the problem of the identity of Zechariah, which has been much debated since early Christian times, see the concise discussion by T. W. Manson, "The Sayings of Jesus," in H. D. Major, T. W. Manson, and C. J. Wright, *The Mission and Message of Jesus* (New York: E. P. Dutton, 1938; reissued separately, London: SCM Press, 1949), pp. 103–05.

Therefore I send you prophets and wise men . . .[20] some of whom you will kill and crucify, and some you will scourge in your synagogues and persecute from town to town, that upon you may come all the righteous blood shed on earth, from the blood of innocent Abel to the blood of Zechariah the son of Barachiah, whom you murdered between the sanctuary and the altar. Truly, I say to you, all this will come upon this generation. Matt. 23:34–36)

Jesus has come as a prophet and wise man,[21] and his followers carry on the eschatological ministry that he launched. But he and they are subject to martyrdom. Their vindication will come in the divine judgment that is to fall "upon this generation."

Three vivid images of conflict are brought together in Luke's version of a Q saying about the fulfillment of Jesus' mission: fire, baptism, and sword (Luke 12:49–53). The fire is the symbol of eschatological judgment, to which Jesus' words point explicitly throughout Q in nonmetaphorical language. The baptism is an apparent allusion to his suffering and death, as it is in the Markan saying (10:39), where in a mixed metaphor Jesus is said to have pointed to his own impending passion under the figures of "drinking the cup" of divinely ordained suffering and undergoing the "baptism" of messianic woes. The division that Jesus' ministry effects will cause rifts in families, setting parents against children and vice versa. Given the fact that in Jewish households the solidarity of the family is the foundation of psychological and sociological stability, the familial disruptions predicted here are catastrophic, though they might not seem so in our day of family tensions and "the generation gap." The conflict foreseen here is an inevitable, even necessary, stage in the final, wrenching struggle that will bring to an end the old age and inaugurate the new.

The obtuseness of Jesus' generation is indicated in his scathing observation that they can predict the next day's weather, but they cannot discern the infinitely more significant change that is

[20] The term "scribe," a characteristic of Matthew's own reworking of the tradition, has been omitted. See pp. 157–60.
[21] See pp. 105–06 and 111–16 for discussion of Q's view of Jesus' role as revealer. Cf. also J. M. Robinson, "Logoi Sophon," in *Trajectories*, and M. J. Suggs, *Wisdom, Christology and Law in Matthew* (Cambridge, Mass.: Harvard University Press, 1970), pp. 31–61.

taking place through Jesus: the inbreaking of the Kingdom of God
(Luke 12:54–56). Preoccupied with workaday affairs, they are
more concerned about the rain clouds blowing in off the Mediterranean and the searing winds from the desert to the southeast
than they are about the breakup of the present order implicit in
the words and works of Jesus.

The advice about bribing your accuser before he can take
you to court (Luke 12:57–59) is intended not as moral counsel
but as a parabolic warning to Jesus' hearers that they are about
to stand before God's judgment throne. The point is this: If an
admittedly guilty man being dragged to justice by his victim has
the foresight to meet his crisis situation, how much more should
Jesus' hearers prepare themselves for the eschatological crisis that
is about to befall them.[22]

A series of sayings that have in common the figure of "enter-
ing in," that is, into the Kingdom of God, is given by Luke in
what is probably the Q form and order (Luke 13:24–29), although the sayings have been scattered by Matthew (7:14; 25:10–
12; 7:22–23; 8:11). Matthew's version of the first of these has
been accommodated to the familiar Jewish teaching about the
two ways, and therefore has taken on the character of a general
moral injunction to seek the less-traveled way of righteousness.
But Luke preserves the saying with an eschatological force that is
more likely original: Engage in the struggle that enables you to
enter into the life of the Age to Come. Not many will be able to
enter. Immediately following (Luke 13:25–29) is the short parable of the householder who has closed the door and will allow no
one else to enter, which suggests that the time when one may
enter the New Age will soon pass; thereafter no second chance
exists, even though men may try to appeal to previous pleasant
associations with Jesus ("We ate and drank in your presence").
Their pleas will be without avail once the time of decision has
passed. Their anguish will be made the greater by the sight of
men "from east and west"—presumably Gentiles—who will have

---

[22] See the discussion by Joachim Jeremias in *The Parables of Jesus*, rev. ed.,
trans. S. H. Hooke (New York: Scribner's, 1963), pp. 42–48.

a share in the eschatological fellowship when God gathers his people in the New Age.

The familiar lament over Jerusalem (Luke 13:34–35) is a prophetic oracle, uttered by Jesus as the final messenger of God to Israel and probably understood to be the fulfillment of the promise in Deuteronomy 18:15–19. The passage directly appealed to, however, is Psalm 118:26, a text widely used in first-century Judaism to refer to the consummation of Israel's hope of the establishment of God's Kingdom,[23] and as such an important feature of the Jewish Feast of Tabernacles. Although Luke understands the lament—or wants his readers to understand it—as a prediction of Jesus' appearance on the occasion of his entry into Jerusalem, Q probably intended it as a mingled lament and warning by Jesus to the nation, represented here by Jerusalem, where the leadership and symbolic center of Judaism were found. If the Jewish leaders did not hear God's message through Jesus, they would have no further opportunity until the Coming One (perhaps God himself) appeared in their midst to judge the faithless and to vindicate the faithful. The city's rejection of Jesus and his message was of a piece with the murders of the prophets that had occurred over the centuries. Although the people of Jerusalem spurn him now, God will vindicate him in the Age to Come.

The sudden coming of the Day of the Lord is stressed in the cluster of words from Q that Luke places immediately after the account of the Pharisee's question to Jesus about the time of the coming of the Kingdom (Luke 17:20–21). The introduction to the Q sayings, "And he said to the disciples" (17:22), is a form of editorial connection frequently used by the evangelists.[24] From Q come verses 24, 26–27, and 33–37. The appearance of the Son of Man, God's eschatological judge, will be as instantaneous and as public as a flash of lightning; it will not be a hidden event, as

---

[23] For the evangelists' adaptation of this saying to the entry of Jesus into Jerusalem and/or the resurrection, see Barnabas Lindars, New Testament Apologetic (Philadelphia: Westminster, 1962), pp. 171–74.

[24] On this phrase as a characteristic editorial device, see Jeremias, The Parables of Jesus, pp. 97–98.

some Jewish sectaries expected or claimed with their "Lo, here!" Under the influence of Markan thought, Luke inserts at this point (17:25) a qualification of the unpredictability of the coming of the Son of Man by asserting the apocalyptic necessity of his suffering prior to his revelation as Son of Man. But this viewpoint is not present in Q, which concerns rather the cataclysmic nature of the coming of judgment.

Allied with the theme of the suddenness of the Judge's coming is that of the complacent, preoccupied attitude of the mass of the people. With judgment about to fall, they are concerned only about preserving their possessions. Like the "decent godless people" of T. S. Eliot's "Choruses from *The Rock*," they go about their daily routines oblivious of the catastrophe that is about to destroy the entire present order. So insensitive and self-centered are they that someone must point out to them the vultures swirling about the carcass of a world that passed away without their having noticed.

Eschatological Conflict

Closely linked with the theme of judgment in Q is the portrayal of conflict with the demonic as an essential factor in the fulfillment of God's redemptive purpose through Jesus. As in Mark (1:12-13), the story of Jesus' baptism leads directly into the section dealing with his being tested by the Devil (Luke 4:1-13 = Matt. 4:1-11). The Q version may have had its own narrative introduction, but both Matthew and Luke have incorporated the Markan setting of the incident. The more extensive treatment in Q, however, shows the greater importance attached to this conflict, which sets the tone and the issues for the whole of Jesus' ministry. Whereas in Mark the temptation is only a preparatory experience for Jesus' public activity (analogous to those of Moses, Elijah, and the prophets of the Hebrew Scriptures), in Q it is made the occasion for laying out what is at stake throughout Jesus' ministry: Will Jesus follow God's will in preparing for the coming of the Kingdom, or will he submit to the Devil's schemes for a counterfeit of the Kingdom of God? The temptations are not tests of Jesus' morality but of his dedication to the fulfillment of his mission at whatever cost.

The first temptation calls on him to use his extraordinary powers for his personal comfort by turning stones into bread when he is hungry. In the second testing he is offered immediate access to authority over the kingdoms of this world, if he will only acknowledge the Devil as his sovereign. This temptation not only tests Jesus' dedication to God but also defines his mission: He has been called not to assume power over this world's kingdom but to prepare men for the coming of God's Kingdom. The third temptation is a proposal that Jesus perform a kind of carnival stunt by leaping from a pinnacle of the temple in order to demonstrate God's special care over him, but Jesus would no more put God to the test than he would himself yield to the Devil's testings. The Q material portrays Jesus engaged in a cosmic conflict, and the stake is nothing less than God's rule over his creation. The fact that Q places these accounts in what we would call a mythological rather than a historical setting in no way diminishes the importance that the tradition attaches to them. Indeed, the vague mention of locale, "in the wilderness," heightens the sense of mystery and awe that surrounds these vivid vignettes.[25]

The implication of the temptation stories is made explicit in the Q version of the Beelzebul controversy (Luke 11:14–22 = Matt. 12:22–29). Q adds to the Markan story the detail that the controversy about the source of Jesus' power arose in connection with his having healed a deaf mute. But the more important difference between Mark's and Q's versions of the incident is the fact that in Q the significance of Jesus' exorcisms is made explicit. In Mark, Jesus responds to the accusation that he can perform exorcisms because he is in league with Beelzebul, the prince of demons, by pointing out how foolish it would be for Satan to work through him, since he will bring about Satan's downfall. In the Q account Jesus goes on to say that if everyone who performed

[25] Cf. Ulrich Mauser, *Christ in the Wilderness* (Naperville, Ill.: Allenson, 1963), and R. W. Funk, "The Wilderness," *Journal of Biblical Literature* 78 (1959):207.

exorcisms were in league with Satan, then the same would have to be said of the Jewish exorcists, including those associated with Jesus' accusers ("By whom do your sons cast them out?"). Although in its present form Luke 11:19 may reflect controversy between the primitive church and Judaism,[26] verse 20 is one of the fundamental passages in the entire gospel tradition for understanding the importance of Jesus' ministry of exorcisms:[27]

> But if it is by the finger of God that I cast out demons, then the kingdom of God has come upon you.

To the extent that Jesus is defeating the hosts of Satan by liberating men from demonic control, the reign of God over his creation is already becoming an accomplished fact. The exorcisms are signs that the New Age of Israel's eschatological hope is already manifesting its powers in the present through the ministry of Jesus. This is the unequivocal claim embedded in the Q document at this point.

It is not sufficient for a man to be freed from demonic domination, however, for if there were not some superior power to replace the satanic control, he might end up worse off than before—with eight demons instead of one, according to Luke 11:24–26 (= Matt. 12:43–45). Although it is not specifically stated, the implication of the pericope is that the rule of God must assume sway in a human life if the former demoniac is not to slip back under Satan's domination. If that were to occur, the possibility of remedy would be even more difficult than before. Thus Jesus' ministry is concerned not merely with removal of Satan's sway but also with replacement of the demonic scheme by the divine will, through the inbreaking of the Kingdom of God.

In the story of the Healing of the Centurion's Servant (Luke

---

[26] So Rudolf Bultmann, *History of the Synoptic Tradition*, trans. John Marsh (New York: Harper & Row, 1963), p. 52.

[27] Although it is not a primary concern for studying Q to distinguish authentic sayings of Jesus from those that arose in the early church, Bultmann's observation about Luke 11:20 is noteworthy here: "The latter [Luke 11:20] can, in my view, claim the highest degree of authenticity which we can make for any saying of Jesus" (*ibid.*, pp. 162–63).

7:1–10 = Matt. 8:5–13) there is, in addition to the matter of Gentile faith, an important element in the account: the authority of Jesus' word. The centurion can appreciate the power of the word of command, since he is himself a man accustomed to authority, presumably both to obeying it and exercising it: "I am a man under authority, with soldiers under me" (Matt. 8:9). But the thrust of the pericope is to depict Jesus as an authoritative figure, who is able to heal disease with a word and thereby to triumph over the powers at work in human life that stand in the way of the fulfillment of God's purpose. Although the terminology is not used, Jesus' healing word is a sign of the inbreaking of the Kingdom of God, as is true in his exorcisms.

Eschatological Promise

In both Luke and Matthew, Jesus' Sermon opens with a series of beatitudes. Although Luke added some material of his own (the woes on the rich, for example—Luke 6:24–26), he seems to have reproduced the Q version of the Sermon more faithfully on the whole than did Matthew, who considerably expanded and modified the tradition.[28] Whereas in Matthew the Beatitudes (5:3–12) are addressed to general categories of persons—"the poor in spirit," "those who mourn," "those who hunger and thirst after righteousness"—in Luke (6:20–23) they are spoken in direct address—"you poor"—and promise future rectification of present injustice. The contrast between present and future has been subdued in Matthew, but it stands out starkly in Luke: "You that hunger now . . . shall be satisfied."

Even where in the English translation the announcement of the blessedness of the poor is linked with the statement "yours is the kingdom of God," the point is not that the poor already possess the Kingdom; it is rather that their future possession of the Kingdom is even now assured. The coming of God's Kingdom will reverse all the ordinary human values. Those who are now

[28] Matthew's version of the Sermon runs to three chapters (5, 6, 7) and incorporates extensive material from his own source. See Chapter 5.

deprived and despised will be vindicated by God when he establishes his rule in the earth. To say "you shall be satisfied" means "God will satisfy you." The reward in heaven is great, Jesus says; his hearers can count on that, even though they will not enter into the reward until the Day of Judgment when God set things right in his creation. "That day" refers to the day of vindication. The disciples rejoice now at the prospect of the coming events that will set things right.

In the present situation of conflict the followers of Jesus can expect rejection and persecution at the hands of those who consider themselves God's people. To "cast out one's name as evil" is a Semitic expression that means to speak ill of someone. The calumny heaped on Jesus' disciples is not for their own sake but because they are publicly identified with the Son of Man (Luke 6:22).[29] The use of the term "Son of man" here heightens the significance of the persecution and suffering that the followers of Jesus are passing through. They are a part of the redemptive suffering that must precede the End of the Age and the coming of God's Kingdom. Luke preserves the original force of the Beatitudes, which are not generalized descriptions of the blessedness of humility but eschatological promises to those who are convinced that Jesus is God's messenger of the coming Kingdom and who are willing to undergo persecution if necessary in standing by their conviction.

The moral appeals to love one's enemies and to respond to injustice with actions of grace (Luke 6:27–36 = Matt. 5:39–42, 44–48) are not based on the shrewd calculation that in the long run things may work out for one's own welfare if he offers non-retaliatory responses to personal wrongs. Rather, Jesus bases his moral appeal in this Q material solely on the precept that man is called to act toward others as God has acted toward him. Love is a way of acting, not an emotion or a sentiment. The great para-

[29] Luke 6:22 was probably added in Q to the original set of authentic Beatitudes (that is, from Jesus) in 6:20–21, and comes from a time (1) when conflict between church and synagogue was mounting and (2) when Jesus had been identified by the church as the Son of Man. Our present concern, however, is with the viewpoint of Q, rather than with the authenticity of the sayings of Jesus.

dox lies in the promise that for the man who acts in love toward his enemy and expects no benefit in return, God has in store a great reward (Luke 6:35). This reward is the goal of the moral life, an eschatological goal: to become a son of the Most High. To move toward this goal, man is called upon to demonstrate concretely the works of mercy that correspond to the mercy he has received at the hands of God. The final appraisal of man's response to God's grace is expected to occur in the Day of Judgment, when works of mercy performed with no eye to recompense will receive the appropriate reward.

As was the case with the Beatitudes, the Lord's Prayer in Luke (11:1–4) is given in its more original form; Matthew expanded it and adapted it for liturgical use (6:9–13). Stripped of such additions (for example, "Father" instead of "Our Father who art in heaven"), the prayer as it stood in Q manifests a strong eschatological urgency. To call for the hallowing of the name of God is to appeal for a new situation in which men will give God the honor that is rightfully his by virtue of his having created the world. The more familiar petition for the coming of God's Kingdom is another way of saying the same thing. Both call for the establishment of God's rule in the earth, as Matthew's addition, "on earth as it is in heaven," rightly shows. The requests for bread and forgiveness indicate man's fundamental requirements: sufficient food to sustain life and enough of God's grace to make life bearable. Man can summon up the grace to forgive others who have wronged him because he has himself experienced God's forgiveness. In Matthew's version the prayer includes the petition to be delivered from evil, which has been commonly understood as a request that God keep us free of evil influences or from performing evil deeds. If "temptation" in the next line is interpreted as being tempted to commit sin, then the meaning would be plausible and consistent, but noneschatological. Luke's version, however, expresses only the hope that the petitioner will not be led into temptation, a word that probably means an eschatological time of testing rather than a moment in a man's life when he is tempted to commit a sin. "Temptation" is a technical term for the ordeal through which God's faithful people will pass in the End Time, just prior to the final judgment.

If they hold fast to the faith in spite of persecutions and demonic opposition, they will have demonstrated their right to enter the New Age. Luke's version of the prayer is an understandable expression of hope that it will not be necessary to pass through that time of testing. Matthew's form of the prayer reads like a general request for being kept from lapsing into sin. But if the text of Matthew 6:13 is translated as "from the Evil One" rather than "from evil," the force is the same: The simple human petition is that one might be spared the eschatological woes that will fall upon the earth in the closing days of the present age.

The theme of prayer continues in the same eschatological vein in Luke 11:9–13 (= Matt. 7:7–11). In this Q pericope what is being asked for is admission to the Kingdom of God, not merely some generalized spiritual benefits. The needs of the faithful will be met in the interim. God will give them the "good things" they require.[30] Similar advice is given in Luke 12:22–31 (= Matt. 6:25–33): Man should settle for the bare necessities of day-to-day living in the present age in order to enter into the Age to Come. No goal concerned with sustaining life or with making life more comfortable or carefree is to be compared with the highest aim of man's existence: seeking God's Kingdom.[31] In Luke 6:33–34 (= Matt. 6:19–21) the disciples are told to rid themselves of earthly possessions, which inevitably become the object of the affections and the force that inclines the will ("where your heart is"). Instead, they are to adopt poverty as a way of life in order that they may devote themselves entirely to effecting the will of God. Only thus can they claim enduring treasure.

Finally, there is an eschatological promise of vindication contained in a saying attributed to Jesus, found in two quite different forms in Luke 22:29–30 and in Matthew 19:28. Some scholars have expressed doubt that it stood in Q at all.[32] For our

---

[30] "The Holy Spirit" in Luke 11:13 is probably Luke's own addition to the Q saying, which otherwise he preserved quite faithfully.

[31] Matthew adds a moralistic touch in "his kingdom *and his righteousness*" (6:33). By contrast, Luke's added saying about the Kingdom as God's gift for "the little flock" is wholly in keeping with the intent of the Q saying to which it is appended.

[32] Manson, for example, maintains that these passages came from Luke's and Matthew's special sources (*The Sayings of Jesus*, pp. 216–17, 337–39).

purpose, it is enough to focus attention on the main idea of the saying, which is present in both versions: The twelve faithful disciples will participate in the judgment of God's people in the New Age. In Matthew, Jesus addresses his disciples simply as "you who have followed me"; in Luke, however, Jesus calls the disciples "you . . . who have continued with me in my [eschatological] trials." Matthew promises participation in the renewal of the world; Luke announces a guaranteed place in the Kingdom. But both agree that the twelve disciples will play the role of judge, as the faithful were promised in Daniel 7:22 and Wisdom 3:8. Discipleship, therefore, involves participation in the work of Jesus, both in this age and in the Age to Come. Jesus is not merely a preacher of the Kingdom's coming; he has a vital role in its establishment.

Eschatological Knowledge

The Q tradition contains not only promises of what God intended to do for his faithful children but also expressions of gratitude to God for having made known these promises. The best known of such passages in Q is in Luke 10:21–24 (= Matt. 11:25–27; 13:16–17).[33] This pericope as found in Luke may consist of what were originally two separate sayings, as Matthew's separation of them suggests. But for Q they belonged together, since they constitute an affirmation that God has given to the inner circle knowledge that prophets and kings have long wanted to possess but have been unable to lay hold of. Knowledge of God resides primarily with Jesus, who alone knows the Father. But he has chosen to reveal this knowledge to his own faithful followers, whose special blessedness is announced here. Although the content of the privileged knowledge is not disclosed, we can infer that it is insight into God's eschatological purpose, which is being achieved through Jesus, his Son. It is important to note that for Jesus to be "Son of God" is not a matter of his supernatural birth or origin but of his revelatory knowledge of the

---

[33] For an interpretation of this material as proto-Gnostic, see M. J. Suggs, *Wisdom, Christology and Law*, pp. 85–95.

divine intention for the world, an intention hidden from even the wisest and noblest of earlier generations. The clear implication is that the last days are approaching, in which God's plan is finally to be disclosed.

Eschatological Discipleship

The completeness of identity between Jesus and his followers is the chief mark of discipleship in the Q tradition. To follow Jesus is to give up the security and comfort of one's home (Luke 9:57–58 = Matt. 8:19–20), as well as the obligation to one's family that was from the beginning a central feature of Israel's societal structure (Exod. 20:12). Every other responsibility, however noble and worthy in itself, must take second place to the demands of discipleship. It is significant that in Luke 9:58 and Matthew 8:20, in a context where the radical nature of discipleship is depicted, Jesus is reported to have referred to himself as Son of Man. In Mark and Q (Mark 8:38; Luke 17:22–30) the term is used of the coming Son of Man who will execute judgment on disobedient, preoccupied mankind. Here, however, "Son of man" is used of Jesus in reference to his earthly rejection by mankind. Although he comes as an authoritative figure, summoning men to leave all and follow him, the widespread rejection he meets means that he cannot offer even a home to his followers:[34] "The Son of man has nowhere to lay his head." Acknowledgment of this hostile reception does not undercut the authority of Jesus; it serves to make his demand more rigorous and to restrict the promise of vindication to the future. There is no ground for encouragement or compensation in the present situation out of which Jesus calls men to discipleship.

The claims of discipleship are set forth in Luke 14:25–27 (= Matt. 10:37–38) in absolute terms. First, there is the demand that one who would follow Jesus "hate" his family. (Matthew

[34] H. E. Tödt, *The Son of Man in the Synoptic Tradition*, trans. D. M. Barton (Philadelphia: Westminster, 1965), discusses the origin and significance of this Son of Man saying. Precisely because authenticity is not our concern, we can see how useful for Q's viewpoint is such a saying, pointing up as it does the eschatological urgency surrounding the ministry of Jesus.

tones this down by substituting "does not love more" for "hate," as Luke has it.) In view of the sense of family solidarity that has traditionally characterized Jewish life, it is evident that a demand that would not merely transcend but even violate family ties was about as radical a requirement for discipleship as can be conceived. But Jesus even went beyond that: He called on his followers to be willing to surrender their lives in fulfilling their discipleship. That the writer of Q understood taking up the cross to mean acceptance of martyrdom is obvious from his setting that theme alongside the call to hate life.[35] To take up the cross is to share in the eschatological sufferings that are a necessary prelude to the coming of the Kingdom of God.

Although Matthew (9:37–38; 10:7–15) and Luke (10:1–16) have divergent accounts of Jesus' sending out of the disciples to preach and heal,[36] they agree on the context of the disciples' ministry, the content of their message, and the purpose of their activity. The context is the sense of urgency created by the expectation of "the harvest," that is, the judgment that is about to take place in preparation for the coming of the Kingdom. In light of the imminence of the End of the Age, the disciples are not to concern themselves at all with funds or equipment, with the comfort of their living accommodations, or with the quality of their food. Everything else must move into the background in light of the overwhelming expectation that the end is to come very soon. A single theme is to be the content of their message

---

[35] Erich Dinkler has tried to blunt the force of this demand by proposing that the "cross" originally meant merely an identifying mark, used metaphorically by Jesus in appealing to would-be disciples to identify themselves with him publicly. Only after the crucifixion of Jesus did "mark" become "cross." The theory is scarcely convincing. (See Dinkler, "Jesu Wort vom Kreuztragen" [Jesus' saying about bearing the cross], in Walter Eltester, ed., *Neutestamentliche Studien für Rudolf Bultmann zu seinem siebzigsten Gebürtstag* [New Testament studies for Rudolf Bultmann on his seventieth birthday], 2nd ed. [Berlin: Töpelmann, 1957], pp. 110–29.) More plausible is the origin of the saying in the early church as a way of understanding martyrdom. The Markan version of this saying (8:34) supports this interpretation; see Chapter 4, pp. 140–42.

[36] There are two accounts in Luke (9:1–6 and 10:1–16): The first account mentions twelve disciples; the second mentions seventy. See the discussion in Chapter 6, pp. 198–99.

and to provide the interpretation for the healings and exorcisms they perform: "The kingdom of God has come near to you." Anyone who spurns them or their message invites disaster in the Day of Judgment that is about to come upon the earth. The town that rejects Jesus or his disciples will be worse off than Sodom in the day of its destruction by fire and brimstone.

In a string of sayings (Luke 12:2–12 = Matt. 10:26–33; 12:32) Q brings together warnings and encouragements for the followers of Jesus. For example, it is futile for them to try to hide from God their words or actions: That which they now may suppose can be hidden, God will reveal in the last days. (Matthew interprets this saying to mean that the disciples are to be free of fear, since even works hidden in darkness will be revealed at the End of the Age.) Their real fear is not those who may put them to death, but those who will cause them to dishonor God and thereby bring about their condemnation. In Luke 12, verses 6 and 7 attest to the loving concern of God for all his creatures, not least of all his own children; therefore they are to be free of fear. But verses 8–10 return to the theme of the Judgment. On the one hand, those who publicly confess Jesus as Son of Man will be vindicated by God on the Last Day; on the other hand, those who deny Jesus will stand condemned before God's throne.

In Luke 12:10 (= Matt. 12:32) we have an unusual phenomenon: Q contains a saying of Jesus that appears in an older form in Mark (3:28–30). Mark explains that an insult to one's fellow man is forgivable but blasphemy against Jesus, specifically the charge that Satan, not the Holy Spirit, is the source of Jesus' power, cannot be forgiven. In Q the Markan phrase "sons of men" has been replaced by "men," only to appear in the next verse transformed into a christological title for Jesus, "Son of man." Here the penalties for insulting Jesus and for insulting the Holy Spirit are contrasted: The first can be forgiven, the second cannot. The aim of the Q tradition here seems to have been to glorify Jesus by identifying him as Son of Man. But the most meaningful aspect of the saying is the seriousness of the consequences of man's response to Jesus now for his fate in the eschatological judgment. In Luke 12:11–12 (= Matt. 10:19), however, divine aid is promised those who are persecuted in the last days.

The Holy Spirit will guide them as they seek to bear their witness during the time of the eschatological woes.

Eschatological Parables

Three closely related parables (Luke 12:39–40, 42–46 = Matt. 24:43–50) make a common point: The coming of the Son of Man cannot be predicted precisely, so it behooves every follower of Jesus to be always ready for his appearance. The owner of the house could have been on guard if he had known the hour that the thief would break in, but he did not know and was robbed. If the servant had known the hour of his master's return, he would not have abused those over whom he had been given authority, but he did not know and was caught. Reward awaits the fully responsible steward, who discharges his duties faithfully in the absence of his master. The lesson is obvious: When the Son of Man comes, he will punish the irresponsible and the disobedient. Sayings that were presumably spoken by Jesus as parables of the eschatological crisis[37] have become allegories of the coming of Christ and the faithfulness of the church's leadership. Although the Q writer has shifted the meaning of these parabolic sayings, he has not lost the eschatological force that they originally possessed; he has only redirected it to the church's situation in his own time.

To the familiar Parable of the Mustard Seed, Q has appended the Parable of the Leaven, since both make the same point: From the most unobtrusive beginnings, wholly unexpected results are certain to come.[38] The parables could also be intended to declare that now that the eschatological process has been launched, its outcome is certain.[39] These two themes are complementary rather than contradictory. Both parables, and both interpretations, look forward to the day when God's purpose is complete, when all the meal will have been leavened.

The Parable of the Great Supper tells the story of the poor

---

[37] Jeremias, *The Parables of Jesus*, pp. 48–51.
[38] *Ibid.*, pp. 146–49.
[39] Manson, *The Sayings of Jesus*, p. 123.

and the outcasts who accept an invitation to a feast; those originally invited are too preoccupied with worldly affairs to come. The parable has been preserved in three different forms: Matthew 25:1–10; Luke 14:16–24; and Logion 64 in the gospel of Thomas.[40] (There is some evidence that the parable is based on an actual incident reported in the Palestinian Talmud: When a tax collector's invitation to the town leaders was declined, he invited the poor of the city to be his guests.) Luke probably has best preserved the original form of the parable, although he seems to have introduced a two-stage invitation to the outcasts as a way of providing sanction in the teaching of Jesus for the shift of evangelistic focus from outcast Jews during Jesus' ministry to Gentiles in the ministry of the apostles.[41] The narrative setting Luke gives for the parable (14:15) is suitable and may even be original. Whether original with Jesus or not, it rightly sets the stage for the parable, since it introduces the theme of eschatological fulfillment, depicted under the familiar image of the banquet. The reaction to the invitation is consistent with the

---

[40] In the translation of Antoine Guillaumont, H. C. Puech, and others, *The Gospel According to Thomas* (New York: Harper & Row, 1959), pp. 35, 37, the parable reads as follows:

> Jesus said: A man had guest-friends, and when he had prepared the dinner, he sent his servant to invite the guest-friends. He went to the first, he said to him: "My master invites thee." He said: "I have some claims against some merchants; they will come to me in the evening; I will go and give them my orders. I pray to be excused from the dinner." He went to another, he said to him: "My master has invited thee." He said to him: "I have bought a house and they request me for a day. I will have no time." He came to another, he said to him: "My master invites thee." He said to him: "My friend is to be married and I am to arrange a dinner; I shall not be able to come. I pray to be excused from the dinner." He went to another, he said to him: "My master invites thee." He said to him: "I have bought a farm, I go to collect the rent. I shall not be able to come. I pray to be excused." The servant came, he said to his master: "Those whom thou hast invited to the dinner have excused themselves." The master said to his servant: "Go out to the roads, bring those whom thou shalt find, so that they may dine. Tradesmen and merchants [shall] not [enter] the places of my Father."

[41] The special interest of Luke in the Gentile mission is discussed in Chapter 6.

response of those who hear the gospel, described elsewhere in Q:
Men are too occupied with their own daily affairs to heed the
call to prepare for the coming Kingdom of God.

Similarly, there is an implied justification for extending the
gospel invitation to the outsiders—the lost sheep—in the Parable
of the Joyous Shepherd (Luke 15:4-7 = Matt. 18:12-14). The
basis of this justification, or vindication of the mission to the
Gentiles in the face of opposition on the part of strict Jewish
Christians, is the nature of God himself, who, like the rejoicing
shepherd, is depicted as filled with joy when even a single estranged person repentantly takes his place within the fellowship
of God's flock. Apart from the parable's declaration about the
attitude of God toward penitents, this pericope implies a criticism of those who pride themselves on being part of the in-group
and scorn the religious outsiders with whom Jesus, in Q, is primarily concerned. There is a 99 to 1 ratio between the insiders
and the outcast, but it is over the single penitent that God re-
joices. This revolutionary understanding of the nature of God is
in keeping with the redefinition of the people of God that this
parable, along with other Q material, implies.

Jesus as Eschatological Messenger and Salvation-Bringer

After beginning his presentation of the ministry of Jesus with
the coming and preaching of John the Baptist, the Q writer appropriately gives his first direct statement of the significance of
Jesus in words describing his relationship to John (Luke 7:19-23
= Matt. 11:3-6). The question as to who Jesus is, is raised by
John himself: "Are you he who is to come?" In itself the phrase
"he who is to come" does not connote a messianic figure but
simply indicates someone whose coming has eschatological significance. Jesus' reported reply recalls portions of the Isaiah apocalypse and of 2 Isaiah (29:18-19; 35:5-6; 61:1), where in each
case the prophets are pointing ahead to the last days, when God
will establish justice in the land and the oppressed will obtain
release from sickness and injustice. The claim of Jesus, according
to this Q material, is that the eschatological fulfillment is already
taking place in his ministry. The significance of his activity is en-

hanced by the fact that it is in fulfillment of Scripture; that is, Jesus' ministry is a part of the unfolding of God's redemptive purpose in and for his creation.

Jesus' words about John the Baptist confirm this interpretation of Jesus' activity reported in Q (Luke 7:24–35 = Matt. 11:7–19). Here it is implied that John is the one who prepares the way for Jesus' coming. Matthew makes the explicit claim that John the Baptist is Elijah, whose coming in the last days was predicted in Malachi 4:5 and was widely expected in various forms in the rabbinic and apocalyptic literature.[42] Whereas in Malachi the messenger is to prepare the way for God's, rather than the Messiah's, coming, in Q's quotation of Malachi the pronouns have been changed ("thy" face instead of "my" face) to imply that the messenger prepares the way for Jesus' coming. Whether we think of Q as representing Jesus to be the kingly Messiah or the prophetic figure of Elijah returned to earth (as Mark seems to have done), he has here a primary role in the coming of the Kingdom of God, whereas John the Baptist has only a secondary and preparatory function.

Accordingly, John is worthy of high praise: There is none greater than John among those born of women. Yet John represents the end of the old era, the epoch of the Law and the prophets. He was the one who pointed to the coming Kingdom, but he was not a part of it. The analogy has often been drawn between this view of John and the Old Testament picture of Moses, who was able to see the Promised Land but not to enter it. With the transition from the ministry of John to that of Jesus, there began a new era of conflict. Only through powerful efforts will the Kingdom of God be opened for men to enter. The implication is that Jesus' ministry of exorcisms and healings, with the attendant defeat of the demonic powers, is an essential element in the effective manifestation of God's power defeating his adversaries.

---

[42] A compendious presentation of Jewish traditions about Elijah is given by Joachim Jeremias, " Ἠλ(ε)ιας" [El(e)ias = Elijah], in Gerhard Kittel and Gerhard Friedrich, eds., *Theological Dictionary of the New Testament*, Vol. 2 (Grand Rapids, Mich.: Eerdmans, 1965), pp. 928–41. See p. 928, "No biblical figure so exercised the religious thinking of post-biblical Judaism as that of the prophet Elijah."

Tragically, many of Jesus' contemporaries fail to realize what is taking place in their midst through him. Like petulant children, they are moved neither by the fun of a dance nor by funereal games (Luke 7:32). They are repulsed by both the asceticism of John the Baptist and the conviviality of Jesus, identified here as Son of Man. But as is the case in Luke 9:58 (= Matt. 8:20), the Son of Man is a designation of Jesus not as an apocalyptic figure in disguise but as a sovereign agent of God, whose fellowship with religious outcasts implies a redefinition of the people of God and a new interpretation of God's Law.[43] The new Law and the new people will alike be vindicated when Jesus is publicly revealed as the Son of Man in the End Time.

The concluding comment (Luke 7:35 = Matt. 11:19), "Yet wisdom is justified by all her children," is an enigmatic statement; not even Matthew ("deeds") and Luke ("children") agree. More is intended here than that both John and Jesus have their places in God's plan and that their roles will be demonstrated by the results of their work.[44] "Wisdom" here means the out-working of God's redemptive scheme for his creation. Knowledge of that plan has been disclosed by Jesus to his followers alone (Luke 10:21–22 = Matt. 11:25–27). The results of the redemptive work launched by Jesus, building on the eschatological message and appeal of John the Baptist, will vindicate Jesus and the wisdom of which he claimed to be the bearer, according to Q. Whoever listens to Jesus, therefore, is giving heed to God's wisdom; whoever rejects Jesus is repudiating God and his redemptive purpose (Luke 10:16 = Matt. 10:40).

This inference is confirmed in the Q version (Luke 11:29b–32 = Matt. 12:39–41) of the incident when Jesus' opponents urge him to perform a sign in order to authenticate himself as the agent of God (Mark 8:11–12). Jesus responds by saying he will give none but the sign of Jonah:[45] Jonah came to preach to the

---

[43] See Tödt, *The Son of Man in the Synoptic Tradition*, pp. 114–18.

[44] So Manson, *The Sayings of Jesus*, p. 71.

[45] The interpretation of the sign of Jonah offered by Matthew is awkward, and is uniquely his own. The explanation offered (Jonah's three-day submarine voyage, ending in an attack of seasickness, as a prefiguring of Jesus' burial and resurrection after three days and nights) does not fit the Easter tradition of the resurrection "on the third day."

Ninevites without credentials or signs to attest to the divine origin of his message of impending judgment. The Ninevites repented because of the power of Jonah's person and message, not because he demonstrated his authority by means of signs.

Jonah is not specifically identified as a prophet in Q, but his role as proclaimer of God's eschatological message and his function as a sign to his generation are both in the prophetic tradition. Nor is Jesus portrayed as another Jonah-like prophetic figure. Rather, he is said to be greater than Jonah, whose preaching was so effective that men repented without his performing any signs to confirm his testimony as originating with God. Further, Jesus is equated by the Q tradition with the Son of Man, who is depicted here as God's final messenger to what is presumably thought of as the final generation, that is, the last one to have an opportunity to repent now that God's ultimate messenger has come.

Paralleling the role of prophet assigned to Jesus in the Q material is the role of wise man. Jesus is greater than Solomon, whose fabulous wisdom the queen of Sheba had come from South Arabia to hear at first hand (1 Kings 10:1–13). In late Judaism, Solomon had been venerated even more than in the Old Testament tradition, so that we have a widely influential book called the Wisdom of Solomon, purporting to be the product of David's kingly son but actually reflecting an understanding of wisdom as a quasi-personal agent by which God created and even now orders the world (Wisd. of Sol. 7:17–8:6). In the Q tradition Jesus is greater than Solomon, or at least the enterprise that Jesus represents is greater than that associated with Solomon. The implication is that Jesus is the one through whom the prophetic and wisdom traditions are moving to their divinely ordained consummation, when the Son of Man is revealed as God's eschatological redeemer. The ancients who in their time heeded God's messengers will give testimony against this generation for having failed to respond in faith to the reality, greater than that of Jonah or Solomon, that Jesus preached and embodied.

In the section of this chapter dealing with eschatological promise we examined the pericope (Luke 22:28–30) in which Jesus speaks of the coming Kingdom, in which he and his disciples will be joined in fellowship and in function. Appropriately, Luke placed this saying in the setting of the Last Supper, the occasion on which Jesus is reported to have told the disciples that he would not again share "the fruit of the vine" with them until the Kingdom of God had come (Luke 22:18). Even if Luke had not inserted the promise of participation in the eschatological supper and of the role of judge in the eucharistic passage, the import of the saying would be clear: The Kingdom of God will provide continuity with and consummation of the work that Jesus began during his ministry and that he committed to his faithful followers. Whether one accepts Matthew's "glorious throne" (19:28) of the Son of Man or Luke's "my" appointed Kingdom (22:30) as the original Q form of the saying, Jesus is in either tradition more than the announcer of the Kingdom's coming: He is the one who has the central role in its establishment. It is by identification with him in his trials that the disciples demonstrate their qualification to share in the exercise of authority when the Kingdom is established.

Whether the pericope of Jesus' lament over Jerusalem (Luke 13:34–35) was originally connected with the Jewish Feast of Tabernacles or not,[46] it includes a passage (Ps. 118:26) that was a central element in the Jewish liturgy for the Feast of Tabernacles, which was celebrated in late Judaism as an anticipation of the rule of God in the future rather than as a mere recollection of the wilderness sojourn.[47] Closely associated in the liturgy was Zechariah 14, where the judgment of God on the nation and its chief city, as well as the appearance of God in the midst of his people, are announced. Although in the mind of the Psalmist, and probably of Jesus (if these are his words), the Coming One

---

[46] Maurice Goguel uses this link between Psalm 118 and the Feast of Tabernacles as the basis for his chronological reconstruction, according to which Jesus came first to Jerusalem at the time of Tabernacles—that is, in September or October—and then returned for the final fatal occasion at Passover—that is, on April 7, A.D. 30 (according to the synoptics) or on April 3, A.D. 33 (according to John). See Goguel's *Life of Jesus*, trans. Olive Wyon (New York: Macmillan, 1946), pp. 226, 250–51.

[47] See the article on the "Feast of Tabernacles" by J. C. Rylaarsdam in G. A. Buttrick, ed., *The Interpreter's Dictionary of the Bible* (Nashville: Abingdon, 1962).

was God himself,[48] Q and the gospel tradition generally understood this saying as a reference to the vindication of Jesus, either in the resurrection or on the Last Day. Jesus' appearing in fulfillment of the hope of the coming rule of God will mark the consummation of that hope and the establishment of God's Kingdom in the earth. For Q, therefore, the decisive role in the eschatological fulfillment God has assigned to Jesus. He is God's final messenger, so man's eschatological destiny is determined by response to him. He is both the bearer of the Good News about the Kingdom's coming and the one who brings to pass that promised Kingdom.

Q has no need of a theological interpretation of the death of Jesus. The passion of Jesus is for Q a sad fact, since it demonstrates the resistance of Israel to the messengers of God and it breaks off the fellowship of Jesus with his faithful disciples. But the Q tradition looks beyond Jesus' death to the vindication that is to come in the Day of Consummation.

Even more surprising than the absence of a theology of the cross is the lack of any reference to the resurrection in Q. It is probable that the restoration of the fellowship between Jesus and the disciples that was believed to have taken place in the post-resurrection appearances[49] and that was continued in the church's celebration of the Eucharist, at which Christ was regarded as present, led to the conviction that Jesus was the Son of Man and to the hope that he would return, vindicated by God and in vindication of his followers. This is, however, nowhere explicitly stated in Q. The explanation of the absence of references to the cross and the resurrection probably lies in the belief represented by Q that the two central factors in God's eschatological purpose were the coming of Jesus as authoritative teacher and agent and God's public confirmation of him as Son of Man at the End of the Age. The scheme of apocalyptically necessary events, including the suffering, death, and resurrection, essential for Mark, has no place in Q. This is not because Q is concerned only about

---

[48] See the discussion in Lindars, *New Testament Apologetic*, pp. 172–73.
[49] Tödt, *The Son of Man in the Synoptic Tradition*, pp. 251–52, 273.

moral instruction,[50] but because for Q even moral instruction is subordinate to and dependent on the eschatological vindication of Jesus when the present struggle against demonic and unbelieving human forces is at an end. History is reduced to three periods: the old era of the Law and the prophets, which terminated with John the Baptist; the present era, in which Jesus inaugurated the eschatological fellowship and in which man's major responsibility is to recognize in the message and the activity of Jesus God's final word to man; and the Age to Come, in which Jesus will be reunited with his followers as Son of Man and they and he will be vindicated by God.

THE VALUE OF Q AS A HISTORICAL SOURCE

The tradition embodied in Q is more concerned with presenting Jesus as bearer of the eschatological message than as someone whose primary function is to perform deeds that effect salvation. Jesus brings salvation by evoking the response of faith to the word from God that he offers, not by virtue of his saving actions. The result of this emphasis is that while Jesus is pictured in the Q source as historical and as a person rather than a faceless spokesman for God, there is not sufficient narrative in Q to reconstruct anything like a biographical sequence or even the course of his public career. We have in Q one of our best sources—along with the special source used by Luke—for recovering the message of Jesus. This is, of course, of primary historical value. But the main

---

[50] See Tödt's summary of this view in *ibid.*, pp. 232–44. A thorough but unconvincing description of Q as a collection of sayings brought together for hortatory purposes is given by Martin Dibelius in *From Tradition to Gospel*, 3rd ed., trans. B. L. Woolf (New York: Scribner's, 1965), pp. 233–49, esp. p. 246: "The sayings of Jesus were originally gathered together for a hortatory end, to give the Churches advice, help and commandment by means of the Master's words. This typical interest was dominant both in the origin of this special source [i.e., Q] and also in the gathering together of the words of Jesus everywhere."

thrust of the Jesus tradition in Q is to point forward to the future Kingdom of God rather than to depict the historical life of Jesus.

THE COMMUNITY BEHIND Q

The segment of primitive Christianity by and for whom Q was produced stood firmly in the tradition of charismatic prophets, with a keen expectation of impending judgment and eschatological vindication. There seems to have been little concern about legal issues; ethical questions were decided more on the basis of wisdom tradition and mutuality within the community than by appeal to legal precepts from Torah. The view of the world that prevailed was sharply dualistic: the powers of Satan were already in process of being overcome by the power at work through Jesus and transmitted by him to his faithful followers. Healings and exorcisms were signs that the era dominated by the devil was coming to an end and that the New Age was dawning. The religious leadership of Judaism was regarded as hypocritical and nitpicking, as exclusive in its attitude toward Gentiles and nonconforming Jews, and as hostile toward Jesus and his followers. The Q community, following Jesus' example, was lax in observation of the Law, open and hospitable toward Gentiles, and ready to accept even martyrdom at the hands of the authorities, confident that God would vindicate the faithful in the End Time.

The absence of specific geographical or cultural allusions makes it impossible to locate the community. The fact that the Q material is preserved in Greek and was probably composed in that language—though with traces of Semitic idiom beneath the surface—suggests Syria, but Greek was widely used in Palestine in this period, as the fragments of Greek manuscripts found at Qumran attest.

We know from the letters of Paul (1 Cor. 15:9; Gal. 1:13; Phil. 3:6) that persecution of the church by Jews began early—as early as the year 30, perhaps.[51] Since it presumably did not stop with the conversion of Paul, we can suppose that by the 40s it was a severe problem; this supposition is confirmed by the evidence that conflict within the Jewish community at Rome over the coming of Christian missionaries was so intense as to require imperial intervention and expulsion of the Jews.[52] The concern of the community about persecution and martyrdom was not paranoia but realism. The most honored virtue in the Q tradition is fidelity or perseverance in the face of hostility. For that, the martyred eschatological prophet, Jesus—soon to be vindicated by God—is the paradigm.

SUGGESTIONS FOR FURTHER READING

A basic necessity for the study of the gospel tradition is *Gospel Parallels: A Synopsis of the First Three Gospels*, ed. B. H. Throckmorton (Camden, N.J.: Thomas Nelson, 1957). Various editions of the Greek text arranged in synoptic form are available; the most recent and most complete (including the noncanonical gospel traditions) is *Synopsis Quattor Evangeliorum* available in the United States from the American Bible Society in New York City.

Reconstructions of Q together with commentary on its contents have been prepared by F. W. Beare, *Earliest Records of Jesus* (Nashville: Abingdon, 1962), who includes Markan, Matthean, and Lukan material as well as Q, and by T. W. Manson, "The Sayings of Jesus," in H. D. Major, T. W. Manson, and C. H. Wright, *The Mission and Message of Jesus* (New York: Dutton, 1938).

Special interest in the Q tradition is shown by H. E. Tödt,

[51] See A. J. Hultgren, "Paul's Pre-Christian Persecutions of the Church: Their Purpose, Locale, and Nature," *Journal of Biblical Literature* 95 (1976): 97–111.

[52] Attested in the decree of Claudius; text and discussion in H. C. Kee, *The Origins of Christianity* (Englewood Cliffs, N.J.: Prentice-Hall, 1973), pp. 258–60.

The Son of Man in the Synoptic Tradition (Philadelphia: Westminster, 1965), and Norman Perrin, *Rediscovering the Teaching of Jesus* (New York: Harper & Row, 1967). The Q parables, as well as all the others, are discussed in detail in Joachim Jeremias, *The Parables of Jesus,* rev. ed. (New York: Scribner's, 1963). A detailed reconstruction of the theology of Q is offered by R. A. Edwards, *A Theology of Q: Eschatology, Prophecy and Wisdom* (Philadelphia: Fortress, 1976). For a recent survey of studies of Q, see R. D. Worden, "Redaction Criticism of Q: A Survey," *Journal of Biblical Literature* 94 (1975): 532–46.

Jesus as the Culmination of Apocalyptic History: The Gospel of Mark

The term "gospel" as a designation for the early Christian claims about Jesus had been in use for nearly four decades before Mark wrote a work that became known as a gospel, and to which he prefixed the words, "The beginning of the gospel of Jesus Christ . . ." (Mark 1:1). He was apparently the first to write a more or less sequential account of the career of Jesus. Q included only sayings and probably no more than a single narrative, as we have seen. Paul gives no indication of knowing the gospels, does not quote from them, and disavows interest in Christ "from a human point of view" (2 Cor. 5:16).[1] Why did Mark write such a gospel? What purposes did he intend it to serve? Why is it—unlike Paul and Q—concerned with the life and activity of Jesus prior to his death and resurrection? Why did Mark link what he wrote with the term "gospel"? Our search for answers to these questions requires us to face up to the fact of diversity in the early Christian understandings of Jesus.

---

[1] Paul alludes to or quotes from sayings of Jesus, but there is no indication that he knew this material from the gospels. Rather, it was part of the oral Jesus tradition. See D. L. Dungan, *The Sayings of Jesus in the Letters of Paul* (Philadelphia: Fortress, 1971).

THE MESSAGE OF MARK
AND THE MESSAGE OF PAUL

The gospel of Mark is an account of the public ministry of word and act performed by the pre-cross and preresurrection Jesus, whereas the letters of Paul are concerned with the understanding of Jesus that is possible through an apprehension of the significance of the crucified and risen Lord. We can postulate the existence of a formal and theological gap in the early church between the message of Paul and that of the gospel tradition if we assume that the second-century Gnostic gospel of Thomas, which relates only Jesus' word without a hint of his deeds or his passion, had precedents, such as Q, in the first century. The Q document presumably competed against Paul's letters as a way of understanding Jesus, though the letters eventually dominated the theological field. It seems likely that the primary focus of Q was on Jesus as eschatological teacher and that Q was an early form of Christian message in which the cross and the resurrection were presented, if at all, as no more than two of a series of important occurrences, which began with the launching of Jesus' public ministry and would one day culminate in his appearance as Son of Man.[2] In Q we have good evidence that before Mark wrote his gospel there were collections of Jesus material that consisted of sayings alone and possibly reports of miracle stories, without reference to the cross-resurrection theology.

Attempts at Reconciling the Differences
Between Mark and Paul

The fact that both the gospels and Paul's letters are, for Christians, Scripture and have been read in the churches as the Word of God since the first century has obscured the differences between them and tended to give them a superficial appearance of uni-

---

[2] See the reconstruction of the theology of Q in H. E. Tödt, *The Son of Man in the Synoptic Tradition*, trans. D. M. Barton (Philadelphia: Westminster, 1965), and in R. A. Edwards, *A Theology of Q* (Philadelphia: Fortress, 1976).

formity. Many scholars and theologians have labored to support this view. Some interpreters of the New Testament have tried to impose unity on the gospels and the letters or have claimed to find a common ground underlying the differences. For example, in *The Apostolic Preaching and Its Development in the New Testament* C. H. Dodd lists certain propositions about Jesus that he claims all New Testament writers affirm despite the differences between them.[3] But it is impossible to fit the gospel narratives and teaching materials into such a scheme, since the "common message" reconstructed by Dodd is based on Paul and Acts, in both of which the cross and the resurrection are central and no place is made for the public ministry and teaching of Jesus. Other historians of early Christianity insist that a choice be made between Jesus and Paul. Some treat the message of Paul as a regrettable development that has been superimposed on the simple ethical message of Jesus, which, it is claimed, can be reconstructed from the sayings portions of the first three gospels. Others think that the message of Jesus in the synoptics does not go beyond the categories of Judaism, and they consider Paul the source of the essential Christian message. There is still another approach—the approach adopted for this book—which is based on the assumption that the attempt to find *the* central Christian message, however useful it may be as a theological undertaking, has hindered recognition of the diversity of interpretations of Jesus embodied in the gospel tradition, and in particular of the distinctive contribution of Mark to Christian understanding of the historical role of Jesus. The inadequacy of approaches that concentrate on the search for *the* central message is evident when we examine the results of investigations of biblical and theological scholars who have taken this message as their goal.

The Search for the Central Element in the Christian Message

In the middle of the nineteenth century F. C. Baur proposed a quite specific solution to the problem of the relationship between the message preached by Jesus and known to us through the

---

[3] (New York: Harper & Row, 1951).

synoptics and the message preached about him by Paul. In Baur's view, the message of Jesus historically was fundamentally one of "absolute moral command,"[4] according to which "the inner is opposed to the outer, the disposition to the act, the spirit to the letter."[5] Jesus' moral ideal was expressed through Jewish concepts, as we would expect of a historical person living under the intellectual and cultural conditions of first-century Judaism. One group of his followers restricted themselves to "the cramping and narrowing influence of the Jewish national Messianic idea" and therefore were never able "to surmount the particularism of Judaism at all."[6] The wing of the church that launched the Gentile mission, on the other hand, of which Paul was the chief representative, built on "the moral universal in [Jesus], the unconfined humanity, the divine exaltation, which gave his person its absolute significance," and thereby "introduced Christianity to its true destination as a religion for the world, and enunciated, with a full sense of its vast significance, the principle of Christian universalism."[7] Baur found Jesus' moral and spiritual ideal set forth in all the gospels, and with particular clarity in Matthew's Sermon on the Mount.[8] In Luke, however, he saw an additional development: Luke emphasized the universal element in Jesus' message, modifying the tradition so as to bring out the universal dimension stressed in Paul's message.[9] (Baur assumed that Luke was a companion and disciple of Paul.) Baur saw the culmination of New Testament universalism in the gospel of John, in which "Christianity is established as a universal principle of salvation; all those antitheses which threatened to detain it within the narrow limits of Jewish particularism are merged in the universalism of Christianity."[10] For Baur there was no essential discontinuity in the conceptual movement from Jesus to Paul and on to the catholic church of the late first and early second centuries. Paul's polemics against the Judaizers were necessary in order to help the church

---

[4] *The Church History of the First Three Centuries*, 3rd ed., vol. 1, trans. Allan Menzies (London: Williams & Norgate, 1878), p. 29.
[5] *Ibid.*, p. 30.
[6] *Ibid.*, p. 49.
[7] *Ibid.*
[8] *Ibid.*, p. 29.
[9] *Ibid.*, pp. 78–81.
[10] *Ibid.*, p. 180.

shed its excess baggage of Jewish images and perspectives. Only through such a conflict could the church emerge to the stage of conceptual reconciliation at which the pure, spiritual intention of Jesus was comprehended and expressed in terms freed of the connotations of Jewish particularism.

With his value judgment that Paul's universalism was good and the Jewish particularism of the synoptic gospels was bad, Baur discouraged serious attention to the interpretations of Jesus embodied in the synoptics. Accordingly, Mark's view of Jesus in history finds no significant place in Baur's critical reconstruction of primitive Christianity, except as it provides evidence of the Jewish particularism that had to be outgrown.

One hundred years after Baur, Rudolf Bultmann was at work on his own formulation of the relationship of the message of Jesus to that of Paul and the later New Testament writers. According to Bultmann, the essential message of the New Testament cannot be found in the message of Jesus in the synoptics; rather, it is to be found in Paul and in the gospel of John. The preaching of Jesus as we have it in the synoptic tradition is only the presupposition of New Testament theology and is not to be considered *kerygma*, or the proclamation of the Christian message.[11] As a historical person, Jesus should be thought of within the sphere of late Judaism[12] and not as the inaugurator of Christian faith. Christian faith began with Easter; that is, in the rise of the belief that God made the crucified one Lord, the church asserted that Jesus was present in the kerygma, in "the proclaiming, accosting, demanding and promising word of preaching."[13]

Although the message of Jesus is by no means to be con-

---

[11] Rudolf Bultmann, *Theology of the New Testament*, vol. 1, trans. Kendrick Grobel (New York: Scribner's, 1951), p. 3. The term *kerygma* (transliterated from Greek) means "that which is proclaimed." It has become a widely used summary term in biblical and theological circles for the essential Christian message.

[12] Bultmann, *Primitive Christianity in Its Contemporary Setting*, trans. R. H. Fuller (Cleveland: World, 1956); see "The Eschatological Preaching of Jesus," pp. 86–93.

[13] Bultmann, *Theology of the New Testament*, vol. 1, pp. 302–03. See also the more recent discussion of the presence of Jesus in the kerygma in Bultmann's essay "The Primitive Christian Kerygma and the Historical Jesus," in C. E. Braaten and R. A. Harrisville, eds., *The Historical Jesus and the Kerygmatic Christ* (Nashville: Abingdon, 1964), pp. 40–42.

sidered kerygma,[14] the synoptics may serve a kerygmatic function: Repetition of Jesus' preaching under the impact of kerygma may make "the past present in such a way that it puts the hearers (or readers) before the decision for (or against) a possibility of self-understanding disclosed in the preaching of the historical Jesus."[15] But it is the Jesus present in the kerygma who is the saving event, not the historical Jesus of the synoptic gospels. Only to the extent that the post-Jesus kerygma influenced and shaped the present form of the synoptic gospels can the synoptics be called kerygmatic.

Bultmann made a brilliant contribution to the study of the gospels through his *History of the Synoptic Tradition*, in which he developed and utilized form criticism to differentiate older from later strata of the tradition incorporated in the synoptic gospels, but he did not close the gap between the message of Jesus and the message about him. For example, he made no attempt to show the continuity between Jesus' proclamation of the Kingdom of God and Paul's proclamation of Jesus as eschatological event.

That he failed to close this gap is evident too in his brief but highly suggestive analysis of the distinctive features of Mark's editing of the tradition.[16] In discussing Mark's purpose, Bultmann states only that Mark combined the tradition of the story about Jesus with the Hellenistic, or Pauline, kerygma.[17] Thus, according to Bultmann, even in Mark the Pauline message is basic, and the Jesus tradition is little more than an embellishment. He remarks that Mark was "not sufficiently master of his material to venture on a systematic construction himself."[18] As we shall see in this chapter, Bultmann seems not to have recognized that Mark did in fact present a theological construction of his own—one

---

[14] Bultmann, *Jesus and the Word*, trans. L. P. Smith and E. H. Lantero (New York: Scribner's, 1934), gives a reconstruction of Jesus' message, but in *Theology of the New Testament*, vol. 1, pp. 33–34, Bultmann asserts categorically that Jesus' message is not kerygma.
[15] Bultmann, "The Primitive Christian Kerygma," pp. 40–41.
[16] Bultmann, *History of the Synoptic Tradition*, trans. John Marsh (New York: Harper & Row, 1963), pp. 338–50.
[17] *Ibid.*, p. 347.
[18] *Ibid.*, p. 350.

that has some elements in common with the Pauline kerygma, though it does not adopt Paul's cross-resurrection theology as its basis.

In the so-called new quest of the historical Jesus, New Testament scholars have reversed their direction in their search for an answer to the problem of the relationship between Jesus and Paul. Instead of moving from Jesus to Paul, they move from Paul back toward Jesus. Of course, this sequence is required by the fact that in terms of literary chronology alone, the documentation of the cross-resurrection kerygma antedates by thirty-five years the earliest gospel writing. If Paul's claim is accurate that there was no difference between his kerygma and that of the original group of apostle-disciples—Peter and the twelve—is it possible that they too had no more interest than Paul in the kind of material that someone later incorporated in the gospels? This theory would suggest that the real Christian message was to be found only in the gospel preached by Paul, a message that he shared with the apostles. But then we should be completely at a loss to know why the gospels were ever written, or why they were included in the same collection—the New Testament—that contained the letters of Paul. Certainly Paul has only a few allusions to sayings of Jesus (for example, 1 Cor. 7:10); Acts attributes to Paul a quotation from the teaching of Jesus that is not otherwise known (Acts 20:35). But Baur long ago recognized the foolishness of those who try to demonstrate Paul's reliance on the Jesus tradition.[19]

Most attempts to trace the links between Paul and the gospels have proved to be evasions of the problem or blind alleys. Baur's suggestion that Luke was a Paulinized gospel,[20] as well as more recent theories about Mark that depict this gospel as filled with Paulinisms, does not bear up under critical scrutiny.[21] Both the theological concepts and the distinctive vocabulary of Paul are missing from all the gospels. The extended treatment of the

[19] Baur, *Church History*, p. 50.
[20] *Ibid.*, p. 81.
[21] A brief discussion and critique of the theory that Mark is a Pauline-oriented document is offered in W. G. Kümmel, *Introduction to the New Testament*, 17th ed., trans. H. C. Kee (Nashville: Abingdon, 1975), pp. 94–95.

public ministry of Jesus, which is central to the synoptic tradition, has no place in Paul's letters, and seems clearly to have no place in his understanding of the central Christian beliefs about Jesus. Even when Paul appeals to a saying of Jesus for parenetic purposes, as in 1 Corinthians 7:10 ("I give the charge, not I but the Lord"), he quotes himself with equal authority in the next breath ("I say, not the Lord"—1 Cor. 7:11).

Given the fact that leading historical critics have not differentiated between the Markan message and the message of Paul, it is not surprising that theologians have perpetuated this confusion. For example, Martin Kähler, whose rejection of the attempt to reconstruct a historical picture of Jesus we considered in the first chapter, took a position that has exercised wide influence on the issue of the relationship between the understanding of Jesus recoverable from critical assessment of the gospels and the understanding of him set forth in the church's kerygma. Having taken as his theological foundation "the kerygma"—which means for Kähler the message of Paul—he declares it invalid even to investigate the differences between Paul and the gospel tradition or to look behind the tradition to its possible historical origins.

> From these fragmentary traditions, these half-understood recollections, these portrayals colored by the writers' individual personalities, these heartfelt confessions, these sermons proclaiming him as Savior, there gazes upon us a vivid and coherent image of a Man, an image we never fail to recognize. Hence, we may conclude that in his unique and powerful personality and by his incomparable deeds and life (including his resurrection appearances) this man has engraved his image on the mind and memory of his followers with such sharp and deeply etched features that it could be neither obliterated nor distorted.[22]

But Kähler's subsequent remarks show that however "deeply etched" the features may be, it is not legitimate for faith to inquire into any of the details with which the gospel portraits have been traced: "It is . . . erroneous to make [faith] depend on

---

[22] Martin Kähler, *The So-called Historical Jesus and the Historic, Biblical Christ*, trans. and ed. C. E. Braaten (Philadelphia: Fortress, 1964), pp. 89–90.

uncertain statements about an allegedly reliable picture of Jesus that has been torturously extracted by the modern methods of historical research."[23] It is obvious that Kähler is interested in the gospel accounts only as they transmit to the hearts of believers "the mind of Christ."[24] Indeed, the more uncertain the historical reconstruction, the more discernible is the inspiration of the gospel writers. As Kähler puts it, "The more obscure the course of events remains which have preceded the literary activity, all the more certainly can we sense the invisible hand of Providence over the primitive community's carefreeness in the transmission of the tradition."[25]

The systematic theologian Paul Tillich had a more positive attitude than Kähler about historical research, but his conclusions concerning the results of gospel criticism and the differences between the gospels and Paul are paradoxical, if not downright contradictory. On the one hand, he praises Protestantism for its courage in subjecting its holy writings to critical analysis[26] and for "the immense historical material which has been discovered and often empirically verified by a universally used method of research."[27] He also asserts that it is not enough to reconstruct a *Gestalt* of Jesus after all questionable details have been eliminated; an essential picture "remains dependent on details."[28] But when he speaks of the transforming power of the biblical picture of Jesus as the Christ, through which the New Being is transmitted, he declares: "No special trait of this picture can be verified

---

[23] *Ibid.*, pp. 72–73. The intention of historical criticism in relation to faith is a large question in itself, and one that such recent discussions as Gerhard Ebeling's ("the uncertainty created by historical criticism is the reverse side of justification by faith") have scarcely dealt with adequately; see the English edition of Ebeling's collected essays, *Word and Faith*, trans. J. W. Leitch (Philadelphia: Fortress, 1963), pp. 17–61. But historical criticism has the necessary function of bringing into focus the issues that faith alone can decide. One must distinguish between clarity as to what the promise is and certainty that God will fulfill it. The former may be aided by the work of the historian; the latter can rest solely on faith.

[24] Kähler, *The So-called Historical Jesus*, p. 91.

[25] *Ibid.*, p. 90.

[26] *Systematic Theology*, vol. 2 (Chicago: University of Chicago Press, 1957), p. 107.

[27] *Ibid.*, p. 103.

[28] *Ibid.*

with certainty. But it can be definitely asserted that through this picture the New Being has power to transform those who are transformed by it."[29] With how little seriousness Tillich took the work of historical criticism—in spite of his commendatory generalities—is evident in this statement: "Harnack was wrong . . . when he contrasted the message given by Jesus with the message about Jesus. There is no substantial difference between the message given by the Synoptic Jesus and the message about Jesus given in Paul's Epistles."[30]

The Different Perspectives of Mark and Paul

By such approaches as these, the problem remains not only unanswered but unaddressed. The problem is not merely one of historical continuity from Jesus to Paul or from Paul back to Jesus. Theologians have made the easy assumption that there is no fundamental difference between Paul's kerygma and the kerygmatic significance of Jesus in Mark, and this assumption has prevented them from seeing clearly Mark's perspective. To make the distinction between Mark's perspective and Paul's, it may be useful to take up Bultmann's contention that the kerygma announces that a historical event has become an eschatological event. Bultmann uses the words "historical" and "eschatological" in a special way that derives from existentialist philosophy. "Historical" concerns not the past, but what he calls the historicity of self, which is constituted by an event or a word by which man finds the meaning of his own existence. Similarly, "eschatological" does not deal with the end of the world at some future date, but describes any moment in the present when man is called to make a fundamental decision that requires him to free himself from reliance on the institutions and powers of the past and to open himself to the future. In making the decision, he experiences an event that transforms his outlook on himself and his world, on which he has relied for standards and stability. As he makes this radical decision, he "dies." But God gives him a new life, so that, in the

---

[29] *Ibid.*, p. 114.
[30] *Ibid.*, pp. 117–18.

language of the New Testament, he enters "the life of the Age to Come." For Bultmann, Jesus' summons to individuals to follow him, in light of his own decision to accept death rather than conform his life to the political and even the religious institutions of his time, constitutes a historical event that for faith becomes an eschatological event.

Bultmann considers the gospel of John (in its expurgated form) the purest version of the kerygma: It is the simple declaration *that* God addresses man in a historical man, Jesus of Nazareth.[31] Paul has approached the purity of this insight by leaving out of consideration the ethical and eschatological teaching of Jesus, locating Jesus' obedience in a decision to do God's will made by him as the heavenly Christ before he took the form of the earthly Jesus (Phil. 2:5–8) and limiting his kerygma to the " 'that' of the life of Jesus and the fact of his crucifixion."[32] Through the cross, God announces the end of the old age and the coming of the new; therefore, to accept God's Word through the cross is to enter the life of the Age to Come. Having died to the old world, one is raised by faith to the new life.

Bultmann's representation of Jesus as historical event become eschatological event is appropriate and illuminating for understanding some of the major aspects of Paul's and John's thought, although it does not provide a satisfactory perspective for dealing with their beliefs about the eschatological future. But for Mark, the axiom is wholly inadequate. It would be useful in interpreting Mark only if both "historical" and "eschatological" were assigned meanings quite different from those Bultmann intends.

Although Paul does not repudiate the apocalyptic element in the gospel he preaches, he does not give it a central place. Or more accurately, even when he includes the apocalyptic elements of the Christian message, he does so without reference to the past ministry or message of Jesus. The only roles Jesus plays in Paul's eschatological scheme are those of the crucified-exalted Lord and

---

[31] *Theology of the New Testament*, vol. 2, p. 66.
[32] "The Primitive Christian Kerygma," p. 20. For Bultmann, the essential Christian message resides in *dass* ("that"), the fact that Jesus came, not in *was* ("what"), facts about Jesus.

the agent who will bring the cosmos into subjection to the will of God. There is no appeal to precedent or guideline in the activity or message of the earthly Jesus.

For the gospel tradition, as for late Judaism and particularly for Jewish apocalypticism, the coming of the New Age was a far more complicated matter than a shift of self-understanding. Whatever one may think of Albert Schweitzer's reconstruction of the life and message of Jesus, Schweitzer has shown beyond doubt the thoroughly eschatological, and indeed apocalyptic, outlook of Jesus, in terms of which his message of the Kingdom of God was formulated.[33]

In the synoptic tradition the central concerns are precisely what is missing in Paul: Jesus is seen as the eschatological salvation-bringer in the context of his *historical* public ministry and without reference to his heavenly existence prior to his appearance as man or to his *parousia*, his future coming in glory. No one before Mark had bothered to bring together the tradition in a sequential way; what pre-Markan documents there were seem to have been structured by topical or mnemonic arrangement. Thus, in any study of the gospels, Mark poses this problem: How in a church that (to judge from most of the New Testament) was dominated by Paul and his kerygma and whose major concern was to proclaim the crucified and risen Lord, did there arise a literary creation like the gospel of Mark, with the theological understanding of Jesus it embodies?

---

[33] Schweitzer's position is sketched in *The Quest of the Historical Jesus*, trans. William Montgomery (New York: Macmillan, 1910), Chapter 19. This work is a translation of *Von Reimarus zu Wrede* [From Reimarus to Wrede] (1906). But his basic study of the gospel texts is set out in *The Mystery of the Kingdom of God*, trans. Walter Lowrie (London: A. & C. Black, 1926), which is the second part of *Das Abendmahl im Zusammenhang mit dem Leben Jesu und der Geschichte des Urchristentums* [The Eucharist in relation to the life of Jesus and the history of primitive Christianity] (Tübingen: J. C. B. Mohr, 1901). A posthumously published work of Schweitzer's on the theme of Jesus' eschatology is *Reich Gottes und Christentum* [The Kingdom of God and Christianity] (Tübingen: J. C. B. Mohr, 1967). A critique of Schweitzer's position is given by W. G. Kümmel, now available in his collected essays, *Heilsgeschehen und Geschichte* [Salvation-event and history] (Marburg: Elwert, 1965), pp. 328–29.

WHAT IS A GOSPEL?

The Meaning of *Euangelion*

The problem of what "gospel" means becomes apparent immediately when we recognize that *euangelion,* or gospel, the word Mark (or the early church for which he was a spokesman) chose as the heading for his little book was Paul's favorite term for his kerygma. For Paul the word meant the announcement of the eschatological event effected by God through the crucifixion and resurrection of Jesus. Therefore, the one who preaches the gospel could be associated with the Deutero-Isaianic messenger of Yahweh, who "proclaims the victory of Yahweh over the whole world."[34] He not only announces it, but his word of good tidings brings about salvation. "By the fact that he declares the restoration of Israel, the new creation of the world, the inauguration of the eschatological age, he brings them to pass."[35]

The noun *euangelion* as used by Mark (1:1) may carry some of the connotation of the verb in Second Isaiah, but its meaning and use lie closer to the term as it was employed in the imperial Roman cult: It meant an announcement of the benefits the empire enjoyed through the gracious authority of Caesar, the divinely appointed ruler of Rome. Although the fuller documentation for this meaning of *euangelion* comes in part from post–New Testament writers, such as Plutarch (A.D. 46?–120?) in *De Fortuna Romanorum,*[36] there is inscriptional evidence going back to the time of Augustus for the use of *euangelion* in connection with the imperial cult: "The birthday of the god was for the world the beginning of tidings of joy [*euangelion*] on his account."[37] Gerhard Friedrich has summarized what the term im-

---

[34] Gerhard Friedrich, "εὐαγγελίζεσθαι" [*evangelizesthai,* "to proclaim good news"], in *Theological Dictionary of the New Testament,* vol. 2, trans. G. W. Bromiley (Grand Rapids, Mich.: Eerdmans, 1965), p. 708.
[35] *Ibid.,* pp. 708–09.
[36] In the Loeb edition of Plutarch the treatise is found in *Moralia,* vol. 2, trans. F. C. Babbitt (New York: Putnam's, 1928), pp. 73–89.
[37] A photograph, transcription, and translation of this 9 B.C. text from Priene can be found in Adolf Deissmann, *Light from the Ancient East,* rev. ed.,

plied when associated with the saving power and person of the emperor:

> The ruler is divine by nature. His power extends to men, to animals, to the earth and to the sea. Nature belongs to him; the wind and the waves are subject to him. He works miracles and heals men. He is the savior of the world who also redeems individuals from their difficulties.[38]

The emperor's divinity was attested by signs in the heavens at both his birth and his death that showed he belonged among the gods. Although some leading scholars have denied the link between the meaning of *euangelion* as applied to the first four books of the New Testament and the connotation it carries in the imperial cult,[39] the connection has recently and rightly been reaffirmed in an important study of gospel origins by Wilhelm Schneemelcher.[40]

It would be wrong to assume, however, that the primary meaning of *euangelion* was taken over from the Hellenistic conceptual world and that the Old Testament belief in the significance of Yahweh's saving acts as set forth in Second Isaiah was added later. The likelihood is rather the reverse. For Mark the Hellenistic term was a useful propaganda tool for setting forth his understanding of Jesus' divine kingship, a form of rulership that rested on conceptions of power and divine purpose in the world entirely different from those in non-Christian circles. This radical divergence is explicitly declared in Mark 10:42–45:

---

trans. L. R. M. Strachan (New York: Harper & Row, n.d.), p. 366 and Figure 70. Whether the εὐαγγέλιον (*evangelion*) is understood to be the announcement of his birth (so Deissmann) or the fulfillment of the Sibylline prophecies about Augustus (so Eduard Norden in Deissmann, p. 366, n. 8), the analogy with the use of the term by Mark and the other evangelists is evident. The full Greek text is in Wilhelm Dittenberger, *Orientis Graeci Inscriptiones Selectae* [Selected Greek inscriptions from the Orient], vol. 2, no. 458 (reprinted, Hildesheim: Olms, 1960), lines 40–79 (the point at which the passage under study appears).

[38] Friedrich, "εὐαγγελίζεσθαι," p. 724.

[39] For example, Bultmann, *Theology of the New Testament*, vol. 1, p. 87.

[40] In *New Testament Apocrypha*, trans. R. McL. Wilson and others (Philadelphia: Westminster, 1963), pp. 72–73.

You know that those who are supposed to rule over the Gentiles lord it over them, and their great men exercise authority over them. But it shall not be so among you; but whoever would be great among you must be your servant, and whoever would be first among you must be slave of all. For the Son of man came not to be served but to serve, and to give his life as a ransom for many.

Without assuming that Mark 10:45 is a direct allusion to the Suffering Servant theme of Isaiah 53 (this cannot be demonstrated on philological grounds),[41] we can see that casting Jesus in the role of a servant on the eve of his entry into Jerusalem as a kingly figure (Mark 11:1–10) is clearly intentional. Mark wants to use the terminology of Gentile kingship—including *euangelion*—but to redefine in a radical way what kingship involves. This redefinition, reflecting his understanding of Yahweh's sovereignty, is drawn not from imperial Rome but from the eschatological kingship of Second Isaiah and the later prophets and apocalyptists.

Although Paul refers to Jesus' turning over "the kingdom" to God after the defeat of the evil powers is complete (1 Cor. 15:24–28), this phrase is not central in Paul's thought. Indeed, he uses it at times in a way that sounds more like early twentieth-century Protestant liberals than like Mark: "The kingdom of God does not mean food and drink but righteousness and peace and joy in the Holy Spirit" (Rom. 14:17). Apart from the 1 Corinthians 15 passage, in which Paul sets forth a kind of eschatological calendar of events, the Kingdom plays no significant role in Paul's thought as we know it from his letters. It may be that the eschatological wisdom was kept for the inner core of the theologically mature believers in the Pauline churches,[42] which could account for the brief attention it receives in his public letters. But even if

---

41 See the discussion by C. K. Barrett in his essay in A. J. B. Higgins, ed., *New Testament Essays* (Manchester: Manchester University Press, 1959).
42 See an important article by Robin Scroggs, "Paul: Σοφὸς καὶ Πνευματικός" [*sophos kai pneumatikos*, "wise and spiritual"], in *New Testament Studies* 14, 1 (1967): 33–55. Scroggs suggests that the wisdom issue concerns the merely human wisdom of the Corinthians and "an esoteric Christian apocalyptic-wisdom teaching which [Paul] carefully guarded from immature Christians."

this were the case—and the hypothesis has great plausibility—the central concern for Paul was the cross-resurrection kerygma.[43]

What we are confronted with, therefore, is not merely a difference between "gospel" as message in Paul and as a narrative account in Mark, but a different understanding of the meaning of Jesus for faith. The problem is not only the relationship of Jesus' message to that of Paul, but also the understandings of Jesus that underlie the synoptic tradition on the one hand and Paul on the other. It is not enough to say that the gospel form developed by a process of enriching the basic message about the cross and resurrection.[44] Kähler's oft-quoted dictum that the gospels are passion stories with extended introductions[45] is likewise inadequate. Although the story of the passion is an essential element in Mark's scheme, it is not the main event for which the events of Jesus' ministry are no more than inconsequential preliminaries. Nor is Kähler any closer to the truth of Mark's intention when he says that the gospels are interested not in *what* happened but in *who* acted and *how*.[46]

Mark's Unique Literary Contribution

What led Mark to arrange the Jesus tradition in the literary form we know as a gospel? Answers to this question were already being offered by the early second century, although there is a certain speciousness about them. Papias of Hierapolis, famed for the low estimate of his intellect advanced by Eusebius[47] and for the tantalizing bits of information about gospel origins attributed to him,[48] reports that Mark is said to have written down the sayings of Jesus as he "remembered [ἀπεμνημόνευσε, apemnēmóneuse] hearing them from Peter."[49] Justin Martyr (A.D. 100?–165?), rely-

---

[43] As Scroggs acknowledges, *ibid.*, p. 54.
[44] So Schneemelcher, *New Testament Apocrypha*, p. 77.
[45] *The So-called Historical Jesus*, p. 80, n. 11.
[46] *Ibid.*, p. 81.
[47] *Ecclesiastical History* 3.39.13, Loeb edition, vol. 1, trans. K. Lake (Cambridge: Harvard University Press, 1949).
[48] *Ibid.* 3.39.1–17. For a critical evaluation of the significance of the Papias tradition concerning gospel origins, see Kümmel, *Introduction to the New Testament*, pp. 42–44.
[49] *Ibid.* 3.39.15.

ing on the testimony of Papias, refers to the gospel of Mark as the "memoir" of Peter.[50] By the very choice of this designation, Justin elevates the gospel as a literary form into the realm of known types of Hellenistic literature. The implication seems to be that before the apostolic generation passed away, Peter and other apostles (or apostolic associates, such as Luke) authorized or allowed their followers to produce memoirs of their associations with Jesus. These memoirs would guarantee an immediacy of witness to what Jesus had said and done and would serve as the last possible eyewitness accounts. As much as a twentieth-century scholar interested in the origins of Christianity might wish to have access to such documents, it must be acknowledged that the gospels do not match the description that Justin Martyr offered for them in the middle of the second century A.D. The gospel of Mark is not a "memoir" of Peter, either in the sense that it recounts in a special way the associations of Peter with Jesus or in the sense that Mark reports first-hand recollections about Jesus. The material on which Mark drew passed through a long process of re-telling and modification and interpretation, and it reflects less special interest in Peter than does Matthew's gospel. (See, for example, Matt. 16:13–20; verses 17–19, in which Peter is singled out for a special place of authority, have no parallel in the other gospel accounts of this incident.)

The memoir as a literary type, *apomnēmóneuma*, is best exemplified by the *Memorabilia of Socrates*, written by Xenophon 434?–355? B.C.). The analogy between this life of Socrates and the gospels, first developed by Justin Martyr in his apologetic writings, has been widely discussed for the past century and a half by biblical scholars.[51] Although the theory of apostolic memoirs has been appealed to as a way of ensuring the reliability

---

[50] Justin uses the phrase "Memoirs of the Apostles" with great frequency in his writings; in Chapters 99–107 of the *Dialogue with Trypho* the term appears twelve times. The "memoirs" are specifically described as documents drawn up by Jesus' apostles and those who followed them (Chapter 103). In *Saint Justin Martyr* (New York: Fathers of the Church, 1949).

[51] A summary of this discussion is given by K. L. Schmidt in his essay "Die Stellung der Evangelien in der allgemeinen Literaturgeschichte" [The place of the gospels in the general history of literature], in Hans Schmidt, ed., *Eucharisterion* [essays presented to Hermann Gunkel on his sixtieth birthday] (Göttingen: Vandenhoek & Ruprecht, 1923), pp. 50–134.

of the gospel accounts, it does not in fact provide any such guarantee. Indeed, the analogy is not even an appropriate one, since Xenophon's *Memorabilia* represents a conscious literary effort, rather than the popular kind of writing that makes no pretensions of being "literature." The distinction is accurately brought out in the contrast between the two German words *Hochliteratur* and *Kleinliteratur*. To make such a distinction is in no way to dismiss the gospel of Mark as beneath academic notice; it is rather to recognize it for what it is: a propaganda writing produced by and for a community that made no cultural claims for itself and offered its writings as a direct appeal for adherents rather than as a way of attracting the attention of intellectuals or literati of the day.

Recently an attempt has been made to place the gospels, especially Luke—the use of contemporary literary conventions shows that the writer of Luke wished to be considered an author and a historian[52]—within a genre of literature produced in the late Hellenistic–early Roman period (150 B.C.–A.D. 150): the aretalogy.[53] Though the term is not used in Greek, it appears in a Latinized form, *aretalogus*, to designate "one who (professionally) speaks the wondrous deeds of a deity or a divinely gifted human."[54] The aretalogy, then, is the narrative in which a heroic figure is portrayed. Plato's portrayal of Socrates is considered by some scholars, most notably Moses Hadas and Morton Smith, "the source for all subsequent aretalogies, pagan and Christian."[55] As artist and teacher, Plato presented Socrates in the *Phaedo* and the *Apology* in such a way as to establish a kind of archetype, in terms of which subsequent ages represented "certain saintly figures, who, like Socrates, had selflessly devoted themselves to the spiritual improvement of the community and had accepted the suffering, sometimes the martyrdom [that Socrates had]."[56]

[52] See Martin Dibelius, "The First Christian Historian" and "The Speeches in Acts and Ancient Historiography," in his *Studies in the Acts of the Apostles*, trans. Mary Ling (London: SCM Press, 1956), pp. 123–85. See also H. J. Cadbury, *The Making of Luke-Acts*, 2nd ed. (Naperville, Ill.: Allenson, 1958).

[53] Moses Hadas and Morton Smith, *Heroes and Gods* (New York: Harper & Row, 1965).

[54] *Ibid.*, p. 61.

[55] *Ibid.*, p. 63.

[56] *Ibid.*, p. 56. My detailed critique of the aretalogy hypothesis is offered in "Aretalogy and Gospel," *Journal of Biblical Literature* 93 (1973):408–16.

When the detailed evidence is adduced to support this thesis, however, it turns out not to be persuasive. There is no pattern discernible that can be called a common literary element in the "aretalogies" summarized by Morton Smith, nor do three of them —Porphyry's *Life of Pythagoras*, Philo Judaeus' *Life of Moses*, and Philostratus' *Life of Apollonius of Tyana*—depict their respective heroes dying a martyr's death. This is something of a letdown after the moving description of the martyred Socrates as the archetypal subject of the aretalogy. The two elements that seem to be shared by the four biographies are that miracles were attributed to all the heroes and that each had his own kind of divine wisdom to offer his faithful followers. The form and content of these four lives do not demonstrate sufficient similarities as a literary genre to consider the aretalogy—if indeed it is a literary form—as the model for the gospel of Mark or the other gospels.

The conclusion reached by K. L. Schmidt in his study of this subject a half-century ago is the only one warranted by the evidence: that the writer of the first gospel, Mark, had no model or precedent to follow. In writing his gospel, he created a new genre of literature for which, as a whole, there was no precedent.[57] He followed the patterns of neither the literary memoirs nor the popular biographies of his time,[58] although analogies to the narrative style can be found in collections of anecdotes in Jewish and pagan folk literature.[59] The chief feature of both the gospel writers (with the exception of Luke) and the authors of anecdotes and miracle stories is the lack of consciousness of being an author or

---

[57] Schmidt, "Die Stellung der Evangelien." Also Siegfried Schulz, *Die Stunde der Botschaft* [The hour of the message] (Hamburg: Furche, 1967), p. 36. The nature of this book's contents is described by its subtitle: *Introduction to the Theology of the Four Evangelists.* For a brilliant discussion of the uniqueness of the gospels among Hellenistic literature, see Erich Auerbach, *Mimesis* (Princeton: Princeton University Press, [1953] 1974), pp. 40–49. Analogies have been noted between certain features of the gospels and Hellenistic literary conventions (see, for example, C. H. Talbert's *Literary Patterns, Theological Themes and the Genre of Luke-Acts* [Missoula, Mont.: Scholars Press, 1974]), but what is demonstrated is (1) that the gospels do share certain stylistic conventions with other writings of the Hellenistic period, and (2) that the composite product, a gospel, has no real analogy in Hellenistic literature.

[58] Schmidt, "Die Stellung der Evangelien," p. 60.

[59] *Ibid.*, pp. 60–61, 65.

of creating a literature.[60] Stated another way, for the preliterary stages of the origin of the gospel tradition, parallels can be shown in Jewish and pagan sources; for the gospel as a literary whole, there is no real precedent.[61] The impact of the pagan miracle stories is most evident at the written stage of the development of the synoptic tradition, so it is possible to distinguish in Mark between what was probably the original intent of the tradition that he incorporated and what it had come to mean to him. But even where this pagan influence can be observed, as in the heightening of the miraculous element, it is apparent in details of stories and sayings, not in the structure of the gospel or in Mark's goals in writing it.

Chief among Mark's goals was the determination to show that the meaning of Jesus for faith was manifest in the arena of world history. His view of history was derived from that of Jewish apocalypticism, especially from the Book of Daniel. He was not content with the notion that God's purpose for creation was disclosed through the words of Jesus; he wanted to demonstrate that the revelation came through a public person performing public acts in interaction with the civil and religious authorities of his time. For Mark faith did not offer an escape from the world but the divinely granted key to the meaning of the past, the present, and the future of the world. It is in that cosmic context that his report of Jesus is placed. And in the interests of that goal he appropriates the Jesus tradition.

MARK'S USE OF THE JESUS TRADITION

The Sources Available to Mark

The theory that Mark is the oldest gospel, as well as the oldest extant gospel, seems to be the most plausible explanation for the literary relationships among the synoptics.[62] As for sources, Mark

---

[60] *Ibid.*, pp. 74–75.
[61] Schulz, *Die Stunde der Botschaft*, p. 37; A. N. Wilder, *Early Christian Rhetoric* (New York: Harper & Row, 1964), p. 36.
[62] Kümmel, *Introduction to the New Testament*, pp. 38–63.

may have had collections of stories about or sayings of Jesus, but there is no evidence that, before Mark did so, they were woven into a continuous narrative as we now have them. The parables may have constituted one such group of sayings, just as the cluster of shorter miracle stories in Mark 2 and 3 and of longer stories in Mark 4 and 5 may have constituted collections of narratives on which Mark drew. A similar case could be made for sayings or collections offering criticism of the Jewish tradition (Mark 7 and 10), presenting accounts of controversies with Jews (Mark 12), and containing eschatological themes (Mark 13); on the other hand, the present topical grouping could come from Mark. Theories proposed for written sources of Mark are dubious, with the possible exception of collections of miracle stories.[63] Even in the case of the passion narrative—the only extended narrative sequence in the gospels—there is no sure evidence (as form critics have assumed)[64] that Mark had access to an existing document for Mark 11–16, or for any part of it. The same characteristics are evident there as are to be found in other parts of Mark. In Mark 11–16 there is pervasive stress on the events that occur as the fulfillment of Scripture, so that the critical reader cannot tell whether the events have been conformed to Scripture or (as seems likely in several cases) the Scripture has been modified to fit the event. Almost everywhere in Mark the connective tissue by which Mark has joined together the sayings and narrative units is secondary; that is, it is the work of Mark himself. Almost certainly he had no sequential or chronological framework available to him, other than the obvious fact that the baptism of Jesus came at the outset of Jesus' ministry and the crucifixion came at the end. C. H.

---

[63] The most elaborate attempt to reconstruct sources behind Mark is that of W. L. Knox, *The Sources of the Synoptic Gospels*, Vol. 1: *St. Mark*, ed. Henry Chadwick (London: Cambridge University Press, 1953). P. J. Achtemeier, "Pre-Markan Miracle Catenae," *Journal of Biblical Literature* 89 (1970): 265–91, makes an excellent case for Mark's having used collections of miracle stories.

[64] Bultmann, *History of the Synoptic Tradition*, pp. 275, 279; Martin Dibelius, *From Tradition to Gospel*, 3rd ed., trans. B. L. Woolf (New York: Scribner's, 1965), pp. 22–23, 178–217. For evidence that Mark has created this sequential narrative, see my essay, "The Function of Scriptural Quotations and Allusions in Mk 11–16," E. E. Ellis and E. Grässer, eds., *Jesus and Paulus* (Göttingen: Vandenhoeck B. Ruprecht, 1975).

Dodd's attempt to prove otherwise is not persuasive.[65] There are a few points at which place names may have been preserved in the tradition on the basis of actual historical memory, as in the scene of the confession of Peter, which is located in the theologically and dogmatically insignificant vicinity of Caesarea Philippi (Mark 8:27).[66]

The freedom felt by the gospel writers to rearrange the order of events in the gospel tradition for programmatic or literary purposes is shown by Luke's placing Jesus' rejection at Nazareth at the outset of his public ministry (Luke 4), whereas in Mark it comes in the middle of the story of Jesus' activity (Mark 6:1). The miracle stories of Mark (Mark 1 and 2) are moved by Matthew to a point following the Sermon on the Mount (Matt. 5, 6, and 7) because that best suited Matthew's arrangement of material in alternating panels of activity and discourse.[67] The sense of movement and sequence that the reader receives in Mark's gospel comes from Mark's own arrangement of the tradition, as K. L. Schmidt showed in his pioneering form-critical study *Der Rahmen der Geschichte Jesu* [The framework of the history of Jesus]. Schmidt points out that "in Mark's introductions to the pericopes, there can still be traced vestiges of an itinerary."[68] But only traces of an itinerary remain, and these are confused as a result of Mark's lack of detailed knowledge of Palestinian geography: The report that Jesus went from Tyre and Sidon through the cities of the Decapolis on his way back to the Sea of Galilee

[65] "The Framework of the Gospel Narrative," in his *New Testament Studies* (Manchester: Manchester University Press, 1953), pp. 1–11.
[66] In contrast, for example, to references to Galilee, which R. H. Lightfoot and Ernst Lohmeyer suppose to have reflected a special interest of a hypothetical Galilean wing of the primitive church that was clearly differentiated, theologically and otherwise, from the Jerusalem church. For details, see R. H. Lightfoot, *Locality and Doctrine in the Gospels* (New York: Harper & Row, 1938).
[67] A summary of Matthew's rearrangement of Markan material is given in H. C. Kee, F. W. Young, and Karlfried Fröhlich, *Understanding the New Testament*, 3rd ed. (Englewood Cliffs, N.J.: Prentice-Hall, 1973), pp. 318–19. Details can be found in W. G. Kümmel, *Introduction to the New Testament*, pp. 59–61, 106–09.
[68] *Der Rahmen der Geschichte Jesu* (Berlin: Trowitsch & Sohn, 1919; reprinted, 1964), p. 317.

sounds as odd to one who knows Palestine as to say that a man stopped off in Boston on his way from New York to Philadelphia. Designations of temporal connections are rare, but where they do occur, as in Mark 9:1—"after six days," that is, one week later— they show us only that Mark may have preserved the few temporal links that he found in the tradition,[69] although these phrases could as well be Markan stylizations intended to impart dramatic movement to the story sequence.

Mark received his material in a period of oral transmission, or perhaps when pregospel documents were available in addition to the oral transmission process, which continued even after the gospels had been written.[70] But what Mark received came to him in isolated pericopes of two main types: sayings tradition and narrative tradition.

SAYINGS TRADITION

1. Aphorisms. Example: "He who has ears to hear, let him hear" (Mark 4:9). Mark positioned this type of saying where he thought it fit, a judgment that does not always correspond with the opinion of modern commentators and critics.

2. Parables. Example: the Parable of the Productive Seed (= the Parable of the Sower) (Mark 4:3–8). Mark interprets this parable as an allegory of the hearers in the church (Mark 4:14–20).

3. Sayings clusters. These are of two types:
   a. Topical groupings. Example: the salt words (Matt. 5:13–16).
   b. Formal groupings. Example: the Beatitudes and woes (Luke 6:20–26).

NARRATIVE TRADITION

1. Anecdotes. Example: the story of the demoniac in the synagogue at Capernaum (Mark 1:23–26). These are brief biographical narratives.

---

[69] *Ibid.*, pp. 222–24.
[70] So H. Köster, *Synoptische Überlieferungen bei den apostolischen Vätern* [Synoptic traditions in the apostolic fathers] (Berlin: Akademie Verlag, 1957).

2. Aphoristic narratives. Example: the plucking of grain on the Sabbath (Mark 2:23–28). A mixture of narrative and sayings material, these are narratives that culminate in pithy sayings.

3. Wonder stories. Example: Mark 5:1–20. In these stories the main point is the wonder itself, the miraculous as such.

4. Legends. These are narratives in which the divine is directly or publicly manifest. They are of two types:
   a. Biographical legends. Example: the temptation story, especially in the Q form found in Matthew and Luke. The main interest is in the divine as disclosed in Jesus' life or activity.
   b. Cult legends. Example: the Feeding of the Five Thousand (Mark 6:30–44). The main interest is in authorization of or grounding for the church's cult.

5. Passion story. In its present form this is the only extended sequential account preserved in the gospel tradition. The extent to which it preserves pre-Markan reports of the course of events or to which it has been given this continuity by Mark in the interest of demonstrating Jesus' trial and death as the fulfillment of Scripture is difficult to determine (see page 304).

Working with these disconnected elements, it would not have been possible to infer a series of cause-and-effect links that would offer an explanation for the dynamics of Jesus' ministry or the sequence in the events that led to his crucifixion. Nor is there the slightest possibility of reconstructing the process by which Jesus came to understand his own role in God's plan or in what terms he came to view his own impending death. To the extent that such a developmental pattern can be discerned in the gospel of Mark, it is to be attributed to Mark himself and to the literary method by which he presents and expands his basic themes.

One must distinguish between Mark's themes and the gospel outline he uses to give what is mostly the appearance, but in part also the substance, of a historical sequence of events. Mark placed the traditional material on the following structural framework:

1. Preparation for Ministry (1:1–20)
2. The Kingdom Announced in Word and Act (1:21—8:26)

3. What Messiahship and Discipleship Mean (8:27—10:45)
4. Preparation for the Events of the End (11:1—14:25)
5. The Passion and the Parousia (14:26—16:8)

The sense of urgency and tension in Mark's account is heightened not only in mechanical ways, such as his twelve-times-repeated "immediately," but also in the recurrent juxtaposition of challenge and rejection, of confession and denial, which highlights both the feeling of eschatological imminence and the importance of a faith decision.

Intertwined in the gospel of Mark (so that more than one theme may be present in a single pericope) are the following major themes:

1. Fulfillment of Scripture
2. Jesus as Son of God and/or Coming Son of Man
3. Coming of the Kingdom and/or Judgment
4. Passion and Parousia
5. Ministry, Ethics, and Cultus in the New Community

Each of these themes, as we shall see, is fundamental to Mark's overall thesis that the eschatological event proclaimed in the kerygma had its beginning in the historical figure of Jesus of Nazareth.[71]

Jesus as the Fulfillment of Scripture

It is tempting to suppose that the gospel writers appealed so frequently to Scripture in their portrayals of Jesus as an apologetic tactic, in order to lend authority to the claim of the early church

---

[71] Hans Conzelmann, "Gegenwart und Zukunft in der synoptischen Tradition" [Present and future in the synoptic tradition], in *Zeitschrift für Theologie und Kirche* 54 (1957): 288–96 (see esp. p. 294), adopts a view of Mark that is formally similar to the one proposed here; the substantial difference lies in the understanding of the aim of the wonder stories. It is not to present Jesus as a θεῖος ἀνήρ (*theios anēr*), but to show him as the bearer of the eschatological power to defeat Satan. On the imprecision of the term *theios anēr* (divine man), see D. L. Tiede, *The Charismatic Figure as Miracle Worker* (Missoula, Mont.: Scholars Press, 1972).

to be the new people of God. This somewhat condescending estimate is made the more appealing by the fact that, gauged by modern interpretive standards, the New Testament writers exercised an embarrassing degree of freedom in applying an Old Testament text to their situation. The fact that the rabbis were performing the same sort of exegetical sleight of hand (or even that similarly fanciful essays in Old Testament hermeneutics have been discovered at Qumran)[72] does not dispel the impression that the methods are artificial. Historically trained Christian interpreters are made more than a little uncomfortable by what they find the New Testament claiming to have happened "according to the Scriptures."[73]

But far more important than the documentation provided by Scripture was the power of the belief, shared by the Qumran Essenes and the early church, that the Scriptures were not so much chronicles of the past as blueprints for the future that God had in store for his creation in general and his people in particular. It was the actualization of the eschatological plan laid down in the Scriptures, and now being rightly interpreted in and through contemporary events, that was the ground of the importance of Scripture in the first century A.D. Thus Mark launches into "the beginning of the gospel" (Mark 1:1) with the claim that through Jesus' baptism at the hand of John were fulfilled both the promise of an eschatological messenger (Mal. 3:1) and the announcement of the one who would prepare for the Lord's coming (Isa. 40:3). The fact that the quotation as a whole is wrongly attributed to Isaiah and that Second Isaiah's expectation was of the coming of Yahweh, not Jesus Christ as Lord, does not obscure the theological assertion that is being made: It is for God's Son, Jesus of Nazareth, that John the Baptist was sent to prepare the way. In a way that could not have been anticipated by the human author of these prophecies, the promise of God is

[72] See Krister Stendahl, *The School of St. Matthew* (Philadelphia: Fortress, 1966), where the use of Scripture in the first-discovered Qumran documents is discussed.
[73] A candid and illuminating discussion of this problem has been written by Barnabas Lindars in his *New Testament Apologetic* (Philadelphia: Westminster, 1961), a book that probably owes to its misleading title its failure to receive the attention it merits.

seen as being fulfilled through Jesus.[74] It is impossible to tell how much of the detail given in the tradition concerning John the Baptist is historical recollection about him that is being passed on and how much is Christian interpretation of his role in the light of the Old Testament. If the former, then the Baptist may have modeled his attire after Elijah (2 Kings 1:8), whose coming is announced as an eschatological promise in Malachi 4:5 and was widely expected in late Judaism.[75] If the latter—that is, if Mark shaped his picture of John by recalling the Old Testament allusions to the Lord's forerunner—then we see that in this case also it was the belief that God's redemptive plan was nearing completion that motivated Mark's and the tradition's appeal to Scripture. Early Christian faith deemed it essential that there be discernible correspondence between what the Scriptures announced and what was actually occurring, since the apocalyptic view of history required that the outworking of the divine purpose be seen in current events or in the recent past. Whether the modern reader finds the alleged correspondence convincing is not the point; what was essential at Qumran and for the author of Mark was the demonstration in the realm of observable history of the fulfillment of what God had announced beforehand through the prophets. Only in this way could one be certain that the eschatological schedule was leading on to the redemptive climax.

The form of appeal to the Old Testament in Mark varies widely. In most instances a passage is directly quoted or alluded to quite explicitly. At other times the correspondence between the narrative of the gospel and a prophetic passage must be inferred, as in Mark 11:1–9, where the details of the lowly king's entry match the prophecy of Zechariah 9:9; the link is made explicit in Matthew's expanded version of the incident (Matt.

---

[74] This lack of exact correspondence between the prophetic promise and the Christian claim of fulfillment has been stressed by Wolfhart Pannenberg in his contributions to Pannenberg, ed., *Revelation as History*, 3rd ed., trans. David Granskou (New York: Macmillan, 1968).

[75] See the excursus on Elijah in H. L. Strack and Paul Billerbeck, *Kommentar zum Neuen Testament* [Commentary on the New Testament], vol. 4 (Munich: Beck, 1922–61), pp. 792–98. Also Joachim Jeremias, " 'Ηλ(ε)ιας" [*El(e)ias*, "Elijah"], in *Theological Dictionary of the New Testament*, vol. 2 pp. 928–34; further discussion of the Son of Man is found on pp. 92–140.

21:1–9). The apocalyptic discourse in Mark 13 is filled with direct and indirect allusions to Old Testament passages. The passion story also corresponds closely with the Old Testament; indeed, there are more Old Testament allusions here than elsewhere in Mark. In the details of the crucifixion alone (Mark 15:24–34) there are at least three recollections of Psalm 22. Thus, the Old Testament may have helped to shape the narrative, although the incidents must have been in some way analogous to Old Testament stories or prophecies from the outset in order for the parallels ever to have been noticed. One gospel passage, however, Mark 9:12, refers to what is "written," as though alluding to Scripture, but no known Jewish writing contains such a prophecy (that is, of the suffering of the Son of Man).

The three major subjects pointed to by the Old Testament quotations in Mark are: (1) the judgment on Israel, (2) the reinterpretation of the commandments of God, and (3) the fulfillment of messianic hopes. All these are eschatological functions, of course, since the repristination of the Law of God was one of the eschatological functions expected in late Judaism to occur in the End Time. At Qumran it was the Teacher of Righteousness, or the eschatological prophet, who was to fulfill this role. In Mark, Jesus performs this function in denouncing the blindness of the faithless (Mark 4:12 = Isa. 6:9–10); in criticizing the practice of allowing human traditions to supersede the divine command (Mark 7:6 = Isa. 29:13); and in defending the belief in the resurrection (Mark 12:18–27 = Exod. 3:6), even though in this case the weight of the argument is lost on the modern reader. No matter whether the arguments are persuasive or not, the fact remains that Mark presents Jesus as one whose ministry among men was characterized by the work of interpreting anew God's Law, and doing so not in continuity with rabbinic methods of interpretation (1:22) but with his own unprecedented authority. Clearly, Mark wants his reader to see in Jesus of Nazareth the eschatological messenger who restores the true understanding of God's will in the End Time.

Mark spells out this role in relation to specific issues: the precedence of human need over Sabbath observance (2:26 = 1 Sam. 21:1–6) and the priority of marriage in the created order over divorce, which is a concession to human frailty (10:2–12 = Gen. 1:27; Deut. 24:1–4).

Most important of all, however, is the correspondence that Mark and his tradition see between the Old Testament messianic hopes (as set forth in Psalms 110 and 118 in particular) and the meaning of Jesus. Both these psalms were interpreted eschatologically in Judaism;[76] by pointing out the fulfillment of them in Jesus' teachings (12:10) and actions (11:9), Mark shows his readers that Jesus, who is worshipped as Lord in the church, was already the eschatological king in the days of his historical ministry, as reported in the synoptic tradition. Something of the difficulties that the early church had in interpreting Jesus in relation to these messianic categories is to be observed in the inconclusive controversy story that Mark pushed back into the ministry of Jesus (12:35–37). Anachronistically, Jesus is thereby depicted struggling with christological questions about himself only a few days before the crucifixion. But what Mark wants to show is that the christological issue was already implicit in the authoritative earthly ministry of Jesus. The historical critic knows, however, that the struggle over titles did not take shape until after Easter.

Jesus as Messiah

The disciples regularly refer to Jesus as "Rabbi" ($\dot{\rho}\alpha\beta\beta\dot{\iota}$) or "Teacher" ($\Delta\iota\delta\dot{\alpha}\sigma\kappa\alpha\lambda$ος, *didaskalos*), even in such circumstances as the storm on the lake, when, presumably, their thoughts were not on instructional matters (Mark 4:38). Mark's use of these terms may show that he has preserved the actual titles conferred on Jesus by his followers. Paul's favorite title for Jesus, Lord ($\kappa\dot{\nu}\rho\iota$ος, *kurios*), is rare in Mark (5:19 and 11:3); the occurrences probably betray an unconscious shift to the terminology of the church's post-Easter kerygma: "Jesus is Lord" (Phil. 2:11, 1 Cor. 12:3), which even on Mark's terms is not appropriate until after the resurrection. Mark's clear preferences as titles for Jesus are Son of God and Son of Man.

---

[76] See Sigmund Mowinckel, *He That Cometh*, trans. G. W. Anderson (Nashville: Abingdon, 1956), esp. pp. 155–86.

Son of God. Because Mark is convinced that the Kingdom of God began to break into the old age in the person and ministry of Jesus, it is wholly fitting for him to locate the eschatological titles, Son of God and Son of Man, in Jesus' earthly ministry. In addition to sounding forth the title of Jesus as "Son of God" in his opening words (Mark 1:1), Mark reports that at Jesus' baptism he was acclaimed by a private, divine disclosure to be Son of God (Mark 1:11). The words of the voice of God form a blend of phrases from Psalm 2 and from Isaiah 42: The first was addressed to David (or his successors) as those who ruled in God's stead; the second was uttered to the Servant of Yahweh, who is commended for his humility and persistence and endowed with God's Spirit to enable him to establish justice in the earth among the nations (Isa. 42:1–4). Mark 10:42–45 expresses the view that the one chosen by God to establish the Kingdom of God on the earth accomplishes his mission not by the exercise of brute force but by humble self-sacrificing service. No claim is offered in either Psalm 2 or Isaiah 42 that God's agent of redemption is a divine being, so "Son of God" in Mark 1:1 is not a metaphysical term. Mark gives no hint of a supernatural birth for Jesus; if there is any belief in the virgin birth abroad, Mary gives no hint of it in Mark's narrative. Indeed, she and her other sons are so unprepared for his authoritative way of commissioning disciples, expelling demons, and accepting acclaim as God's Son (3:11, 14) that they conclude he is crazy (3:21) and try to remove him from the public scene (3:31).[77]

Although the term Son of God is not given (as in Matthew) in connection with the confession of Peter (Mark 8:29), the title used, Christ, refers to the anointed figure or figures who were to reestablish the true kingship and the true cultus in the End Time. The Christian faith in Jesus as a single kingly figure, to whom priestly functions are assigned in a peripheral manner (except in Hebrews, which is itself near the periphery of the canon), cannot obscure the fact that in late Judaism there was

---

[77] The phrase οἱ παρ' αὐτοῦ (hoi par' autou) in Mark 3:21 is wrongly translated in some editions of the RSV as "his friends." It means "his family," as 3:31–35 shows and as TEV accurately renders the phrase.

widespread belief in two anointed figures: the kingly figure from Judah and the priestly figure from Levi.[78] First attested in Zechariah 4 and 6, the theme of two anointed eschatological figures is a dominant one in the Testaments of the Twelve Patriarchs, especially the Testament of Levi (fragments of which have been found at Qumran).[79] However, since no contrary evidence is present in Mark, we can assume that for him the terms King, Son of God, and Christ are interchangeable: All point to the man divinely appointed to establish God's rule over his people and, through them, over the whole creation. What is new in Mark is his linking this kingly hope with the eschatological servant of Second Isaiah. The importance for Mark of the servant role of Isaiah 42 is stressed by the fact that Mark sees in Jesus' baptism the fulfillment of the prediction in 42:1, which describes God's pouring out of his Spirit upon the servant to enable him to carry out his redemptive role. At Jesus' baptism he is acclaimed Son of God by a heavenly utterance (Mark 1:10–11).

The other crucial text in which the term "Son of God" is used is Mark 15:39. At the cross, having observed the darkness that covered the earth, the cry of Jesus, the scorn of the crowd, and the ripping of the temple veil, the centurion said: "Truly this man was a son of God!" Although the definite article is not used (not "*the* Son of God"), the pagan soldier's testimony is central for Mark: Through the cross, even Gentiles will recognize in Jesus the redeemer of mankind. The term Son of God seems to have carried quite different connotations in Gentile thinking, and Mark's account is not uninfluenced by these. The practice of

[78] The fundamental essay on this subject is by K. G. Kuhn, "The Two Messiahs of Aaron and Israel," in Krister Stendahl, ed., *The Scrolls and the New Testament* (New York: Harper & Row, 1957), pp. 54–64. Subsequent criticism of Kuhn's interpretation has not set aside his basic position. See Matthew Black, *The Scrolls and Christian Origins* (New York: Scribner's, 1961).

[79] On the theory that the Testaments of the Twelve Patriarchs originated at Qumran, see F. M. Cross, *The Ancient Library of Qumran*, rev. ed. (Garden City, N.Y.: Doubleday, 1961), pp. 198–206. On the background of the Testaments, see my introduction in the forthcoming edition of the Pseudepigrapha to be published by Duke University–Doubleday, J. H. Charlesworth, editor.

deifying a great leader or wise man of the past is common throughout the Hellenistic and Roman worlds. It is almost surely too much to claim that there was a fixed type, the *theios anēr*,[80] to which Mark conformed the image of Jesus. This notion, which arose in the heyday of the history of religions school, has been repeated so often that it has come to be accepted as a fact.[81] But in truth, except for a widespread fondness for apotheosis of great men, there is no set type or model of *theios anēr*. That is not to say, however, that the tendency toward apotheosizing Jesus is not at work in Mark, nor in the tradition on which he drew. What is clear is that this does not constitute a major, conscious aim of Mark. The basic function of Jesus as Son of God in Mark is as bringer of the eschatological salvation, in keeping with the expectations of late Jewish apocalypticism.

Son of Man. The influence of apocalypticism is even more apparent in Mark's use of the title Son of Man. Scholarly opinions about the use of this term in the gospel tradition vary widely:[82] Some scholars think that only the future Son of Man words are authentic;[83] some are convinced that only the present Son of Man sayings go back to Jesus;[84] others are persuaded that all or nearly all the sayings are genuine;[85] and a few think that none of the

[80] It is treated along with christological titles by Ferdinand Hahn in *Christologische Hoheitstitel* [Christological titles] (Göttingen: Vandenhoek & Ruprecht, 1963).
[81] See my discussion of aretalogy and *theios anēr* in "Aretalogy and Gospel," *Journal of Biblical Literature* 93 (1973): 408–16, and in "Aretalogies, Hellenistic 'Lives' and the Sources of Mark," *12th Colloquy of the Center for Hermeneutical Studies in Hellenistic and Modern Culture* (Berkeley, Calif.: Center for Hermeneutical Studies in Hellenistic and Modern Culture, 1975).
[82] The three groupings of the Son of Man sayings are conveniently summarized in Bultmann's *Theology of the New Testament*, vol. 1, pp. 30–32.
[83] So Bultmann, *ibid.*
[84] Eduard Schweizer, "Son of Man," *Journal of Biblical Literature* 79 (1960): 119–29. Also Norman Perrin, *The New Testament: An Introduction* (New York: Harcourt Brace Jovanovich, 1974), pp. 76–77, 156–57.
[85] For example, Vincent Taylor, *The Names of Jesus* (New York: St. Martin's, 1953). With many Anglo-Saxon scholars, Taylor believes that Jesus' messianic consciousness was formulated through his combining the traditional kingly messianic idea of Israel with the apocalyptic Son of Man notion and the Suffering Servant concept of II Isaiah.

sayings can be attributed to Jesus.[86] The background of the term, whether used by Jesus of himself or by the synoptic tradition in its interpretation of him, is Jewish apocalypticism.[87]

The hypothesis with the greatest potential for explaining the development of the various categories of Son of Man words as we now find them in the gospel tradition is the one advanced by H. E. Tödt.[88] According to Tödt, Jesus gathered around himself an eschatological community to whom he announced the coming of the Son of Man, who would judge men on the basis of their response to him and his ministry. His message of the coming Kingdom of God and the signs of its inbreaking, evident in his healings and exorcisms, called men to decision; the Son of Man would confirm that decision in the eschatological judgment (Mark 8:38). When Jesus' fellowship with his own followers was reconstituted in the postresurrection appearances, they came to believe that Jesus was himself the Son of Man, whose coming as judge they still awaited. In the light of this conviction, the gospel tradition read back into his earthly ministry this insight into who Jesus was: the Son of Man. The pre-Markan tradition went on from that interpretive point to consider Jesus' suffering as a necessary part of his role as Son of Man (Mark 8:31; 9:31; 10:32–34). But before examining the eschatological framework in which Mark presents the passion of Jesus, we must look more closely at the description of his public ministry and his message.

Jesus as Salvation-Bringer in His Public Ministry

Mark's understanding of the intention of Jesus' public ministry is expressed succinctly in Mark 1:15: "The time [*kairos*] is fulfilled,

---

[86] Philip Vielhauer, "Gottesreich und Menschensohn in der Verkündigung Jesu" [Kingdom of God and Son of Man in the preaching of Jesus], in his *Aufsätze zum Neuen Testament* [Essays on the New Testament] (Munich: 1965), pp. 55–91. Also H. B. Sharman, *Son of Man and Kingdom of God* (New York: Harper & Row, 1943).

[87] See the most thorough and convincing survey of the history-of-religions backgrounds of υἱὸς τοῦ ἀνθρώπου ("Son of Man") in Carsten Colpe's article on the term in *Theological Dictionary of the New Testament*, vol. 8, pp. 400–77.

[88] *The Son of Man in the Synoptic Tradition*, esp. pp. 222–83.

and the kingdom of God is at hand; repent, and believe in the gospel [good news]." What is involved in Jesus' gospel is made clear immediately in the story of the demoniac in the synagogue at Capernaum (Mark 1:23–26). A central element in the story is the question of the demon (or the demoniac as his spokesman), "Have you come to destroy us?" The tradition could scarcely make its point more forcefully: To destroy Satan and his hosts is precisely what Jesus has come to do. The interrogative style is replaced by straight declarative in a related passage (Mark 3:22–27) in which a series of sayings points to Jesus' role as the agent through whom Satan's dynasty will be shattered and his posessions plundered. The Q version of this incident makes the point even more explicitly: "If it is by the finger of God that I cast out demons, then the kingdom of God has come upon you" (Luke 11:20). Mark, however, uses a technical term in the exorcism accounts, *epitimáō*, which translates a Semitic word meaning "to utter a commanding word by which an enemy is subjugated."[89] This is the significance attached to Jesus' exorcisms, and perhaps to his healings, in the earliest tradition: By Jesus' powerful acts, Satan's control over the creation was being wrested from him as a necessary step toward the establishment of God's rule. Mark modified this intention of the miracle stories somewhat by shifting the focus at times (especially in Mark 5:1–20) to the thaumaturgic, or wonder-working, technique and to the person of the wonder-worker, as in pagan miracle tales. But Mark's changes do not obscure or conflict with his own overall aim of presenting Jesus as the bringer of the message and the signs of the New Age.

Mark shares with Q the belief that Jesus is the eschatological bringer of salvation, but he lays great stress on Jesus' "mighty works" as manifestations of the inbreaking of the rule of God. Q, as we have observed, holds the same view of the meaning of Jesus' exorcisms, but in fact the Q material is almost wholly limited to sayings tradition. Mark differs from Q also in the sense of apocalyptic urgency that pervades his gospel.

The message of the coming Kingdom is directly set out in

[89] See my article on this term in *New Testament Studies* 14, 2 (1968): 232–46.

the apocalyptic discourse (Mark 13) and metaphorically proclaimed in the parables of the Kingdom (Mark 4). Although
Mark reproduced the older—and almost certainly original—form
and intent of these parables, with their encouragement to the
messengers of the Kingdom to carry out their work without cal-
culating the results (which are, after all, in God's hands), he also
added allegorical explanations that turn attention to the inner
state of the eschatological community.[90] But the apocalyptic
images of the harvest still predominate; by retaining the emphasis
on the Judgment, Mark kept the parables within their original
eschatological atmosphere. The shorter parabolic sayings, such as
those dealing with the bridegroom and the wineskins, are likewise
built on apocalyptic imagery and remind the hearer or reader of
the day of reckoning that lies ahead (Mark 2:18–22). As a result,
the churchly question about whether or not to fast is settled on
the basis of an eschatological pronouncement: "The days will
come. . . ."

In the context of the announcement by Jesus of his passion
(8:27–31), Mark introduces the apocalyptic prediction of the
coming in glory of the Son of Man (8:38) and the coming with
power of the Kingdom of God (9:1). Precisely because this section of Mark is composite in its present form, we can be sure that
Mark placed these materials together with full intent: Jesus' acceptance of the cross and Peter's satanically originated remonstra-
tion (8:32–33) are linked with the prophetic words about the
coming Son of Man and the coming with power of God's Kingdom. Jesus' message and ministry, as well as his passion and death,
are set by Mark within a sequence of apocalyptic events, a schedule of eschatological actions by which God will establish his rule
over creation. The direct pronouncement of the apocalyptic role
of Jesus is given in Mark 13, which is likewise composite. How
much of this apocalyptic discourse goes back to Jesus is variously
assessed,[91] but Mark placed it in a strategic spot—just before the

---

[90] The fundamental work here is Joachim Jeremias, *Parables of Jesus*, rev. ed.,
trans. S. H. Hooke (New York: Scribner's, 1963).
[91] See Bultmann, *History of the Synoptic Tradition*, pp. 120–30. G. R.
Beasley-Murray has written a *Commentary on Mark 13* (New York: St.
Martin's, 1957).

passion narrative and just after the prediction of the destruction of the Temple—in order to show Jesus' crucial role in the apocalyptic scheme of things: After all these catastrophes have occurred on earth and in the cosmos, "the Son of man" will be seen "coming in clouds with great power and glory" (Mark 13:26). In keeping with the conventions of apocalyptists, Mark asserts that the end will be soon, within the lifetime of Jesus' hearers (13:30), but that the exact time is known only to God (13:32).

Thus, it is in the interest of documenting his reading of the event of Jesus that Mark, or the tradition on which he drew, assigns to the earthly Jesus throughout his gospel the titles Son of God (king) and Son of Man (eschatological salvation-bringer).

The Apocalyptic Necessity of Jesus' Death

Mark presents Jesus' passion as an essential element in a series of eschatological events rather than as the ground of a developed doctrine of the atonement. From the first prediction of the passion onward, Mark reports Jesus as describing his impending death in terms of apocalyptic necessity (δεῖ, *dei*),[92] or simply as certain to occur in the apocalyptic scheme of things ("how is it written of the Son of man, that he should suffer many things . . . ?"—Mark 9:12). Although we know of no such apocalyptic document in which the suffering of the Son of Man is predicted, Mark's appeal to what is "written" suggests that he either had such a document or assumed its existence. In any case, he makes no claim for having originated the idea of the Son of Man who must suffer. From this hypothetical document Mark concluded that the passion of Jesus was a necessary event in the working out of the divinely determined apocalyptic scheme of "history," both past and future.

The apocalyptic necessity of Jesus' death is underscored in Mark not only in the explicit predictions of the passion[93] but also in metaphorical allusions to it: the bridegroom taken away (2:20), the cup and the baptism to be endured (10:38). The nearest

[92] The relevant texts are 8:31 ("must suffer"), 9:11 ("Elijah must come first"), and 13:10 ("the gospel must first be preached to all nations," i.e., before the End).

[93] Mark 8:31; 9:12; 9:31; 10:33–34.

Mark comes to an interpretation of Jesus' death as an atonement is in 10:45, where the life of the Son of Man is said to be given "as a ransom for many." In spite of learned efforts to link this phrase with Paul or with Isaiah 53,[94] the fact remains that the verse says only that in some unspecified way the death of Jesus will effect release "for many." This notion of the redemptive benefits of the death of a righteous man could be understood in terms of the cult of the martyrs,[95] or simply as a part of the messianic woes that "must" occur before the New Age dawns (Mark 13:7–8). The closest one can come to an interpretation of the death of Jesus in Mark is in the eucharistic word (Mark 14:24–25) and in the Parable of the Vineyard Workers (12:1–11). In the first instance, the life given ("blood . . . poured out") is associated with the covenant,[96] a term that is given eschatological significance by Mark's placing beside it the saying about Jesus drinking the fruit of the vine on "that day . . . in the kingdom of God." Similar positive meaning is given to the death of Jesus

[94] See note 85, above.
[95] Edward Lohse, *Märtyrer und Gottesknecht* [Martyr and servant of God] (Göttingen: Vandenhoek & Ruprecht, 1955).
[96] Although the King James Version and a great many of the Greek and other ancient manuscripts read "new testament" (= covenant) at Mark 14:24, the Revised Standard Version follows the oldest and best Greek manuscripts in omitting the word "new." Nevertheless, the implication of this saying of Jesus is that the new basis of man's relationship to God that Jesus is establishing will replace the basis of the Jewish covenant. Whether the claim of newness arose with Jesus or with the early church, it is clearly dependent on Jeremiah 31:31–34:

> Behold, the days are coming, says the Lord, when I will make a new covenant with the house of Israel and the house of Judah, not like the covenant which I made with their fathers when I took them by the hand to bring them out of the land of Egypt, my covenant which they broke, though I was their husband, says the Lord. But this is the covenant which I will make with the house of Israel after those days, says the Lord: I will put my law within them, and I will write it upon their hearts; and I will be their God, and they shall be my people. And no longer shall each man teach his neighbor and each his brother, saying, "Know the Lord," for they shall all know me, from the least of them to the greatest, says the Lord; for I will forgive their iniquity, and I will remember their sin no more.

Read against the background of these words of Jeremiah, the implication of this saying of Jesus (Mark 14:24) is that his death in some way seals or ratifies the (new) covenant and effects the forgiveness of sin.

in the Parable of the Vineyard Workers, where his rejection is presented as a necessary step prior to his becoming the "head of the corner," in fulfillment of Psalm 118:22–23. What is at stake, as is shown by (Jesus'? Mark's? the tradition's?) use of the allegorical representation of Israel (Isa. 5:1–7), is the founding of a new people, an eschatological community. In rejecting Jesus as God's final Word, the Jewish nation is unwittingly laying the foundation for the new community. This seems to be the fundamental meaning given by Mark, and/or the tradition on which he drew, to the death of Jesus.

Because the cross is not in Mark the basis for a doctrine of the atonement, there is no problem of correlating it with the parousia or of correlating the parousia with the resurrection. Both resurrection and parousia are terms Mark uses to represent a single, central apocalyptic event: the vindication of Jesus as triumphant Son of Man and founder of the eschatological community. The explicit predictions of the passion are also always announcements of the resurrection (8:31; 9:31; 10:32–33). Jesus' metaphorical warning, couched in apocalyptic language, that the shepherd is about to be struck (14:27)[97] leads directly on to an announcement of his resurrection and the reassembling of the eschatological community under Peter (14:28), a promise recalled by the supernatural messenger in the postresurrection scene (16:6–7) in which the cross is once more presented as a prelude to the reconstitution of the circle of followers: "Do not be amazed; you seek Jesus of Nazareth, who was crucified. He has risen, he is not here. . . . But go, tell his disciples and Peter that he is going before you to Galilee; there you will see him, as he told you."

Jesus' Relationship to Judaism: A New Understanding of Divine Will

Because Mark regards history as the chain of events by which the divine purpose is worked out through struggle and seeming defeat,

---

[97] This passage is built on the imagery of the proto-apocalyptic book of Ezekiel (esp. Ezek. 34) and the apocalyptic oracle of Zechariah 13:7.

it is not surprising that he can discover authorization in the period of Jesus' earthly ministry for the practices that are the concern of the eschatological community as it awaits the final, victorious disclosure of God's redemptive agent, Jesus, the Son of Man. Accordingly, the ethical norms, the missionary practices and pitfalls, and the cultic life of the community are all read out of—or back into —the lifetime of Jesus.

In the course of setting forth his account of Jesus' ministry, Mark addresses himself to the specific problems the early Christian church faced in relation to the conventions and circumstances of the day. Since the church of Mark was so deeply conscious of itself as heir to the promises made to Israel, it could not merely brush aside the distinctive features of Jewish piety. What should the attitude of the church be toward Sabbath observance, fasting, prayer, dietary laws, eating a meal with those who are ceremonially or religiously impure? In addition, problems arose from the historical circumstances of life in first-century Palestine. What should be the relationship of the Christians to Roman authorities? Further, how was a Christian to understand God's seeming judgment on Judaism, as evidenced by the destruction of the Temple? What right had the church to announce the forgiveness of sins? What lay behind the sacraments of Baptism and the Eucharist? Why had not Jesus' claims, which were now so obviously—to the Christians' way of thinking—the fulfillment of Scripture, been recognized by the Jews who knew and searched the Scriptures?

The question of Sabbath observance is dealt with through several stories about Jesus' healings (Mark 1:21–28; 3:1–5): The answer is, meeting human needs takes precedence over Sabbath observance, although the tradition makes the point that Jesus was faithful in worship on the Sabbath. The argument moves beyond the question of human need, however, when Jesus is reported as asserting that, first, the Sabbath was made for man and, second, the Son of Man (= Jesus) is lord of the Sabbath. Even if one assumes that in Mark 2:28 "Son of man" originally meant simply "man,"[98] the verse still shows that for Mark Jesus has the authority to set aside the venerable Sabbath law and that, indeed, he

---

[98] So Colpe, "$\upsilon\grave{\iota}\grave{o}\varsigma$ $\tau o\hat{\upsilon}$ $'\alpha\nu\theta\rho\acute{\omega}\pi o\upsilon$." See note 87.

has done so. Neither the dietary laws nor those forbidding eating a meal with impure or unworthy persons are any longer in effect: Jesus has come as the physician for those who are in need and know it, not to confirm the religiously complacent. The dietary laws are unconditionally set aside (7:18–19). This dictum is given in a private session with the disciples, a device that Mark regularly uses for providing his readers with special insight into the intention of Jesus as Mark understands it.[99] The concern of the church, here attributed to Jesus, is for moral qualities (7:20–23), not for ceremonial purity. The clue to the shift away from the laws and traditions in terms of which Judaism understood the will of God is given in 2:21–22: A new and powerful reality has come into being in the person and message of Jesus; this reality cannot be pressed into old containers or merely tacked on to what already exists. The eschatological community requires a new understanding of the divine will. Jesus, as Mark represents him, is the bearer of that new morality.

The Markan Jesus refuses to become identified with Jewish national or racial exclusiveness. He is willing to perform healings and exorcisms among and in behalf of Gentiles (5:1–20; 7:24–30); he refuses to arouse Jewish national hopes by encouraging disobedience to Roman law (12:17). He will not engage in typical rabbinic debate about the interpretation of the Law; instead, he confronts man directly with God's radical demand (10:1–12; 10:17–27; 12:28–34). Similarly, the demand of discipleship is total (8:34–37; 9:42–50; 10:28–30), although its reward will be known only in the eschatological judgment.

The ministry to which the disciples are called is an extension of Jesus' own eschatological activity: preaching and casting out demons (3:13–14). Both exorcisms (9:14–29) and simple acts of mercy (9:38–41) are to be performed in the name of and by the authority of Jesus. Such works will receive their appropriate reward in the eschatological judgment.

The eschatological significance of Christian baptism is suggested by the words of John the Baptist (1:7–8); the eschatological meaning of the Eucharist is made explicit in Jesus' words about

---

[99] On this Markan characteristic, see Jeremias, *Parables of Jesus*, pp. 97–98.

drinking wine in the Kingdom of God (14:25). The church's eucharistic practice is reflected—and therefore, as Mark intended, authorized in advance—by the twice-told story of the miraculous feeding of the multitudes (6:30–44; 8:1–10). The fact that there is no hint of redemptive or memorial significance in these meals suggests that they are regarded, as is the Last Supper itself, as anticipations of the great eschatological banquet. The blueprint for the life of the eschatological community, therefore, from cultus to ethics, is provided by Mark, and is placed for purposes of authorization within the ministry of Jesus.

MARK'S APOCALYPTIC VIEW OF HISTORY

We shall now consider two questions that have been set aside up to this point: What was Mark's historical aim? What historical value does his book have? In juxtaposing these questions, we must recognize that in the first we are asking about Mark's own understanding of history; in the second, about history in terms of modern historiography. Some scholars have attempted to merge these two issues by theorizing that there is identity between a modern conception of historicity as a mode of man's self-understanding and Jesus' summons to man to find his true life (or self) by deciding for the will of God and against the world (Mark 8:35). This view implies that by turning away from being obsessed with facts and toward helping man gain self-understanding, the historian is heading toward the same goal as that to which Jesus invited men in his gospel preaching: the achievement of a true understanding of human existence.[100] The existentialist approach, however, is a distortion of modern historical work, with its attention to factual evidence and its attempt to reconstruct the

---

[100] Thus J. M. Robinson in *A New Quest of the Historical Jesus* (Naperville, Ill.: Allenson, 1959). Norman Perrin's discussion of Mark as "apocalyptic drama," in *The New Testament: An Introduction*, pp. 143–66, serves as a valuable corrective to the attempt to convert ancient historical categories into those of modern times.

past, just as the exclusive concentration on self-understanding in the message of Jesus is inadequate for dealing with the wider range of the gospel tradition.

What must be recognized is that Mark did not have, and could not have had, a view of history concerned with cause and effect in a universe governed by natural law, or with the sociological and psychological factors that shape human decisions and therefore affect human and social movements. The kind of "history" that Mark knew was the apocalyptic variety as it has been preserved for us in such works as the Book of Enoch, the Book of Jubilees, and the Book of Daniel. These works deal with actual events of the past (or events believed to have occurred, such as the experiences of the patriarchs); they set them in a framework of divine purpose, in the light of which the meaning of the present is grasped and illumined and the hope for the future is specified. Thus Daniel looks back over the fall of world powers—Babylon, Persia, the Hellenistic kingdoms—that had seemed formidable in their time; he encourages his contemporaries not to be intimidated by the present power, the second-century B.C. Seleucid king Antiochus IV, for he has confidence that theirs is the final struggle, out of which will come the triumph of God's will and purpose in his cosmos. Both the Apocalypse of Weeks and the Dream Visions included in the Book of Enoch trace the history of Israel from the days of Enoch (who is mentioned in Gen. 5:18–24), through the Exodus and Exile, the restoration and the apostasy, to the founding of what is called the "Plant of Righteousness," (1 En. 10:16), the Essene community at Qumran, in whose behalf God is about to intervene. The angelic hosts will aid the earthly army, and Belial will go down in defeat; the Kingdom of God will be established in the earth.

It would be easy and natural to dismiss these accounts as fantasy, lacking all claim to be historical documents. Yet the writers believed that they were reporting the past truly; the neat, chronological schematizations were considered not distortions but testimony to the divine order of things. Mark took the synoptic tradition as he found it, largely in scattered units, and worked it into a consecutive account of "history" in which past, present, and future are viewed apocalyptically. He did not have to do violence to his material to set it in this mold, since the basic outlook of Jesus and what seems to have been his understanding of his own exorcisms and healings were also apocalyptically oriented. What was required was for Mark to shift the focus of the record from the implicit meaning of the eschatological signs and words of Jesus to the church's explicit christological claims made in his behalf and even attributed to him. It is not correct to say, as does William Wrede, that Mark took nonchristological material and made it appear christological by editing into it his apologetic notion of the messianic secret.[101] Nor is it satisfactory to suppose that Mark tried to historicize the Christians' understanding of Jesus by interpreting the tradition about Jesus' miracles along the lines of the Hellenistic *theios anēr*.[102]

Mark "historicized" the picture of Jesus because his kerygma demanded it. When at Easter the disciples met the risen Christ, they acclaimed him Son of Man. Through these resurrection experiences the church came to the understanding that the resurrection was itself a climactic eschatological sign pointing ahead to the consummation of the Kingdom, and it recognized the necessity of tracing the details of the eschatological meaning of the public ministry of Jesus, including both his acts and his message. As is customary with apocalyptic writing, the symbolic and the factual have a way of merging in Mark, so that the story of the transfiguration, for example, though presented as a historical occurrence, is probably a purely symbolic narrative. Much of the activity of Jesus was public; the fact that not all—or even many— of Jesus' contemporaries saw him as the agent of God's New Age is candidly acknowledged by the tradition and by Mark (3:20– 27). But Mark provides an explanation for this lack of insight: "To you [Jesus' followers] has been given the [mystery][103] of the

---

[101] According to Wrede, the injunctions to silence were Mark's way of explaining the fact that although Jesus had never publicly claimed to be the Messiah, he was so regarded by the early church. *Das Messiasgeheimnis in den Evangelien* (Göttingen: Vandenhoeck & Ruprecht, 1901; reprinted, 1963); English translation by J. C. G. Grieg, *The Messianic Secret* (Greenwood, S.C.: Attic Press, 1971).

[102] So Conzelmann, "Gegenwart und Zukunft."

[103] An important technical term in apocalyptic literature. Cf. 1 En. 16:3; 51:3; 103:2; 104:12; 106:19; Lev. 2:10; 1QS 4. 6; 11. 5; 1QH 1. 21; 2. 13; 1QpHab 7. 5, 8, 14. On the use of this term in the Qumran literature, see Friedrich Nötscher, *Zur theologischen Terminologie der Qumran-Texte* (Bonn: Peter Hanstein, 1956), pp. 71–77.

kingdom of God, but for those outside everything is in [riddles]"[104] (4:11).

THE MARKAN COMMUNITY

The community for which Mark is the spokesman or whose traditions he set forth differs from the community of Q in that the Markan group takes with pronounced seriousness the course of history, and while it shares with Q the expectation of an imminent end of the present age, it is much more conscious of obligations for guiding the life of the community in the interim. Therefore it gives attention to reinterpretation of the Law, even though its members are not fully familiar with such aspects of Mosaic Law as using ritually clean utensils (Mark 7:3–4). There is more emphasis in Mark than in Q on the esoteric nature of the information revealed to the community, but both groups seek to include the Gentiles in the new community of faith. Most striking, however, is the fact that the Markan community stands on the brink of a major confrontation with Judaism and anticipates as the outcome the destruction of the Temple in Jerusalem and the vindication of the faithful by divine act. The details of the passion narrative serve to differentiate the Markan group both from the strict adherents to the Law and from the Jewish revolutionaries who seek to establish the Kingdom of God by their own direct action (Mark 10:35–45; 12:13–17). The role of the community is to bear faithful witness, even if it leads to martyrdom, confident of God's sure and soon vindication.

SUGGESTIONS FOR FURTHER READING

An excellent analysis of the major themes and literary methods of Jewish apocalyptic literature is by D. S. Russell, *The Method*

---

[104] So Jeremias, *Parables of Jesus*, pp. 14–17. Although used by Mark in relation to the parables, this explanation is fittingly applied to the whole of his representation of Jesus.

and Message of Jewish Apocalyptic (Philadelphia: Westminster, 1964). Sigmund Mowinckel, *He That Cometh*, trans. G. W. Anderson (Nashville: Abingdon, 1954), offers a masterful survey of the antecedents of Christian messianic ideas in the Hebrew Scriptures and in Judaism.

In contrast to the attempt of C. H. Dodd in *The Apostolic Preaching and Its Development in the New Testament* (New York: Harper & Row, 1951) to present a unified view of the gospel in early Christianity, W. G. Kümmel, *Promise and Fulfillment** (Naperville, Ill.: Allenson, 1957), shows clearly the distinctive features of Jesus' message of the inbreaking Kingdom of God, as reflected in the synoptic tradition. An early attempt to locate the specifics in Mark's interpretation of that message is J. M. Robinson, *The Problem of History in Mark** (Naperville, Ill.: Allenson, 1957). A comprehensive survey and discerning analysis of the christological themes of the New Testament, including the synoptic tradition, is R. H. Fuller, *The Foundations of New Testament Christology* (New York: Scribner's, 1965).

Of the commentaries on Mark, the finest is by Vincent Taylor, *The Gospel According to St. Mark* (London: Macmillan, 1953). The best popular commentary is that of D. E. Nineham, *The Gospel of St. Mark** (Baltimore: Penguin, 1964).

My detailed study of the Markan community, *Community of the New Age* (Philadelphia: Westminster, 1977), develops the Markan themes more fully. Surveys of critical questions relating to Mark are available in W. G. Kümmel, *Introduction to the New Testament* (Nashville: Abingdon, 1975), esp. pp. 80–101 (and bibliography); and Ralph Martin, *Mark: Evangelist and Theologian* (Grand Rapids, Mich.: Zondervan, 1973).

* *Available in a paperback edition.*

5 Jesus in the History of the Church: The Gospel of Matthew

In the last two decades of the first century A.D., at least three writers in addition to Mark undertook to produce gospels of their own, utilizing Mark's literary form, but modifying it each in his own way. Two of these evangelists, Matthew and Luke, not only adopted the literary genre but took over nearly the whole of Mark's content as well, expanding it with Q and other traditions to which they had access and shaping the Markan material to suit their own special ends. John, however, borrowed the genre but utilized the substance of Mark's traditions hardly at all. Questions of the literary dependence of the gospel writers have often been explored;[1] less frequently discussed is the fact that Matthew, Luke, and John modified for their own purposes Mark's understanding of history.

None of the other gospel writers took over unchanged Mark's apocalyptic view of history. Matthew carried over, and at

---

[1] The classic statement of Matthew's and Luke's dependence on Mark is B. H. Streeter, *The Four Gospels* (New York: Macmillan, 1925). For a recent comprehensive analysis, with bibliography, see W. G. Kümmel, *Introduction to the New Testament*, 17th ed., trans. H. C. Kee (Nashville: Abingdon, 1975), pp. 105–19.

some points intensified, the apocalyptic language and the sense of urgent expectancy, but significantly altered the historical outlook, as we shall see. Luke introduced into the gospel tradition sayings that lay even more stress on the coming Son of Man than does Mark, but his schematic view of history is far removed from Mark's apocalypticism. The *language* of apocalypticism is scattered throughout John's gospel, but with almost none of its substance. In each case, the evangelist recast the tradition in such a way as to present his own understanding of the place of Jesus in history.

One of the important elements that contributed to the reshaping in each case was the fact that the church was now an organized community. In Mark and Q we find a strong sense of community, expressed in recognition of the community as the eschatological people to whom God has granted special wisdom and promised redemption; but there is little evidence of concern for the organized, ongoing life of the community. Only in the few scattered bits of parenetic material and in the challenge to the tasks of discipleship do we have strong hints of the function of the church, and even these strands of the tradition are oriented more toward bringing about the eschatological fulfillment than toward giving guidance to the church as an ongoing institution. In each of the other three gospels, however, the situation of the church with respect to inner organization and external relations has changed, or at least the writer's understanding of the church's situation has altered.

In Matthew the problems of authority within the community and of the moral responsibility of its members are explicitly raised, and the question about the nature of the continuity between the Christian church and Judaism is directly addressed. Closely related to this is Matthew's concern for the place of Jesus and his community in God's historical plan for creation—an interest he shares with Luke, although the two gospels differ in important detail, as we shall see. Matthew emphasizes the church as the ongoing instrument through which God is calling the nations of the world to repentance and faith (Matt. 25:32; 28:19), even though there is full acknowledgment that not all will respond in faith (25:32, 41–46). The outreach to the world began within

Judaism itself (10:5-6). Because those who first heard the gospel message rejected it (22:5) and participated in the death of Jesus, God's messenger, the missionary call now goes out to those who would be regarded by Mosaic Law as unworthy (22:9). The community of Christians for Matthew is a mixed group, ethnically and ethically (22:10). Luke has less to say about the church as community, but much more to say concerning the present age as the epoch of the church in the divine plan of the ages. He does, however, stress Gentile participation in the church as a major factor in the outworking of the plan of redemption.

John evidences no interest in the organizational aspects of the church's life, preferring to portray the church under a series of metaphors or images—children, flock, vine—in which dependence on God and on others is the chief characteristic of the people of God. His view of history might be called existential: man comes to understand himself as moment-by-moment participant in, rather than as spectator of, historical events. As will become evident in the more detailed analyses of the three gospels presented in this chapter and the next two, the distinctions sketched here are in many instances differences of emphasis, and common elements are shared by all three writers.

THE CONTINUING IMPORTANCE OF JEWISH TRADITION

Matthew's two major convictions, both of which are made explicit in his gospel, are (1) that the Law of God, as given to ancient Israel, is eternally valid and (2) that Jesus is the final agent and plenipotentiary through whom God's purpose in the world is being consummated (Matt. 5:17-18).[2] Putting the two beliefs

[2] Found only in Matthew, although a variant of Matthew 5:17 appears in Luke 16:17. Luke's intention, however, is not so clear. T. W. Manson, "The Sayings of Jesus," in H. D. Major, T. W. Manson, and C. J. Wright, *The Mission and Message of Jesus* (New York: Dutton, 1938; reissued separately, London: SCM Press, 1949), p. 135, thinks it was originally spoken in irony: Jesus was telling the scribes that they would rather have heaven and earth pass away than give up a single ornamental flourish of the calligraphy with which the Law was copied.

together, one can say that for Matthew, Jesus is the inaugurator of the true Israel, the people through and among whom God's ultimate purpose for man is to be achieved.

The Law of Jesus and the Law of Moses

Interpreters have frequently drawn attention to the parallels between Moses in the Old Testament and Jewish tradition and Jesus in the gospel of Matthew. Both appear on mountains to interpret God's Law to his people. In the Sermon on the Mount, Jesus sets his authority over against that of Moses: "You have heard that it was said [that is, by Moses] . . . But I say to you. . . ." The important common element is not the figures of Moses and Jesus, but the Law itself as the expression of God's will for man.

The "book" of Matthew—as it calls itself (1:1)—has been variously outlined by scholars. If one takes as the principal clue to the structure of Matthew the twice-repeated phrase "From that time Jesus began . . ." (4:17 and 16:21), then Matthew has arranged his gospel in a chronological way, beginning in Galilee and culminating in Jerusalem.[3] If, on the other hand, the five-times repeated phrase "when Jesus had finished . . ." is taken as the clue to Matthew's intention, then the book may be divided up thematically, with five major discourse sections, each of which is paired with a narrative section.[4] There are other recurrent phrases throughout the gospel, however, such as the so-called fulfillment quotations from Scripture, in terms of which divine justification or determination is offered for important details in Matthew's account of Jesus' career (1:23; 2:15, 18, 23; 4:15–16; 8:17; 12:18–21; 13:35; 21:5; 27:9–10). Each is prefixed by a variant of the phrase, "This was done in order that it might be fulfilled as was spoken by the prophet." Some have tried to argue from this recurrent phrase that the structure of Matthew's gospel manifests his developing portrait of Jesus as the Christ.[5]

If the five-fold phrase "When Jesus had finished . . ." is

---

[3] Recently developed by J. D. Kingsbury, in *Matthew: Structure, Christology, Kingdom* (Philadelphia: Fortress, 1975).
[4] So B. W. Bacon, *Studies in Matthew* (New York: Holt, Rinehart & Winston, 1930).
[5] So J. D. Kingsbury, *Matthew, passim*, but esp. p. 36.

adopted as the key to the structure of the gospel, then perhaps it is best explained as the result of a conscious imitation of the structure of the Torah, the first five books of the Old Testament, which are attributed by Jewish tradition to Moses. On this theory, Matthew's gospel could be divided as follows:

1. The Coming of Jesus as God's Messiah (1—2)
2. The Ministry of the Messiah and His Followers (3—25)
   - a. Narrative: The Beginning of the Ministry in Galilee (3:1—4:25)
   - Discourse: The Sermon on the Mount (5:1—7:29)
   - b. Narrative: The Authority of Jesus' Ministry (8:1—9:35)
   - Discourse: The Messianic Mission (9:36—10:42)
   - c. Narrative: The Kingdom and Its Coming (11:1—12:50)
   - Discourse: The Parables of the Kingdom (13:1–52)
   - d. Narrative: The Life of the New Community (13:53—17:27)
   - Discourse: Greatness and Responsibility (18:1–35)
   - e. Narrative: Conflict and Consummation (19:1—24:3)
   - Discourse: Revelation of the End (24:4—25:46)
3. The Humiliation and Exaltation of the Messiah (26—28)[6]

Supporting this approach is the fact that transitions from narrative to discourse are marked off at 4:23 and 9:35 by summarizing statements about the healing ministry, although this element is missing elsewhere. Problematical for this structural hypothesis,

---

[6] Based on my analysis of Matthew in the *Interpreter's One Volume Commentary* (Nashville: Abingdon, 1971) and used here by permission. The suggestive analysis of Matthew by Günther Bornkamm, Gerhard Barth, and H. J. Held in *Tradition and Interpretation in Matthew*, trans. Percy Scott (Philadelphia: Westminster, 1963), has, more than any other work, influenced the general interpretation of Matthew that is offered here. This view of Matthew is likewise heavily indebted to Wolfgang Trilling, *Das wahre Israel* [The true Israel] (Leipzig: St. Benno Verlag, 1959). M. J. Suggs considers Matthew's aim to have been to set the true Torah of Israel, regarded as embodied in Jesus as incarnate Wisdom, over against the Pharisaic Torah; see his *Wisdom, Christology and Law in Matthew* (Cambridge, Mass.: Harvard University Press, 1970), pp. 106–08.

however, is the fact that the contrast in 2(d) between narrative and discourse is not at all clear, while 2(e) contains a potent discourse denouncing the Pharisees (23:1–36), one which is separated by theme and locale from the apocalyptic discourse that follows. The pattern is not altogether clear[7] probably because Matthew's purposes are multiple, including apologetics, controversy with Pharisees over interpretation of the Law, and the provision of norms and guidelines for the church as an ongoing institution, especially in view of its mounting conflict with Jewish authorities. The disagreement with Judaism was not over the enduring validity of the Law (which is, in fact, affirmed—5:17–18) but rather over the interpretation of the Law and the purity of heart with which it is obeyed.

The Jewish Law, as analyzed by modern scholarship, falls into two categories: (1) apodictic laws, which are based solely on God's decree ("Thou shalt . . . thou shalt not . . .") and (2) casuistic laws, which state the consequences of obeying or disobeying ("Honor thy father . . . that thy days may be long . . ."). The apodictic form of ethics that Matthew attributes to Jesus, particularly in the Sermon on the Mount, seems to be a conscious paralleling of the giving of the Law through Moses on Mount Sinai, even though the actual contents of the moral declarations may have arisen through the words of Christian prophets in apostolic times.[8] If the ethics in Matthew did, in fact, develop in this way, then their development would parallel the development of Jewish ethics: The process of interpreting the Law of Moses was an ongoing task of the community under the guidance of its authoritative teachers. It was believed, at least in principle, that the link could be traced from an authoritative rabbinic interpretation back through earlier generations of interpreters to Moses himself. In practice, no sharp distinction was made between the Law of Moses and the subsequent inter-

---

[7] The broken patterns in Matthew have been discussed by F. V. Filson, "Broken Patterns in the Gospel of Matthew," *Journal of Biblical Literature* 75 (1956): 227–31.
[8] Treated by Ernst Käsemann, "Sentences of Holy Law in the New Testament," in his *New Testament Questions of Today*, trans. W. J. Montague (Philadelphia: Fortress, 1970), pp. 66–81.

pretation of it: Both were equally binding. Similarly, the words of Jesus and the later interpretations carried an equally authoritative obligation for Matthew's church.

The Outworking of the Divine Purpose

In order to heighten the aura of the supernatural that surrounds Jesus, Matthew portrays his birth as climaxing a development that began with Abraham, the progenitor of the Hebrew people, included such eminent figures in Israel's history as David, the ideal king, and Solomon, the ideal man of wisdom, and culminated in Jesus, born of a virgin in fulfillment of the prophecy of Isaiah 7:14.[9] Even the movement of the stars in the heavens is altered by the appearance of a star that guides the astrologers (Magi) from the East (presumably Mesopotamia, where astrology is supposed to have flourished) to Jesus' birthplace (Matt. 2:1–2), Bethlehem, a city that was predetermined by the divine plan laid down in the Scriptures (cf. Matt. 2:5–6 with Mic. 5:2). It is possible that mention of the star results from Matthew's literal understanding of the prophecy of Numbers 24:17, in which the future ruler of Israel is called a Star from Jacob, a title that figured in the expectations of the Qumran community,[10] as it did in the brief but fervent Jewish nationalism of the Second Revolt against the Romans in A.D. 130–35. The leader of that revolt, Bar Kosibah, took the name Bar Kochbah, meaning "Son of the Star," apparently to associate himself in the popular mind with the promise of Numbers 24. But Matthew's primary interest in the

[9] In Isaiah 7:14 the Greek word for virgin, *parthenós*, is essential for Matthew's representation of Jesus as supernatually born, but the Hebrew text here contains the word *almah*, which means simply "young woman." It is evident that Matthew is writing in and for a Greek-speaking community, since without *parthenós* his citation of the Old Testament quotation would be pointless.

[10] In the document known as 4Q Florilegium, Numbers 24:17 is quoted in connection with the messianic expectations at Qumran. See J. M. Allegro, "Further Messianic References in Qumran Literature," *Journal of Biblical Literature* 75 (1956):174–87. The document is translated in André Dupont-Sommer, *The Essene Writings from Qumran*, trans. Geza Vermes (Cleveland: Meridian, 1962), pp. 311–14.

star at the birth of Jesus is to imply his place, not in Jewish political aspirations, but in the cosmic scheme.

The notion of supernatural preparation for the coming of
Jesus is further heightened by the dreams that Matthew describes:
Joseph is advised about the pregnancy of his betrothed, who is
still a virgin; the Magi are warned against reporting back to Herod
as he had requested them to do (Matt. 2:12); Joseph is counseled
to flee with the child to Egypt in order to escape the wrath of
Herod, as later, after Herod's death, he is instructed to move with
his family to Nazareth in Galilee, where he will be out of the jur-
isdiction of Archelaus, the son of Herod.[11] Unlike Luke, who pictures Joseph as residing in Nazareth but required to go to Bethlehem for enrollment in the Roman census, Matthew mentions
Joseph's "house" in Bethlehem, as though he had lived there per-
manently until forced to flee by Herod's decrees aimed against
Jesus (Matt. 2:11).

Each of these "historical" moves was ultimately dictated
not by the dreams themselves but by the divine plan laid down in
Scripture. The return from Egypt is said to be the fulfillment of
Hosea 11:1. The grief of the mothers whose children were slain
by Herod is seen as predicted in Jeremiah 31:15. The move to
Nazareth accords with "what was spoken by the prophets": "He
shall be called a Nazarene" (Matt. 2:23). Matthew has no interest in the actual historical situation out of which the prophets
spoke these words, nor does he make any attempt to correlate the
actual events with Jesus' situation. Hosea was describing the
exodus from Egypt, when God delivered his people ("my son")
and led them into the land of Palestine. Jeremiah's words probably refer to the fall of the northern kingdom of Israel in 722 B.C.,
some two hundred and fifty years before his own time. (Jeremiah's
prophecies come from the last quarter of the sixth century B.C.,
shortly before Judah, the southern kingdom, likewise fell.) The
word Nazarene does not occur in the Hebrew Bible, but is probably to be traced to Isaiah 11:1, where the shoot (*netser*) from

---

[11] Herod the Great was ruler of the whole of Palestine at the time of Jesus'
birth. It was only after his death that the puppet kingdom was divided among
his sons; Archelaus for a time ruled Judea, and Herod Antipas governed Galilee
(along with Perea, the area east of the Jordan).

the stump of Jesse is mentioned. The metaphor in Isaiah is that of a tree cut down, which signifies the end of the Davidic dynasty. The prophet foresees the appearance, from the seemingly lifeless stump, of a shoot that will both signal and effect the reestablishment of the Kingdom. Conceivably, Matthew could have found in this prophetic word a prediction pointing to the kingly role that was assigned by Christians to Jesus. Instead, Matthew used the Isaiah 11 passage to prove that it was ordained in Scripture that Jesus' residence should be in Nazareth. (The Hebrew letters would be *n–ts–r*; the language was written in consonants, and the reader supplied his own vowels.) The writer of Matthew did not ask what Isaiah intended by his words; he was interested in finding what they might mean to him and his readers. Since the Bible was held to be divinely inspired, its sacred letters were subject to multiple interpretations, limited only by the talent and ingenuity of the interpreter. The discovery of obscure meanings in Scripture was a tribute to its divine origin, not a falsification of the intention of the biblical writer. The question of the Old Testament writers' intentions was for Matthew as well as for Jewish interpreters of his age an irrelevant one, because they believed that the God who had spoken through the prophets in the past was still in control of the affairs of men and was shaping them in accord with his own purpose, which the skillful interpreter of Scripture could discern in the present and correlate with the writings from the ancient past. What was significant was continuity of divine purpose, not precision of historical knowledge.

Because this redemptive purpose of God was seen as being worked out through Jesus, not only in his mission but even in the circumstances of his birth, Matthew gave him in a particularly explicit way superhuman titles and prerogatives. He affirmed Jesus' sinlessness and his superiority to John the Baptist in his brief addition to the baptismal story (3:14–15), in which John acknowledges his inferiority to Jesus and suggests the inappropriateness of Jesus' receiving a baptism for repentance. In the apocryphal gospel of the Hebrews (quoted by Jerome in his fourth-century treatise *Against Pelagius* 3.2), the problem of Jesus' baptism for repentance is handled more explicitly than in the canonical gospels: Jesus directly disclaims any consciousness of having committed sin. In

Matthew the heavenly voice that speaks at the moment of the descent of the Spirit makes a public declaration rather than a private disclosure to Jesus (as is the case in Mark 1:11): "This is my beloved Son, with whom I am well pleased" (3:17). These words are repeated in Matthew 17:54 on the occasion of the transfiguration of Jesus. Again they are uttered by the heavenly voice, and again they are in an expanded form, as compared with the parallel account in Mark 9:7 (Matthew's source!). A similar development occurs in Matthew's account of Peter's confession (16:16): "You are the Christ, the Son of the living God." And in contrast to the parallel passage in Mark (8:30), the term Christ is repeated at the end of the pericope (Matt. 16:20). A still more remarkable expansion in Matthew's version of Peter's confession is the response of Jesus to Peter, in which Peter's blessedness is asserted to be that of one who has received a divine revelation (16:17), and he is promised both a foundational role in the establishment of Christ's church (a word used only by Matthew among the evangelists) and an authoritative function in its administration. Whatever the origins of this passage added by Matthew may have been,[12] he used the pericope to assert unequivocally the messiahship of Jesus and his central place in God's plan as one assigned to establish the new people of God. The Greek word for church, *ekklesia*, has long been recognized as a translation of the Semitic word used in the Old Testament for the covenant community of Israel, *qahal*.[13]

The healing ministry of Jesus is presented by Matthew as prime evidence of Jesus' divine authority, in that the miracles are explicitly linked in Matthew with the fulfillment of Scripture in order to underscore the connection between Jesus' activity and the plan of God. In reproducing Mark's summary of Jesus' healing in Galilee (Mark 1:32–34 = Matt. 8:16–17), Matthew con-

---

[12] For a full interpretation of this passage see Oscar Cullmann, *Peter: Disciple, Apostle, Martyr*, 2nd rev. ed. (Philadelphia: Westminster, 1962). Cullman thinks this is an authentic saying of Jesus spoken at the resurrection appearance of Jesus to Peter.

[13] On the use of *ekklesia* in this passage, and in the New Testament in general, see K. L. Schmidt, "καλέω (Kaléō)," in Gerhard Kittel and Gerhard Friedrich, eds. *Theological Dictionary of the New Testament*, vol. 3 (Grand Rapids, Mich.: Eerdmans, 1965), pp. 487–536.

nects it directly with Isaiah 53:4: "This was to fulfill what was spoken by the prophet Isaiah, 'He took our infirmities and bore our diseases.'" Similarly, in Matthew 12:15–21 there is a parallel with Mark 3:7–12. In Mark a full summary is given of the response to Jesus' ministry in Galilee and the surrounding regions; Matthew added an extended quotation from Isaiah 42:1–4, and the whole passage has the effect of identifying Jesus with the Servant of Yahweh in Second Isaiah and of explaining, by appeal to the Scriptures, the shift from Jewish to Gentile audiences for the hearing of the gospel and the acceptance of its power: "And in his name will the Gentiles hope."

THE DIVINE AUTHORITY OF JESUS

In his handling of the miracle-story aspect of the gospel tradition,[14] Matthew asserts that Jesus is endowed with divine authority and that he exercises his power in relation to the community of faith. Many details are intended to heighten the miraculous element. For example, Matthew reports that Jairus' daughter, whom Jesus makes well, is not just at the point of death (Mark 5:23) but already dead (Matt. 9:18); he doubles a miracle by reporting that in Jericho Jesus healed not one blind man (Mark 10:46) but two (Matt. 20:29). The details of the discovery of the empty tomb in Mark 16:1–8 are expanded to include an earthquake, a descending angel, and a band of soldiers on guard who fall unconscious (Matt. 28:1–4). Matthew also modifies the miracle-story tradition in such a way that the stories deal with problems of faith in the church in his own time. Accordingly, the stories of Jesus stilling the storm (8:23–27) and walking on the water (14:22–33) include a rebuke to the disciples (= the church of Matthew's time) for being men of little faith, an element not found in the Markan and Lukan parallels.

[14] See H. J. Held, "Matthew as Interpreter of the Miracle Stories," in Bornkamm, Barth, and Held, *Tradition and Interpretation in Matthew*, pp. 164–299.

The heightening of the sense of Jesus' authority is further seen in Matthew's allegorical modification and elaboration of the parables. For example, Matthew appended to the Parable of the Weeds (13:24–30) an allegorical explanation in which Jesus is identified as the Son of Man, whose present task of proclamation of the gospel will be brought to completion by the work of judgment that he will carry out at the End of the Age (13:36–43). Indeed, Jesus' teaching in parables is seen by Matthew (13:35) as the fulfillment of a predetermined role announced by the prophets (actually the Psalmist, in Ps. 78:2). Matthew reworked parables that he received from the tradition in such a way as to make more nearly explicit the christological meaning he found in them; for example, the Parable of the Supper (Matt. 22:1–14; cf. Luke 14:16–24) he made into a marriage feast (= the eschatological banquet in the End Time) given by a king (= God) for his son (= Jesus). But Matthew also added from his own source(s) parabolic material that is even more explicit in depicting Jesus as the criterion by which God judged man and as the one designated Judge and Son of Man in the Day of Consummation (Matt. 25:31–46).

JESUS AS PREEMINENT INTERPRETER OF GOD'S WILL

The church of Matthew is faced with problems of identity, discipline, and proper interpretation of Scripture in the interim between its Lord's vindication in the resurrection and the time when he will return to vindicate the faithful, while judging their opponents. Meanwhile, they are to live in obedience to his words and in confidence of both his presence and his return (Matt. 28:20).[15] Thus, Matthew recognizes the crucial role of Jesus in

---

[15] See on this Günther Bornkamm, "End-Expectation and Church in Matthew," in Bornkamm, Barth, and Held, *Tradition and Interpretation in Matthew*, pp. 15–51.

the coming Day of Judgment, but this is not his main point. More important is the fact that Jesus, the Christ, is now authoritatively active in the ongoing life of the true Israel, the church. He is the "one teacher" of the church, its sole "master"[16] (23:7–10). It is therefore primarily as interpreter of the Law of God, regarded by Matthew as the expression of the divine will for man, that Jesus functions in the history of the true gospel.

Matthew sounds this theme near the beginning of his version of the Sermon on the Mount (5:17–20). Jesus' mission under God was not to destroy the Law and the prophets, but to bring to completion the will and purpose of God contained in them. From what follows in the Sermon, it is clear that "fulfill" refers not only to the outworking of a purpose in history—though that is surely an important factor—but also to the obedience of the true Israel to the moral demands of the Law and the prophets. The Pharisees are attacked in Matthew, not because they are too demanding and legalistic, but because there is a hypocritical gap between their demands on others and their own moral performance (5:20; 23:2–

---

[16] The word translated "master" here (*kathēgētēs*) is of special interest since it is primarily a scholastic term. It means "school teacher" in the Greek of New Testament times (see J. H. Moulton and George Milligan, *The Vocabulary of the Greek Testament* [Grand Rapids, Mich.: Eerdmans, 1949], as it did in the patristic period (see G. W. Lampe, ed., *A Patristic Greek Lexicon* [New York: Oxford University Press, 1961–68] and as it does in modern Greek (= professor). When linked with *didaskalos*, as in Matthew 23:8, it is clear that Matthew's aim is to ascribe to Jesus the central role of instructor. The verb from which *kathegetes* is derived means "to explain, show the way." This is precisely what the church of Matthew understands Jesus to be doing in the life of the Christian community, which is another way of saying that it sees its own task as instructional. The school atmosphere of Matthew has been discussed by Krister Stendahl in his *The School of St. Matthew* (Philadelphia: Fortress, 1966). W. D. Davies, in his masterful study *The Setting of the Sermon on the Mount* (London: Cambridge University Press, 1964), pp. 297–98, suggests that the scholastic controversy implicit in Matthew 23:8–10 reflects the historical controversy between Judaism and Christianity that was spearheaded from the Jewish side by a movement, centered at Jamnia on the Palestinian coast, that reacted to the destruction of the Jerusalem Temple by striving to consolidate Jewish faith and to safeguard the integrity of the Hebrew Scriptures against all actual and potential threats. In reaction against the Jamnian exclusivist truth claims, Jesus is declared by the Matthean tradition to be the sole teacher of truth.

4). The rigor of the moral requirement of the Law is not to be relaxed in the slightest degree.

Unique to Matthew is the series of antitheses mentioned earlier, in which Jesus contrasts the words of the Mosaic Law with his own interpretation of God's will: "You have heard that it was said . . . But I say to you . . ." (Matt. 5:21–48). Without exploring the details of Matthew's ethics, we can see two important elements emerge: (1) Jesus is cast in the role of the teacher whose authority transcends and supplants that of Moses, the ultimate interpreter of the divine will in Judaism, and (2) the moral requirements laid down by Jesus exceed the severity of the demands contained in the Torah, the Law of Moses. Not only murder but even anger toward others is outlawed. God requires more than abstention from the act of killing; he requires the positive act of reconciliation (5:21–26). Similarly, it is not enough for Matthew's Jesus that a man refrain from committing adultery. He is to exercise such self-control that he avoids even lustful looks (5:27–30). Divorce and oath-taking are likewise ruled out (5:31–37), on the ground that these practices give a show of honoring the Law and the purpose of God while actually violating God's will (19:4–9). But according to Matthew, Jesus went beyond even this rigid view to enjoin celibacy as a higher way of life (19:10–12). Matthew's call for a righteousness exceeding that of the Pharisees is carried to great lengths. For example, only Matthew reports Jesus as saying, "You must be perfect . . ." (5:48). On the more humane side, Matthew also reports Jesus as calling for acts of kindness in response to maltreatment or exploitation (5:38–42) and for works of love even toward one's enemies. But the standard for man's behavior is nothing less than the perfect character of God himself (5:48).

The true Israel is to be characterized by the same forms of religion that are practiced in Judaism, but the church is to avoid the kinds of display of piety that can make a mockery of true religion. Almsgiving and prayer are purely private matters, not occasions for religious ostentation (6:1–8). Likewise, fasting is to be practiced in secret, as a discipline directed toward God alone, not as a means of drawing attention to one's religious devotion

(6:16–18). The primary aim of the life of the member of the true Israel is to seek God's Kingdom and the righteousness he demands (6:32).

The problem of conflict within the Christian community is obviously one of the most serious for Matthew. In 18:15–35 he has brought together a series of tradition units, some from Q but mostly from his own source(s), through which he describes the conciliatory attitude Christians are to adopt toward one another. On the other hand, he sets forth the structured procedure the church is to follow when dealing with recalcitrant members. Those who refuse to listen to the church face excommunication. What is perhaps surprising here is that Matthew views both the procedure of reconciliation and the exercise of authority as manifestations of the continuing presence of Christ in the midst of his people (18:20). For Matthew the place of Jesus in history is quite specific: His invisible presence is the ground of the fellowship and the exercise of authority that are to characterize the corporate life of the true Israel.

Matthew gives Jesus' assignment of authority to the disciples new force by bringing together not only the parallel passages from Mark (6:6–11; 3:13–19), where the disciples are commissioned by Jesus, but also other pericopes selected from Q and from the apocalyptic discourse of Mark 13. The disciples are specifically called apostles (Matt. 10:2), as they are in Mark 6:30, but the transposition of the material from the apocalyptic section of Mark back into the section on the ministry of Jesus has the effect of establishing an identity between the ministry of Jesus and that of the church in the apostolic age. From the standpoint of the modern historian, one could say that Matthew has falsified the account by depicting Jesus as warning his disciples that they will be required to appear at hearings before kings and governors (10:18), since these circumstances did not arise until apostolic times and even later. But Matthew is making precisely the opposite point: The living Christ is present and active in his church in apostolic times. It is not a matter of placing the history of the church back into the ministry of Jesus, but of placing the history of Jesus within the ongoing life of the church.

THE CHURCH AS THE TRUE ISRAEL

There is a distinction—apparently an intentional one—between the limitation of the disciples' mission in Matthew 10:6 to the "lost sheep of the house of Israel"[17] and the command of the resurrected Christ to the disciples to undertake worldwide evangelism in 28:19. Possibly Matthew had in mind the geographical and ethnic limitations of Jesus' actual ministry and that of the first phases of the church's mission in Judea, in contrast to the Gentile mission launched in the apostolic age. The distinction would be a valid one from the perspective of the modern historian, since, with the possible exception of a few excursions into the region of Tyre (Matt. 15:21) and the cities of the Decapolis (Mark 7:31), Jesus seems to have restricted his activity to Jewish territory and his audience to Jewish people. Only in the time after his death was the wider mission launched into the Gentile world, first Syria and Asia Minor, and then Greece and Rome. For Matthew, however, the attempted evangelism of the Jewish people seems to have been a necessary preliminary phase; its relative lack of success was interpreted as being in keeping with a divine plan. Twice in the report of the teaching of Jesus in the final days before the passion, Matthew introduces the saying, "The first will be last,

[17] This limitation is of fundamental importance for Albert Schweitzer's reconstruction of the career of Jesus, especially when Matthew 10:6 is linked with 10:22 and the inference drawn that Jesus, expecting the End of the Age to occur in a matter of weeks, tried to force God's hand when Israel did not repent. See Schweitzer's *The Quest of the Historical Jesus*, trans. William Montgomery (New York: Macmillan, 1910), p. 357. A fuller development of this position is found in Schweitzer's *The Mystery of the Kingdom of God*, trans. Walter Lowrie (New York: Macmillan, 1956), pp. 219–42. But in the posthumously published work *Reich Gottes und Christentum* [The Kingdom of God and Christianity] (Tübingen: J. C. B. Mohr, 1967), pp. 127–31, Schweitzer puts more stress than in his earlier works on Jesus' voluntary participation in the messianic woes that must precede the coming of the Kingdom, giving less attention to the notion of forcing God's hand. On the "lost sheep" and Jesus' relation to the Gentiles, see the discussion in Joachim Jeremias, *Jesus' Promise to the Nations* (Naperville, Ill.: Allenson, 1958), and T. W. Manson, *Only to the House of Israel? Jesus and the Non-Jews* (Philadelphia: Fortress, 1964).

and the last first" (19:30; 20:16); that is, the Gentiles will replace the Jews as first in divine favor. The second occurrence of the saying leads directly into the third and final prediction of the passion (20:17–19) and thus seems to point to the impending rejection of Jesus by Jewish officialdom in Jerusalem. The conviction that God will open the gospel invitation to the Gentiles when the Jews have spurned it is again expressed in the Parable of the Supper (Matt. 22:1–14). It is made even more explicit in the long and bitter discourse in which Jesus reportedly denounces the scribes and Pharisees (23:1–36) and which culminates in the announcement that judgment for the persistent rejection and murder of God's messengers will fall "on this generation." The acceptance of this responsibility is attributed by Matthew to the Jewish leaders in the dreadful words of Matthew 27:25: "His blood be on us and on our children!"

Matthew took advantage of details in such unlikely places as the miracle stories to strengthen his case for the lack of responsiveness of Israel and the openness to faith of the true Israel. In the story of the Healing of the Centurion's Servant (8:5–13), for example, he took out of another context in Q (= Luke 13:28–30) a pericope that contrasts the participation of Gentiles in the benefits and privileges of the New Age with the outcast state of unrepentant Israel (Matt. 8:9–11). That Matthew placed this tradition at this point is confirmed by his addition of one of his favorite phrases describing the unrepentant, those who "weep and gnash their teeth." What is little more than a hint of the Gentile mission in Q became, at Matthew's hand, a part of his anti-Jewish polemic.

The shift of attention from Jews to Gentiles is directly declared in Matthew's addition to the Parable of the Vineyard Workers (21:43): "Therefore I tell you, the kingdom of God will be taken away from you [Jews] and given to a nation producing the fruits of it." The new "nation" is, of course, the church, composed of Gentiles and believing Jews. To the extent that Matthew is at all interested in what modern man might call the course of history, he seeks to show that the focus of God's concern has shifted from primary occupation with the Jews to a new undertaking in which there is a universal potential for participation in the people of God, or the true Israel.

In the final verses of his gospel (28:16–20), Matthew draws together several strands that run through his work: (1) the worldwide mission for which the disciples are commissioned, (2) the continuing presence of the risen Christ, who is the sole source of the church's authority and the chief agent of its teaching ministry among "all nations," and (3) the reminder that the present age will come to a close when the Kingdom of God is finally established. The present age is designated by Matthew as the Kingdom of the Son of Man, during which time the church is composed of good and bad (13:41); it will end in the judgment (13:49; 25:31–46). The Age to Come will be the Kingdom of God or, as Matthew prefers, the Kingdom of the Father (13:43; 25:34).[18]

Eschatological expectation figures in Matthew's understanding of the course of history, so that heavy stress is laid on the need for being ready when the Last Day comes. For example, Matthew appended to the apocalyptic discourse that he took over from Mark 13 an extended series of sayings (24:37–41); he also included parabolic words (24:42–51) and parables (25:1–46), two of which are found only in Matthew: the Ten Maidens (25:1–13) and the Last Judgment (25:31–46). There are two main themes that run through all this material as Matthew reproduced and edited it: the need to be ready ("Watch therefore, for you know neither the day nor the hour," 25:13) and the severity of punishment of the unworthy:

> For to every one who has will more be given, and he will have abundance; but from him who has not, even what he has will be taken away. And cast the worthless servant into the outer darkness; there men will weep and gnash their teeth. (Matt. 25:29–30)

The inference to be drawn from this representation of the conclusion of Jesus' ministry in these solemn words of warning is

[18] For a succinct analysis of this distinction see Bornkamm, Barth, and Held, *Tradition and Interpretation in Matthew*, p. 44.

that for Matthew the most important consideration is the purity of life and faithfulness in service of the church, the true Israel. The concept of the Judgment is retained from the older tradition, and readiness is repeatedly enjoined, but the aim throughout Matthew's gospel is to encourage by every means righteous living on the part of Christians *in the present*. Mark's eschatological outlook, and even his apocalyptic words and imagery, have been retained. But the focus has shifted from the future consummation to present churchly responsibilities, so that even the announcements of the coming Judgment are an appeal to present moral obligation. For Matthew, Jesus' place is in the history of the church. He is its master; he will be its judge. But its obedience to him and therefore to the Law of God now will determine the outcome of the future judgment at his hands.

THE COMMUNITY BEHIND MATTHEW

In what segment of early Christianity could the gospel of Matthew have originated? Clearly, in a place where the issues and decisions of the burgeoning rabbinic movement were taken seriously, both by the Jewish community and by those who were opposed to the point of view in the process of formulation at Jamnia in Palestine. It is not likely that Matthew was produced in Palestine and it is inconceivable that it was written in Hebrew or Aramaic in an earlier version, since it used the Greek Mark as one of its basic sources. Furthermore, its frequent quotations from Scripture are in the Greek version, and in some instances the argument turns on the details of the text as found in the Septuagint (LXX). The quotation from Psalm 8:2 in Matthew 21:16, for example, makes sense in the Greek wording of the LXX but would not in the Hebrew original. Matthew could have been written in any Greek-speaking Jewish center, although it likely came from a city with close ties to Palestine, since the rabbinic decisions at Jamnia seem to have exerted so great an influence. The earliest witness we have to Matthew's gospel is from Ignatius of Antioch, who died as a martyr in the early second century. A reasonable conjecture for the provenance of Matthew is a city in the eastern Mediterranean, perhaps in Phoenicia or elsewhere in western Syria. Wherever it was, the community was locked in fierce debate with Greek-speaking Jews on the issues as they were being shaped from the Jewish side through the process reflected in the decisions of the School at Jamnia.

SUGGESTIONS FOR FURTHER READING

The most comprehensive and erudite study of the background of Matthew's thought is W. D. Davies, *The Setting of the Sermon on the Mount* (London: Cambridge University Press, 1964). Fundamental essays on the theology of Matthew are in Günther Bornkamm, Gerhard Barth, and H. J. Held, *Tradition and Interpretation in Matthew* (Philadelphia: Westminster, 1963). An illuminating study of the early Christian use of the Old Testament, Barnabas Lindars, *New Testament Apologetic** (Philadelphia: Westminster, 1962), is helpful for the study of Matthew, which abounds in Old Testament quotations. Important comparisons between the Qumran community and that of Matthew are in Krister Stendahl, *The School of St. Matthew* (Philadelphia: Fortress, 1968), and A. R. C. Leaney, *The Rule of Qumran and Its Meaning* (Philadelphia: Westminster, 1966). Brief commentaries on Matthew are "Commentary on Matthew" by Krister Stendahl, in *Peake's Commentary on the Bible*, ed. Matthew Black and H. H. Rowley (Camden, N.J.: Thomas Nelson, 1962), and "Commentary on Matthew" by H. C. Kee, in *The Interpreter's One Volume Commentary*, ed. Charles Laymon, (Nashville: Abingdon, 1971).

A comprehensive survey of critical questions on Matthew, with full bibliography, is available in W. G. Kümmel, *Introduction to the New Testament*, 17th ed., trans. H. C. Kee (Nashville: Abingdon, 1975), pp. 101–21; see also Norman Perrin, *The New Testament: An Introduction** (New York: Harcourt Brace Jovanovich, 1974), pp. 169–92.*

* *Available in a paperback edition.*

Jesus and the Church in the History of the World: The Gospel of Luke

Luke has been called "the first Christian historian."[1] In at least two fundamental ways, that is an accurate designation. First, he is the only New Testament writer who set about presenting the story of Jesus in the forms and categories in use among secular historians of the first century. In the gospel of Luke and in the Book of Acts, which from the similarity of style and vocabulary as well as from the specific claims of the opening paragraphs (Luke 1:1–4; Acts 1:1) we recognize to be two parts of a single work, Luke[2] gives an account of events from just before the birth of Jesus to the climax of Paul's missionary activity in Rome, on

---

[1] So Martin Dibelius, *Studies in the Acts of the Apostles*, trans. Mary Ling (London: SCM Press, 1956), p. 136.

[2] "Luke" is used here to designate the writer of the single two-volume work, Luke-Acts, but the authorship of the work is in fact unknown. Attribution to Luke is perhaps nothing more than an ancient conjecture. The assumption that Luke-Acts was written by a companion of Paul (note the "we" passages in Acts 16:10 and 20:5) is an inference from Colossians 4:14 and 2 Timothy 4:11. For a discussion of the work's authorship, see W. G. Kümmel, *Introduction to the New Testament*, 17th ed., trans. H. C. Kee (Nashville: Abingdon, 1975), pp. 122–51. The relation of Luke to Acts is discussed on pp. 156–73.

the eve of his trial (Acts 28). In presenting his historical narrative, Luke uses the methods and conventions of the Hellenistic historians of his time. Writing in an age that lacked a universally accepted absolute chronology, Luke dates certain crucial events in his work by referring to the monarchs and governors in power at the time:

> In the fifteenth year of the reign of Tiberius Caesar, Pontius Pilate being governor of Judea, and Herod[3] being tetrarch of Galilee, and his brother Philip tetrarch of the region of Ituraea and Trachonitis, and Lysanias tetrarch of Abilene, in the high-priesthood of Annas and Caiaphas, the word of God came to John the son of Zechariah. . . . (Luke 3:1–2)

The reference to Lysanias is of no help in establishing the date of the beginning of Jesus' ministry, since we do not know which Lysanias Luke meant.[4] But what the paragraph does show is that Luke wanted to represent the career of Jesus as a real event that occurred in a historical time and place, along with other known and observable events. In Acts he takes pains to describe the conversations of Paul and the other apostolic leaders with various pagan rulers in Cyprus, Corinth, Caesarea (13:7; 18:12; 23:24), and elsewhere. The famous interrogation of Paul by the council of the Areopagus in Athens pictures Paul encountering the leaders of pagan culture as well (Acts 17:16–34). In this synchronization of the history of Jesus with that of the pagan world, Luke is following the literary patterns of his time, and is thereby—at least implicitly—making a claim for Christianity to be considered seriously by pagan observers.

The second aspect of Luke's historical work is more subtle.

---

[3] Not Herod the Great, who died in 4 B.C., but Herod Antipas (r. 4 B.C.–A.D. 39).

[4] Lysanias was the name of a governor of Abilene executed by Mark Antony in 36 B.C. Josephus mentions that "Abila of Lysanias" was assigned to Herod Agrippa I in A.D. 42, thus implying that Lysanias was a recent ruler. But the reference could be to the earlier Lysanias, in which case Luke's reference is an anachronism, not a synchronism. See Josephus, *Antiquities of the Jews* XIX.5.1, in Loeb edition, vol. 9, trans. L. H. Feldman (Cambridge, Mass.: Harvard University Press, 1957).

The very fact that his story line does not end with the death and resurrection of Jesus means that not only literarily but in terms of his view of history he is in a different category from the writers of the other two synoptic gospels. It is true that in the other gospels each author has reworked the tradition so that the significance of the Jesus tradition for the Christian community of the evangelist's own time is evident. However, in Mark and Matthew the focus remains on the End of the Age, at which time the mission will be completed and there will ensue a judgment wherein the faithful will be vindicated, the wicked punished, and the Rule of God established. Luke's distinctive interests are in the church's ongoing work in the present age, its expansion to the ends of the earth (Acts 1:6), and its image as a literate, appealing enterprise. For Luke, God's redemptive purpose in history is evident not only through present appropriation of the effects of events in the past (Jesus' teaching, miracles, death, and resurrection), but also through the progress of the gospel in the widening circles of the Roman world. This is portrayed in a mixture of the literal and the symbolic in Luke's two-volume narrative that begins with the divine preparations for the birth of Jesus in Bethlehem and ends with the divine exploitation of Roman judicial process that brings Paul to launch his Christian mission in the capital of the empire itself (Acts 28).

Some scholars have suggested that Luke placed the story of Jesus in this larger historical framework as a way of overcoming the embarrassment felt in the early church when the parousia of Jesus did not occur in the first generation of Christians as expected.[5] The gospels of Mark and Matthew, however, had already

---

[5] At various points in a series of essays under the general title *New Testament Questions of Today* (Philadelphia: Fortress, 1969), Ernst Käsemann declares Luke to be "the first representative of nascent early catholicism." Käsemann thus places Luke in the period of "transition from earliest Christianity to the so-called ancient church, which is completed with the disappearance of the imminent expectation [of Jesus' coming at the End of the Age]." In his view, primitive Christian eschatology, which was the dynamic force of New Testament preaching, is in eclipse in Luke and in other later New Testament writings, where it survives solely as a formal, doctrinal statement about the Last Things. In Luke it is replaced by a concept of redemptive history that centers on the world mission of the church (p. 21).

come to terms with the needs of their respective communities as ongoing enterprises, offering norms and regulation for members and pointing up the correspondences between Jesus' work and their own. The new feature in Luke is the adoption of an epochal view of history, according to which the story of the human race is depicted as moving through successive stages.

LUKE'S EPOCHAL VIEW OF HISTORY

The writing of periodized historical accounts became common in the Hellenistic period, probably through influences from Iran. Already in Hesiod (eighth century B.C.) there appeared a scheme of successive ages of the world. In the Book of Daniel, history is divided into three eras: (1) the history of Israel down to the fall of Jerusalem to the neo-Babylonian armies (587 B.C.); (2) the era of Alexander's world kingdom, which is ruled by the two Hellenistic dynasties of most importance for Jews—the Seleucids in Syria and the Ptolemies in Egypt; and (3) the era of the Rule of God, which will be established solely by divine intervention. Luke represents Jesus as offering a schematic view of history that falls into a roughly comparable set of three periods. The first two epochs are implied in Luke 16:16:

> The law and the prophets were until John; since then the good news of the Kingdom of God is preached, and every one enters it violently.

The first epoch, which is presented as preliminary and anticipatory of later events, covers the time of the Law and the Prophets, the second is the present age, when the coming of the Kingdom of God is being proclaimed in words and acts, first by Jesus (phase one) and then by his emissaries (phase two). It will culminate in the coming of the Son of Man and the judgment of the world, and will be followed by the final epoch: the Kingdom of God.[6]

The final age is variously described as "your redemption" (Luke 21:28), or simply "the Kingdom of God" (21:31) in which Jesus' followers share with him in exercising authority over the twelve tribes of Israel (22:28–30). The transition from the present age into the eschatological age will be marked by the coming or the "day" of the Son of Man (17:22–26; 21:27). Another way of referring to the end of the current age is the fulfillment of "the times of the Gentiles" (21:24). Surprisingly, the destruction of Jerusalem is not seen by Luke as marking the end of this age, as is the case in Mark 13:14–27; rather, the attack on Jerusalem is a warning of its impending destruction (Luke 21:20) and of its continuing occupation by pagan rulers (21:24).

Luke's primary interest is in the present age, during which Jesus' followers carry forward the work of preaching and healing for which he commissioned them. That missionary charge was in two stages: The first concerns Jews exclusively; the second includes Gentiles, as is shown by the narrative accounts in Luke (9:1–6, where twelve are sent, presumably to Israel; 10:1–16, where seventy are sent on the Gentile mission) and also in Luke's variant of the Parable of the Supper (14:15–24), where those first invited refuse and the outsiders are welcomed. These include, presumably, both Jewish outcasts (14:21) and Gentiles (14:23). The central epoch of redemption is inaugurated by the coming of Jesus (Luke 1:2). The redemptive scheme begins with his birth (Luke 2) and will be consummated by his coming in glory (21:27). As we shall see, Luke's two-volume work is occupied with showing how the work of the gospel was launched so that

---

[6] Hans Conzelmann first developed the idea that Luke saw history as the unfolding of God's plan in three successive phases. (See *The Theology of St. Luke* [New York: Harper & Row, 1961], pp. 202–06.) The scheme presented here follows Conzelmann in distinguishing three ages, but differs in considering that Luke's special contribution is his divison of *present age* of redemption into two phases: (1) Jesus' career as the paradigm in word and act of the inbreaking of God's kingdom; and (2) the Spirit-empowered ministry of the Twelve and of Paul as God's means of effecting the consummation of his purpose in the world. Luke describes phase one; Acts displays the pattern for phase two, which is not yet completed.

the objective might be ultimately achieved: "All flesh shall see the salvation of our God" (3:6; cf. Mark 1:3; only Luke continues the quotation from Isaiah 40 that far). In his two opening chapters Luke shows how the epoch of redemption, the present age, began.

THE INAUGURATION OF THE EPOCH OF REDEMPTION: THE BAPTIST AND INFANCY STORIES

Luke opens his gospel with a report about the childlessness of an aged Jewish couple, Zechariah, a priest, and Elizabeth (Luke 1:5–25). The account is reminiscent of the Old Testament story of Elkanah and Hannah (1 Sam. 1). In each case a son is born to a pious priest after it seemed that his wife was barren; in each case the son is especially dedicated to God, although his greatest task is to prepare the way for someone else—Samuel to anoint Israel's first king, Saul, and John to prepare the way for Jesus. The rhetoric of the prophets (specifically the words of Malachi 4:5, which predict the coming of Elijah before the Last Day) is recalled in the hymn of the angel before Zechariah:

> And he [John] will go before him [Jesus?] in the spirit and
>   power of Elijah,
> to turn the hearts of the fathers to the children,
> and the disobedient to the wisdom of the just,
> to make ready for the Lord a people prepared.
>
> (Luke 1:17)

Similarly, the other hymns of Luke's infancy narratives are based on the diction and prophecies of the Old Testament. Mary's Magnificat (1:29–32) closely parallels Hannah's hymn of praise in 1 Samuel 2:1–10. Zechariah's prophesying (Luke 1:67) is patterned after the Psalms of the Old Testament and draws for its content on the prophecies of Isaiah 9 and Malachi 4. Simeon's blessing of God on the occasion of the presentation of the infant Jesus in the Temple incorporates themes from 2 Isaiah:

> Lord, now lettest thou thy servant depart in peace,
>> according to thy word;
> for mine eyes have seen thy salvation
>> which thou hast prepared in the presence of all peoples,
> a light for revelation to the Gentiles,
>> and for glory to thy people Israel.
>
> (Luke 2:29–32)

The point of Simeon's prayer is not merely that prophecy is being fulfilled, but that God's redemptive plan for all mankind—Gentile and Jew—is about to be fulfilled. In short, the long age of preparation that stretched from creation through the days of the prophets is now drawing to a close, not in disappointed hopes, but in eager expectation of fulfillment. Simeon's hymn is not only his own farewell but also a farewell to the age that lived by hope alone. Similarly, John the Baptist[7] has the final role in preparing Israel (Luke 1:80) to receive the one whose coming is to be a source of joy "to all the people" (2:10). The last of these prophetic figures to be described by Luke is Anna, who is God's representative and spokesman to "all who were looking for the redemption of Jerusalem" (2:38).

But Luke goes beyond the theme of prophetic fulfillment in depicting Jesus' place in God's plan of history. Prophecy drawn from the Hebrew Scriptures was, after all, limited to the Jews. Luke sees God's hand at work in the routine Roman requirement for persons to return to their ancestral homes to be enrolled. Caesar Augustus' decree about the census became the occasion for Jesus' birth in Bethlehem in fulfillment of the Hebrew prophecy in Micah 5. God's sovereignty over history is thus fully demonstrated. There is a difficulty with the story, however, since Josephus

---

[7] It has been suggested by C. H. Kraeling, *John the Baptist* (New York: Scribner's, 1951), pp. 16–23, that all the hymns incorporated by Luke into the first two chapters were originally used in the Baptist movement, which saw John as the redemptive figure, but were modified by the Christians so as to place John in the subordinate position and Jesus in the central role. See also C. H. Scobie, *John the Baptist* (Philadelphia: Fortress, 1964), pp. 54–55.

reports[8] that Quirinius was sent by Augustus to Syria to conduct a census in connection with his duties as governor of the province, but this was in A.D. 6, ten years after the supposed date of Jesus' birth. In spite of attempts to explain away Luke's error,[9] it must be concluded that Luke's interest in setting the events of Jesus' life in the context of world history led him to make what is probably an innocent mistake in assigning to the year of Jesus' birth a census that actually occurred a decade later.[10]

THE CENTRAL REDEMPTIVE EVENTS, PHASE ONE: JESUS' PUBLIC CAREER

The launching of the first phase of Luke's second and central epoch, the career of Jesus, is effected in the sermon of Jesus in the synagogue in Nazareth (Luke 4:16–30). It is important to note the Janus-like nature of the sermon and its immediate sequel: The passage looks back to the Old Testament, whose prophecies are seen as being fulfilled in Jesus, and it looks forward to the events of Jesus' ministry, in which the fulfillment itself takes place. With a few quick strokes, Luke paints a picture of Jesus in the synagogue, observing the traditions of worship as they had developed in postexilic Judaism: his habit of regular attendance, his being asked to read and interpret the Scripture as a layman who was presumed by the synagogue community in Nazareth to have something to say worth hearing, the attendant's selection of the scroll of Scripture from its place, the unrolling of the unwieldy scroll to the appropriate point at which to begin reading, and Jesus' sitting down to begin his extemporaneous exposition of the Scripture. More significant than these details, however, is the position of the

---

[8] *Antiquities* 18.1.1.

[9] Such as that by Jack Finegan, *Handbook of Biblical Chronology* (Princeton, N.J.: Princeton University Press, 1964), pp. 235–38, where Quirinius' participation in the earlier census is described as "not unlikely."

[10] See the summary of evidence and bibliography in the notes to Josephus, *Antiquities* 18, Loeb edition, vol. 9, trans. L. H. Feldman. (Cambridge, Mass.: Harvard University Press, 1965), pp. 2–3.

scene in the gospel: By placing this sermon at the beginning of Jesus' public activity (instead of later on, as in Luke's source, Mark 6), Luke provides the context for all that Jesus does. The passage chosen to be read, Isaiah 61:1-2, is one of the great eschatological poems of the Old Testament. Its appropriateness here is heightened by the fact that Jesus reads it shortly after he has been anointed with the Spirit at baptism (Luke 3:21-22); thus the words of 2 Isaiah epitomize the gospel that Jesus preached and enacted:

> The Spirit of the Lord is upon me,
> because he has anointed[11] me to preach good news to the poor.
> He has sent me to proclaim release to the captives
> and recovering of sight to the blind,
> to set at liberty those who are oppressed,
> to proclaim the acceptable year of the Lord.
>
> (Luke 4:18-19)

The quotation that Luke takes from Isaiah serves as a kind of program for the ministry of Jesus as Luke represents it. The final element, proclaiming the acceptable year of the Lord, is important for Luke's schematization of history, which is depicted here as unfolding in accord with the divine plan. The link between the prophecy of Isaiah and the activity of Jesus is made explicit in the words attributed to Jesus (Luke 4:21): "Today this scripture has been fulfilled in your hearing." The details of the miracles, especially specific features of thaumaturgic or exorcistic technique, tend to be played down in Luke, with the result that the emphasis in his miracle stories is more often on the power of faith than on the act of healing (cf. Luke 7:1-10 with Matt. 8:5-13) or on the miracles as the fulfillment of Scripture (as in the location of the string of miracle stories following the report of Jesus' sermon in Nazareth).

Stress on fulfillment of Scriptures makes all the more appropriate Luke's appeal to two of the most familiar miracle-workers of the Old Testament as paradigms for Jesus' activity:

---

[11] The Greek verb here, *chriō*, is the base of the adjectival title "Christ"; the underlying Semitic root is related to "Messiah."

Elijah and Elisha. In the face of the opposition that Jesus' claim immediately arouses, Luke (4:25–27) appeals to two incidents in their lives. Each prophet, rejected in his own land and among his own people, turned to non-Jews (or non-Israelites) as the beneficiaries of the prophetic healing power. It was in the land of Sidon (Phoenicia) that Elijah and the hospitable widow were miraculously sustained during a long drought (1 Kings 17:8–16). It was a leprous Syrian officer who benefited from the restorative powers of Elisha (2 Kings 5:1–14). The illustrations chosen by Jesus, with their implicit criticism of Israel's lack of faith, evoke hostility from the worshipers in the synagogue, who try to destroy Jesus. Thus, at the very outset of Jesus' career, his rejection by the Jews and his acceptance by the Gentiles are portrayed as an outworking of the ancient pattern laid down in Scripture and now fully revealed in "the acceptable year of the Lord."

Just as Elijah and Elisha carried out their work by the power of God's Spirit (1 Kings 18:12; 2 Kings 2:9–16), so the Spirit empowers Jesus and his followers. In the second volume of his work Luke gives a summary of the career of Jesus (Acts 10:36–43) that moves from the launching of Jesus' activity of preaching and healing, through his confrontation with the authorities in Jerusalem, his death and resurrection, and his commissioning of his followers as "witnesses" whose work will continue until he is manifested as "the one ordained by God to be the judge of the living and the dead." This account is placed in a sermon of Peter, which serves as a means for Luke to depict the transition from the ministry of Jesus to that of his apostles: They are sent forth in Jesus' name and in the power of the same Spirit (Acts 1:8) that came upon him at the outset of his career (Luke 3:22; 4:18).

The description of Jesus' ministry begins at 4:31, at the point where Luke resumes the Markan narrative (cf. Mark 1:21). The general strategy of the ministry has already been indicated in the transitional verses, Luke 4:14–15, where Luke turns from the preparatory phases (birth, baptism, temptation) to the appropriate scene of Jesus' activity: Galilee.

> And Jesus returned [that is, from the Jordan Valley] in the power of the Spirit into Galilee, and a report concerning him

went out through all the surrounding country. And he taught in their synagogues, being glorified by all.

The Ministry in Galilee

For Luke, Galilee is the place of public manifestation, just as Jerusalem is the place of rejection and passion. The geographical movement of Jesus, therefore, is not simply historical recollection; nor is it even strictly accurate. Rather, it functions in a symbolic way and as evidence of a predetermined scheme as Luke understands it.[12] We shall see how important for Luke is the shift of scene from Galilee to Jerusalem.

The straightforward Markan account of Jesus' calling of the disciples (Mark 1:16–20), which is reproduced with little change in Matthew (4:18–20), becomes in Luke (5:1–11) an extended miracle story, rich in symbolic detail pointing to the world mission of the church. The nearest parallel in the gospel tradition is in John 21:1–11, where the risen Lord commissions the church to carry out its "fishing" task in obedience to his word, not merely in reliance on its own resources.[13] Far from preserving, as a fiction writer would, the illusion that the ministry of Jesus unfolded in a series of events that could not have been anticipated by the participants, Luke (5:4) tips off his reader well in advance, in Jesus' words to Simon, as to the divinely intended scope of the church's mission: "Put out into the deep. . . ." The rest of Luke-Acts tells how this enlargement of scope came about, first through Jesus and then through the church.

Luke follows without variation Mark's order from 5:12 (= Mark 1:40) to 6:19 (= Mark 3:12), except that just before introducing his Sermon on the Plain (6:20–49), Luke varies the order

---

[12] Luke's knowledge of Palestinian geography is quite vague, as is evident from his reference to Jesus' passing between Galilee and Samaria (Luke 17:11). On the symbolic significance of Galilee and Jerusalem, see R. H. Lightfoot, *Locality and Doctrine in the Gospels* (New York: Harper & Row, 1938) and Hans Conzelmann, *The Theology of St. Luke*, Part I, esp. pp. 60–65.

[13] An informative study of the disciples as fishers of men is Wilhelm Wuellner, *The Meaning of "Fishers of Men"* (Philadelphia: Westminster, 1967).

of Mark's description of the call of the disciples (cf. Mark 3:13–19 with Luke 6:12–16). Although Luke's version of the Q material in the Sermon is not nearly so full as Matthew's (5—7), Luke presents it in the same sequence as Matthew, which suggests that they used a common document as the basis for their reconstructed Sermons. The Q material continues in Luke from 7:1 to 7:35, with the insertion at 7:11–17 of a uniquely Lukan pericope, the first of a long series of stories about women that is found only in Luke. The pericope describes Jesus healing a widow's son and is thus reminiscent, as were Jesus' words at the end of his sermon in the Nazareth synagogue, of the miracles of Elijah and Elisha in 1 Kings 17 and 2 Kings 4. It is not surprising, therefore, that Luke reports that Jesus was acclaimed a "great prophet."

Two more stories about women follow almost immediately. One reads like a variant of the Mark 14:3–9 (= Matt. 26:6–13) narrative in which a woman anoints Jesus on the eve of his crucifixion, "beforehand for burying" (Mark 14:8). But in keeping with Luke's emphasis on Jesus' message of God's gracious forgiveness, the story has become an act of acceptance toward a sinner. Elsewhere in the gospel tradition, "Your faith has saved you" means "Your faith has made possible your being healed." In Luke 7:50, it means "You have been granted divine forgiveness." The theme of forgiveness as the chief feature of salvation was sounded in the prophetic oracle of Zechariah in the infancy narrative (Luke 1:77) and is repeated in the Christian preaching of Acts (10:43; 13:38; 26:18). The theme of penitent Gentiles turning to God brings Acts to a close (28:27–29). In this way Luke underscores the continuity between the message of Jesus and that of his apostolic messengers in the author's own time.

Luke resumes Mark's sequence at the point where the parables of the Kingdom are introduced (Mark 4:1 = Luke 8:4). The section of Mark (3:19–35) that Luke passes over he includes at later points, chiefly where it better serves his purpose of demonstrating the mounting conflict in the period after Jesus turns toward Jerusalem (Luke 9:51). The miracle stories follow in the Markan order, from the Stilling of the Storm (Mark 4:35–41 = Luke 22–25) to the Raising of Jairus' Daughter (Mark 5:43 =

Luke 8:56). And with a few omissions,[14] the sequence continues through the story of the Feeding of the Five Thousand (Luke 9:10–17 = Mark 6:30–44). From that point, Luke leaps over the Markan material to the account of the confession of Peter and the first prediction of the passion.[15]

Luke usually condenses the narrative taken over from Mark, although he underscores the divinity of Jesus, as in 9:20, where Jesus is expressly called "the Christ of God," and in 9:43, the story of the Healing of the Epileptic Child, which is described as a manifestation of "the majesty of God." At one crucial point, however, an extended Lukan addition to Mark (cf. Luke 9:30–31 with Mark 9:4) discloses the subject of the conversation of Jesus, Moses, and Elijah at the transfiguration: Jesus' departure (*exodos*), which he was on the point of accomplishing in Jerusalem. Luke is offering to his reader a clear hint not only of the fact of the passion but also of the place of Jesus' death, in accord with the divinely determined plan. That Moses and Elijah are able to converse on the subject shows that it is predicted in Scripture, which is tantamount to saying it is predetermined by God.

As we have observed, it is in keeping with Luke's conviction that the Jews had the first opportunity to hear the gospel;[16] the twelve disciples are reported as being sent out to preach, to heal, and to perform exorcisms, presumably among Jews, though Luke does not say so explicitly. The number twelve (Luke 9:10–17) is

---

[14] Luke's omission of Mark 6:1–6 is only an apparent one, since he has reworked and expanded the incident into a programmatic event at the outset of Jesus' ministry (Luke 4:16–30). Luke's failure to include the pericope on the death of John the Baptist is more difficult to account for, since it would seem to be precisely the kind of "historical" incident that would serve Luke's aims well.

[15] The longer omission—from Mark 6:45 to 8:10—is probably best explained by assuming that Luke had a defective or incomplete copy of Mark, since elsewhere he either follows it carefully or adapts it to his own purposes.

[16] In addition to the implication of the two-stage invitation in the Parable of the Supper (Luke 14:15–24), the shift from Jews to Gentiles is made explicit in Acts 13:46. This means that Israel's destiny is redefined to include Gentiles, although the evangelism of Jews is regarded in Acts as an activity whose time has passed. See Jacob Jervell, *Luke and the People of God* (Minneapolis: Augsburg, 1972), esp. pp. 42–43; Jewish Christian observance of the Law and Gentile participation in salvation "are the distinguishing marks of the Israel that Moses and the prophets predicted . . ." (p. 147).

probably intended to symbolize the twelve tribes of Israel, as it does in Acts 6:1–2, where the "twelve" are chosen from among the Hebrews. In contrast, after Jesus has begun his final, fateful journey toward Jerusalem, another mission is launched; but this time its intended audience is the Gentiles, as reflected in the selection of seventy disciples, symbolizing the number of Gentile nations according to Jewish tradition of the period (Luke 10:1–20).[17]

The Journey to Jerusalem

The first prediction of the passion (Luke 9:18–22) provides the beginning of the transition to Luke's section on the journey to Jerusalem, but the locale of the passion is not specified until the transfiguration story, as we have seen. It is in Luke 9:51, however, that the journey actually gets under way. Twice in the pericope (9:51–56) Luke declares that Jesus "set his face to go to Jerusalem." Clearly, Jesus is dedicating himself to the outworking of the divine plan, as Luke sees it, which requires that the death of God's messenger occur in Jerusalem. But it is not until 13:31–33 that the link between Jerusalem and the passion is made explicit: "It cannot be that a prophet should perish away from Jerusalem."

The material between these two statements about Jesus' going to Jerusalem is drawn almost entirely from Q and from Luke's own special source.[18] There is very little actual narrative, apart from the story of the sending of the seventy messengers and their return. The pericope about Mary and Martha, the devoted and the diligent sisters, respectively, is more like a parable than a narrative (Luke 10:38–42). The single miracle story (13:10–17) is seemingly less concerned with the health of the woman (that problem is handled in three verses) than with Jesus' setting aside the Sabbath law, since his act of healing was regarded as a form

[17] Some of the ancient manuscripts read "seventy-two" instead of "seventy," but this does not affect the symbolism, since a variant of the Jewish tradition claimed that there were seventy-two nations. The fact that the Greek translation of the Old Testament, the Septuagint (= seventy), was reportedly accomplished by seventy scholars and was intended for Gentile readers is further evidence of the symbolic force of the number.
[18] The only Markan material in this section is (1) the lawyer's question, (2) the Beelzebul controversy, and (3) the Parable of the Mustard Seed.

of work. The story clearly reveals the influence of controversy between church and synagogue in the writer's time, in addition to preserving part of the record of Jesus' healing activity.

The rest of this section contains eight parables—the Good Samaritan (10:29–37), the Friend at Midnight (11:5–8), the Rich Fool (12:13–21), the Faithful Servants (12:35–38), the Servant's Wages (12:47–48), Settlement Out of Court (12:57–59), the Unproductive Fig Tree (13:6–9), and the Late Guest (13:25–27)—in addition to many short parabolic words. One of the main themes of these parables is the need to repent now, a point that is made explicitly in the sayings about the sign of Jonah (11:31–32) and in Jesus' reply to the question about whose sin it was that brought about certain catastrophes (13:1–5): "Unless you repent you will all likewise perish."

Another theme that runs throughout this section is that of the disciples' blessedness, revealed in the special insight into his purpose that God has granted to them. As we might expect, this motif is drawn largely from such Q passages as Luke 10:21–24 and 11:9–13, where the privileges of the true children of God are described. Luke adds to the gifts of grace the promise of the bestowal of the Holy Spirit (11:13). The term Spirit probably did not appear in the Q version, but it does figure prominently and pervasively in Luke's second volume, the Book of Acts, from the promise of the Spirit and the vivid account of the outpouring of the Spirit at Pentecost through the rest of the book. From Acts 2:16–21 we learn that the outpouring of the Spirit is to be regarded as an eschatological sign in fulfillment of the prophecy of Joel 2:28–32. In both Acts and Luke's gospel, the Spirit is accessible for "all flesh," a point that fits nicely with the prominent position Luke gives to the promise of the Spirit in the gospel narrative, just after the mission of the seventy to the Gentiles. Luke follows the pericope with his own modification of the tradition so that it now announces God's offer of the gift of the Spirit:

> How much more will the heavenly Father give the Holy Spirit to those who ask him? (Luke 11:13)

Similar declarations of blessedness are present in sayings unique to Luke. In Luke 11:27–28 Jesus pronounces more blessed than the mother that bore and nurtured him the follower who obeys God's word. In 12:32, the Kingdom is spoken of as a gift of God to his own flock. Mention of God's "good pleasure" recalls the message of the angel (2:14): "Peace among men with whom he is pleased!"[19]

The promise of the Kingdom leads into a series of sayings, widely scattered in the Matthean parallels, which Luke has brought together and in which the recurrent theme is that of preparedness for the coming of the Judgment (12:33–13:9). The urgency of the decision of faith is stressed in parables and sayings, culminating in a final pericope—reportedly spoken by Jesus on the way to Jerusalem (13:22)—in which the finality of the Judgment is depicted under the image of the closed door (13:25). Only the truly faithful will be admitted to the eschatological feast, at which will be gathered the ancient worthies, Abraham and the other patriarchs, and the faithful Gentiles ("from east and west"). But those who heard Jesus—and those who heard his messengers—and failed to repent will not be able to "sit at table in the kingdom of God." Luke is letting his reader know what the end of the final epoch will be like, since one's response to Jesus now will be the decisive factor in how one fares on the Day of Judgment.

The transition to the third phase of Jesus' ministry, the passion in Jerusalem, is extensive. Although there is in the narrative no indication of actual progress from Galilee to Jerusalem once the journey through the Samaritan villages has been described (9:51–56), Luke reminds his readers repeatedly that Jerusalem is now Jesus' goal. The vivid account of the Pharisees' rumor that Herod Antipas intends to kill Jesus and Jesus' response to the rumor suggest that Jesus left Galilee not to escape Herod but to conform to the divine plan:

> At that very hour some Pharisees came, and said to him, "Get away from here, for Herod wants to kill you." And he said to

---

[19] The meaning of the word in 2:14, *eudokía*, sometimes translated as "good-will" (that is, toward men), has been clarified through a parallel expression in the Thanksgiving Hymns of the Essene community of Qumran. See Ernest Vogt, " 'Peace Among Men of God's Good Pleasure': Luke 2:14," in Krister Stendahl, ed., *The Scrolls and the New Testament* (New York: Harper & Row, 1957), pp. 114–17.

> them, "Go and tell that fox, 'Behold, I cast out demons and
> perform cures today and tomorrow, and the third day I finish
> my course. Nevertheless I must go on my way today and tomor-
> row and the day following; for it cannot be that a prophet should
> perish away from Jerusalem.' " (Luke 13:31–33)

By enumerating the days, Luke is depicting the divinely ordained
sequence of events, not presenting a literal timetable. Jesus' ministry must continue until the passion takes place, and the passion
can occur only in Jerusalem. Luke follows the announcement of
the Jerusalem journey with the Q pericope, the lament over Jerusalem (13:34–35), which Matthew included in his expanded version of the prediction of the destruction of the Temple (Matt.
23:37–39). Luke is telling his reader that Jesus' death is part of
the outworking of God's plan of history and that Jesus foresees it
in this way throughout the second half of his ministry. The general implications of the predictions of the passion that Luke takes
over from Mark are made more specific so that in Luke they detail
the inexorable movement from Galilee to the place of the passion,
Jerusalem.

As was true in the section between 9:51 and 13:33, Luke has
strung together parables and sayings (many of which are parabolic), nearly all of which point to eschatological judgment or
blessing. Exceptions are the Healing of the Man with Dropsy
(14:1–6) and the sayings about divorce (16:18), temptations to
sin (17:1–2), forgiveness (17:3–4), faith (17:5–6), and fidelity
(17:7–10). Otherwise, even sayings that seem to concern ethical
questions, such as the parable about humility (14:7–14), the
saying about children (18:15–17 = Mark 10:13–16), and the reply
to the ruler's question (18:18–30 = Mark 10:17–31), are set in a
context where the issue is one's fate in the eschatological judgment. The parables are either explicitly eschatological, as in the
Great Supper (14:15–24), the Prudent Builder and the Prudent
Warrior (14:28–33), the Unjust Steward (16:1–13), the Rich
Man and Lazarus (16:19–31), or else they depict the joy of God
over a sinner's repentance, as in the Joyous Shepherd, the Joyous
Housewife, the Joyous Father (15:1–32). The Parable of the Unjust Judge (18:1–8) is given eschatological connotations by the

addition of the concluding question, "When the Son of man comes, will he find faith on earth?" Similarly, the generalizing conclusion to the pericope about the Pharisee and the Publican (18:9–14) reminds the reader that God is the one who will do the final humbling and exalting of men on the Last Day.

The Passion

The final section of Luke's account of Jesus' ministry begins with the third prediction of the passion (18:31–33), as taken from Mark (10:32–34) and adapted by Luke:

> And taking the twelve, he said to them, "Behold, we are going up to Jerusalem, and everything that is written of the Son of man by the prophets will be accomplished." (Luke 18:31)

The rest of the prediction Luke reproduced without important change, except that he added the statement that the disciples did not and could not understand this prediction because its meaning was "hid from them" (18:34). This implies that God concealed its meaning from them, even though the fate of Jesus (= the Son of Man) was in fulfillment of the words of the prophets. There is nothing in the Old Testament prophets about the suffering of the Son of Man, and in the late (probably first century A.D. or later) apocalyptic writings where the Son of Man appears, he is a triumphant figure and nothing is indicated of his suffering.[20] Luke must be using the Christian title Son of Man for Jesus and read-

---

[20] The Son of Man is mentioned in 1 Enoch and in 4 Ezra ("the Man"), but in each case the term occurs in parts that may be Christian in origin. The fragments found at Qumran include all parts of Enoch (known from later translations into Ethiopic and Greek preserved by Christians) except the section called the Similitudes of Enoch. From this absence, J. T. Milik (*Ten Years of Discovery in the Wilderness of Judea*, trans. John Strugnell [Naperville, Ill.: Allenson, 1959], p. 33) has concluded that the Similitudes are later than the time of Qumran and that they are Christian in origin. That view is challenged by André Dupont-Sommer, *The Essene Writings from Qumran*, trans. Geza Vermes (Cleveland: Meridian, 1962), and by others who assign the Similitudes to the first century B.C. or to the turn of our era. See Barnabas Lindars, "Re-enter the Apocalyptic Son of Man," *New Testament Studies* 22 (1975): 54–60; also Martin Hengel, *Judaism and Hellenism*, vol. 1 (Philadelphia: Fortress, 1974), p. 200.

ing it back into the account of Jesus' earthly ministry. His editing of the saying makes it serve his purpose well, since the fact that it was written by the prophets shows it to be a part of the divine plan for history, and the fact that it is being fulfilled shows that God is achieving his purpose through the death of Jesus and his resurrection "on the third day" (18:33).

On the whole, the narrative of Jesus' journey through Jericho follows that of Mark, but with some highly significant departures. The story of the tax collector, Zacchaeus, who received Jesus (Luke 19:1–10) is an instance of the receptivity to the gospel of the outcasts ("the poor") who hear it and respond in faith. The story stands in sharp contrast to the parable, originally from Q, that Luke inserted at this point (19:11–27) and drastically re-shaped to suit his purpose, adding details about the man who journeyed far to have himself confirmed as king. Matthew's version is probably more original,[21] but Luke tells his reader that the parable is relevant for those who expect the End of the Age immediately (19:11). This can only mean that Luke understands the parable as an allegory in which Jesus has gone to heaven to await his installation on earth as king. The citizens who hate him are unbelieving Jewish leaders who claim to possess for themselves the Kingdom of God. When the king returns at the End of the Age, he will reward the faithful and slay the wicked, "who did not want me to reign over them" (19:27).

For dramatic effect, Luke inserted in the Markan narrative of Jesus' entry into Jerusalem an oracle spoken just as Jesus

---

[21] The parable was probably originally intended as a criticism of the scribes, to whom the Word of God had been entrusted, but who had failed to allow it to work in a fruitful way; thus Joachim Jeremias, *The Parables of Jesus*, 6th ed., trans. S. H. Hooke (New York: Scribner's, 1963), p. 62. Matthew has placed the emphasis on the Day of Reckoning, which suits well his setting of it in 25:14–30, the synoptic apocalypse. The Lukan addition, about the nobleman traveling (to Rome?) to have his kingship confirmed, may reflect an actual occurrence in 4 B.C., when Herod's son, Archelaus, who had gone to Rome to try to gain his official designation as king of Judea from Caesar Augustus, was followed by a Jewish delegation requesting the denial of his appointment (Josephus, *Antiquities* 17.8–11). See T. W. Manson, *The Sayings of Jesus* (London: SCM Press, 1949), pp. 314–15. Augustus compromised by giving Archelaus half his father's realm, but he was so incompetent that he had to be replaced by a Roman governor in A.D. 6.

reached the crest of the Mount of Olives, where he could see the city of Jerusalem spread out below. The prophecy (19:39–44) is very specific about the siege of the city and the ramparts thrown up to prevent the escape of the besieged ("Your enemies will cast up a bank about you and surround you"), a description that coincides with the fate of the city as Josephus depicts it in his *Jewish Wars*.[22] The slaughter of the inhabitants of the city and the destruction of its marvelous buildings are likewise fully attested by Josephus. What Luke did was to amplify the theme in Mark 13:1–2 concerning the destruction of the Temple (which is reproduced in Luke 21:5–6) and thereby make Jesus envision the ruin of the city as a whole. It is clear that this event had already occurred at the time Luke was writing. Far from sensing anything unethical in representing a description of the past as though it were a prediction about the future, Luke seized the opportunity to demonstrate how the course of such visible, worldly events as the sacking of a provincial city by the Roman legions is the outworking of God's plan.

Luke picked up this theme again in his version of the apocalyptic discourse (Luke 21:20 = Mark 13:14), where he replaced Mark's vague reference to "the desolating sacrilege" with the concrete "Jerusalem surrounded by armies." The succeeding verses continue the theme of the destruction of the city, rather than portending the End of the Age. Indeed, there is to be an interval of indefinite extent, "the times of the Gentiles," during which "Jerusalem will be trodden down by the Gentiles" (21:24). Only when this time is "fulfilled" will the end come. The Markan notion of the imminent end has been played down; instead, Luke calls for patient and pious waiting until the Son of Man appears (21:34–36).

It is important for Luke's purpose to report that during the days of Jesus' witness in Jerusalem, "early in the morning all the people came to him in the temple to hear him" (21:38). His testimony was available to the entire populace, Luke suggests, so that Jerusalem can never offer the excuse that it had no oppor-

[22] 5.262, Loeb edition, vol. 3, trans. H. St. John Thackeray, (Cambridge, Mass.: Harvard University Press, 1957).

tunity to hear Jesus' message. This is, of course, an important ingredient in Luke's understanding of the divine scheme of the spread of the gospel, beginning "in Jerusalem . . . and [extending] to the end of the earth" (Acts 1:8).

The detailed differences between Luke's and Mark's passion narratives are such that some interpreters think Luke used a source other than Mark in this part of his gospel.[23] It is more likely that he amplified Mark's account by drawing on his own written or oral sources, and that he modified the whole to suit his theological aims. We can find three "historical" motifs in the service of Luke's theological aims at work in Luke 23:4–16. First, to the Markan account of Jesus' hearing before Pilate (Mark 15:2–5) Luke adds Pilate's remark that he can find no crime in Jesus,[24] thereby strengthening his case that no Gentile ruler was ever able to show that Jesus or his followers were lawbreakers, so that Christianity is not a subversive force in history. The second point is seen in Luke's historical tracing of the geographical movement in the two main phases of Jesus' ministry, which he summarizes for his readers as follows: ". . . teaching throughout all Judea, from Galilee even to this place" (23:5). The third motif is the care with which Luke seeks to show how Jesus and the beginnings of Christianity were involved with the secular rulers of the time; hence, it is important to describe the hearing held by Herod Antipas, who felt authorized on the ground that he was tetrarch of the territory where Jesus' public activity had begun.

Another oracle concerning the destruction of Jerusalem is uttered by Jesus on the way to Golgotha, according to Luke (23:28–31). The doom of the city is certain as a judgment on the nation for its failure to receive Jesus as God's Christ. In his ver-

---

[23] On this see Vincent Taylor, *Behind the Third Gospel* (Oxford: Oxford University Press, 1926), which develops B. H. Streeter's hypothesis that a writer first combined Q and L (Luke's special source, which included a non-Markan passion story) to produce a document that Streeter designated as Proto-Luke. Only later, his thesis runs, was Proto-Luke combined with L to form Luke as we now know it. For the arguments against this hypothesis, see Kümmel, *Introduction to the New Testament*, pp. 131–37.

[24] A similar verdict is attributed—in Luke only—to the centurion at the foot of the cross (Luke 23:47).

sion of the scoffing remark of the rulers, Luke removed the suggestion that Jesus could not save himself:

> He saved others; let him save himself, if he is the Christ of God,
> his Chosen One! (23:35)

It is the refusal to say in faith what is said here in jest that is the
ground of the judgment Luke has Jesus announce here.

In yet another addition to the passion story (23:39–43),
Luke sets forth his own eschatological view that Jesus is to remain
in heaven for a time, after which he will come again to establish
God's Kingdom. This is clearly implied in the correction that
Jesus reportedly offers the penitent thief, who asks to be remembered when Jesus comes "in kingly power." Jesus' emphatic reply
("Truly, I say to you") is that *today* the thief will be with him
in paradise; which is to say Jesus will enter the presence of God
immediately and remain there until the time has arrived for the
consummation of the hope for the Kingdom.

As though to underscore his claim (1:2) that he had access
to eyewitnesses to all of Jesus' ministry, Luke reproduced Mark's
description of the women at the cross as having followed Jesus
from Galilee (Luke 23:49 = Mark 15:41) and then repeated the
detail of their Galilean origin in 23:55, as though intending
through their testimony to bind together the whole story of
Jesus' ministry, from the beginning in Galilee to the passion and
burial (Acts 1:21–22).

PHASE TWO: REJECTION IN JERUSALEM
BRINGS OPPORTUNITY FOR THE WORLD

According to Luke, it was near Jerusalem, not in Galilee, that the
disclosure of the risen Lord occurred (Luke 24:13–53). The obtuseness of the disciples in their initial conversation with Jesus
after the resurrection is apparent: They had thought of him as a

mighty prophet, who might redeem Israel on its own terms. It is in the exposition of the Scriptures that the meaning of Jesus and of God's purpose through him is communicated to the disciples. But, significantly, it is in the Eucharist that he is "made known" to them (24:35). Except for the apologetic lines, which seek to combat a purely spiritual concept of the resurrection of Jesus and which therefore offer proof of the corporeality of the resurrection, the main force of the concluding section of Luke is to affirm the real presence of Christ among his people: in the interpretation of the Scriptures and in the Eucharist. That the three-fold Hebrew canon—Law, prophets, and Psalms—has its fulfillment in Jesus attests that he is the one through whom the redemptive purpose of God is being consummated.

But there is one further evidence of the invisible presence of Christ among his people, as Luke perceives it. This is the Holy Spirit, which is promised to the faithful (24:49) and which will provide the power for them to carry out their world mission, "beginning in Jerusalem." The Book of Acts is the account of how that mission was launched, following the outpouring of the Spirit.

To the modern reader, it is incongruous to alternate accounts of Jesus' postresurrection appearances (Luke 24:13–49; Acts 1:3) with presentations of his ascension (Luke 24:50–53; Acts 1:6–9). It is essential for Luke's purposes, however, that all these elements stand in his report. Of first importance is the ascension, which is an essential element in Luke's scheme, since he must show that Christ is now bodily removed from the earthly scene and bodily present at God's right hand, and that he will bodily return:

> This Jesus, who was taken up from you into heaven, will come in the same way as you saw him go into heaven. (Acts 1:11)

It is in such a framework of space and time that Luke placed Jesus, the central figure in the unfolding of God's plan of history.

In the distinctive narratives of the appearances of the risen Christ are several other motifs that were clearly of special importance for the Lukan community. There is a stress on the bodily nature of the resurrected Jesus, who invites his followers to inspect his hands and his feet as well as to handle him, so that they can be assured that "it is I myself" and not a "ghost." In addition to serving to combat the early heretical view mentioned earlier that Jesus' resurrection was purely spiritual, this story makes all the more emphatic his absence from earth and presence in heaven. That is the point of Acts 1:11: Just as he went up to heaven, so he shall return. Furthermore, by the heavenly vision of a dying martyr, Stephen, he can be seen to be in heaven in the present age of the church (Acts 7:55). This provides a dimension of concreteness to the church's expectation of his appearance in glory at the consummation of the age.

Furthermore, these postresurrection stories show how the community saw itself as sustained in the period of waiting: through sharing in the Eucharist (Luke 24:30, 35) and in the Christian exposition of the Scriptures (24:25–27, 32). The issue of fidelity was a paramount concern for Luke's community, as may be inferred from the special emphasis placed on faithfulness and perseverance (18:8; 12:46; 21:36; 9:57–62). The sufferings of the faithful are pointed to specifically, as in 22:28, and are exemplified by the faithful messengers of Jesus in Acts, from Stephen through Paul, both of whom are martyred (Acts 7:59; 20:18–38).

Finally, Jesus is portrayed as "a prophet mighty in word and deed" (Luke 24:19), who commissions his followers to carry forward his work (24:47–49) by the power of the Spirit. The Kingdom of God, whose consummation is eagerly awaited, was already manifested through the words and acts of Jesus during his earthly ministry (8:1; 11:20; 16:16; 17:20–21). The program sketched in Jesus' sermon in Nazareth ("good news to the poor . . . sight to the blind . . . release to the captives"—Luke 4:18) is assigned to the members of the community. The story of the miraculous catch of fish becomes an allegory of their mission (5:1–11). Yet Luke reckons with the fact that the protraction of the period before the consummation will result in the lapse of many from their commitment (12:42–46) and even in the fall of some into profligate life styles ("weighed down with dissipation and drunkenness and cares of this life . . ."—21:34). The faithful, however, rest confident in God's vindication of them (18:8).

In spite of his call for unswerving devotion to the Kingdom of God and to its earthly consummation, Luke carefully points out that neither Jesus nor the followers whose story is told in Acts were ever accurately charged with political subversion. The details of the trials of Jesus before Jewish and Roman authorities have been modified in detail to remove "any semblance of legitimacy" in the Jewish process and to show that Roman involvement was minimal. The rare lapse in Roman justice that resulted in the death of Jesus was an unusual succumbing "to the chaos of unlawful men," but it occurred "in order to set in motion the plan of God" for human redemption. Whenever Jesus or the apostles were brought up before the civil authorities, political charges could not be made to stick (Acts 16:39; 18:14–16; 19:37; 23:29; 25:8; 25:25; 26:32). This does not suggest that Luke-Acts was written as a political apology for Christianity, but rather that Christians were being counseled to maintain a nonpolitical stance, in keeping with the tradition that went back to Jesus and Paul.[25]

LUKE AS HISTORIAN

Luke had historical interests and skills that went beyond the scheme of theological history outlined in this chapter. He was able to write with verisimilitude, especially in the infancy stories, using an intentionally archaic language in order to give the flavor of an era and a culture—early first-century Palestine—that were not his own. He possessed the historian's imagination. But he also possessed the historian's concern for careful use of his sources. We are under obligation to him for reproducing faithfully most of the Q document, as well as the parables and sayings that he alone has recorded, which give us some of our most important clues concerning the message of Jesus.

Although in a broad way Luke manifests greater kinship

[25] Paul W. Walaskay, "The Trial and Death of Jesus in Luke," *Journal of Biblical Literature* 94 (1975): 93.

with formal literature of his time than do the other evangelists, the material itself was not easily transposed into formal history, but rather was dependent on the traditions and social needs of the community for whom Luke was writing.[26] The stylistic feature by which parallels are drawn implicitly between central characters in the narratives—between Jesus and John the Baptist, between Jesus and Paul, between the activities of Jesus and those of the apostles—suggests that Luke is consciously following the pattern used by Hellenistic writers for presenting the lives of philosophers. But the absence of the typical summaries of the "philosophical doctrines" of Jesus and Paul shows the literary analogy is at most approximate.[27]

In spite of some inaccuracies, Luke furnished what slim evidence we have for correlating the rise of Christianity chronologically with the history of the period. By modifying the tradition to make it more comprehensible for non-Jewish readers, he made more effective the communication of the gospel to Gentiles. But perhaps most important of all, by replacing the Markan apocalyptic scheme of an imminent end of the age with the epochal pattern of an ongoing church with its own place in the economy of God, Luke must have helped to prevent many early Christians from despairing when their apocalyptic hopes were not realized. And his perspectives on the church in the divine plan gave it an understanding of itself and its mission that has enabled it to function in spite of the passing of nearly two millennia since the prediction was uttered, "This generation will not pass away before all these things take place" (Mark 13:30). Whereas Matthew placed Jesus in the history of the church, Luke placed the church and Jesus in the history of the world.

By using the popular narrative and other literary styles of its time, by linking the events of Jesus with those of the empire

---

[26] The classic studies of Lukan style and aims are both by H. J. Cadbury: *The Style and Literary Method of Luke* (Cambridge, Mass.: Harvard University Press, 1919–20) and *The Making of Luke-Acts* 2nd ed. (Naperville, Ill.: Allenson, 1958).

[27] Analyses of these parallel accounts in Luke-Acts, as well as in Hellenistic and Roman literary conventions of the time, are offered by C. H. Talbert, *Literary Patterns, Theological Themes, and the Genre of Luke-Acts* (Missoula, Mont.: Scholars Press, 1974). The details Talbert presents are impressive; the case he seeks to make for Luke-Acts as a Hellenistic *life* is not.

and the wider world, by underscoring the public nature of the life and work of Jesus (and, in Acts, of the apostles), the Lukan community was making the point expressed indirectly in Acts 26: "This did not take place hidden away in corner!"

SUGGESTIONS FOR FURTHER READING

Pioneer work on the special aims of Luke was done by H. J. Cadbury, *The Making of Luke-Acts*, 2nd ed. (Naperville, Ill.: Allenson, 1958), and Martin Dibelius, *Studies in the Acts of the Apostles** (London: SCM Press, 1956). On the theological interests of Luke, see especially Hans Conzelmann, *The Theology of St. Luke* (New York: Harper & Row, 1961), and Helmut Flender, *Saint Luke: Theologian of Redemptive History* (Philadelphia: Fortress, 1967). Jacob Jervell, *Luke and the People of God* (Minneapolis: Augsburg, 1972) stresses that (1) Paul's evaluation of the faith of the local congregations as essential to the spread of the gospel was in line with Luke-Acts' portrayal of a developing apostolic tradition; and that (2) Luke regarded Israel alone as God's people, so that the conversion of Jews provided the essential transition to the inclusion of Gentiles within "Israel." Since the parables are especially revealing of Luke's aims, see the relevant portions of Joachim Jeremias, *The Parables of Jesus,** 6th ed. (New York: Scribner's, 1971); for Luke's special version of the passion narrative, see also Joachim Jeremias, *The Eucharistic Words of Jesus,** 2nd ed. (Naperville, Ill.: Allenson, 1966).

Two good commentaries on Luke are E. E. Ellis, *The Gospel of Luke* (London: Thomas Nelson, 1967), and G. B. Caird, *The Gospel of St. Luke** (Baltimore: Penguin, 1964). *Studies in Luke-Acts*, ed. J. L. Martyn and L. E. Keck (Nashville: Abingdon, 1966), includes essays on Luke and on the relationship between Luke's viewpoint and the viewpoints of other New Testament writers.

* *Available in a paperback edition.*

Theology as the History of Jesus: The Gospel of John

From the moment the reader first encounters the stately cadences of John's hymn to the Word of God (John 1:1–18), it is apparent that this gospel stands apart from the other three, despite the superficial similarity of content. To be sure, all four gospels move through a sequence of events from the launching of Jesus' public career to the report of instructions to his followers after his passion and carry accounts of his teachings. But the radical differences between John and the other three gospels have long been recognized.

The Greek Christian theologian Clement of Alexandria wrote in the second half of the second century that "John, last of all, conscious that the outward facts had been set forth in the other gospels, was urged on by his disciples, and, divinely moved by the Spirit, composed a spiritual gospel."[1] Irenaeus who left his native Asia Minor for Rome and by A.D. 180 was Bishop of Lyons in Gaul, likewise connects the gospel of John with the Spirit,

---

[1] Quoted by Eusebius, *Ecclesiastical History* 6.14.4–9, Loeb edition, vol. 1, trans. Kirsopp Lake (Cambridge, Mass.: Harvard University Press, 1957), from Clement's *Outlines* (of Holy Scripture), preserved only in fragments by other writers.

whose coming John predicts and whose work he describes (John 14–16). According to Irenaeus, the Spirit's activity in the gospel of John is like that of an eagle hovering over the church, protecting it with his wings.[2] But Irenaeus declares that John also aimed to combat the teaching of the Gnostic Cerinthus,[3] by asserting the oneness of the God of creation and redemption. (These functions were assigned to two gods by the Gnostics.) Ironically, however, as Irenaeus is obliged to acknowledge, it was the gospel of John that was seized upon by Valentinus and the later second-century Gnostics to document their own view of Jesus as the heavenly possessor of secret knowledge.[4] John's claim that the purpose of the Holy Spirit's coming was to offer private knowledge to the inner circle of Jesus' followers (14:17; 16:13) was an invitation to the Gnostics to exploit John's gospel for their own ends.

Why did John especially lend itself to exploitation by the heretics, with their claims of superior revelations? Throughout the gospel there are allusions to the heavenly origin of Jesus and to the links he has with a transcendent realm that is inaccessible to most human beings. The heavenly connection is expressed, for example, in the following:

> Truly, truly, I say to you, you will see the heaven opened, and the angels of God ascending and descending upon the Son of Man. (John 1:51)

Jesus affirms here that his ultimate destiny will receive heavenly confirmation. But his heavenly origin is likewise attested, when he declares that he "came down from heaven" (6:38, 41, 62). Indeed, he asserts that his existence is eternal (8:23, 58) and that he is not subject to death (10:17–18; 11:25). Under what circumstances and by what sort of person was such a representation of Jesus produced?

[2] Irenaeus, *Against Heresies* 3.11.8–9, in *The Ante-Nicene Fathers*, vol. 1, Alexander Roberts and James Donaldson (New York: 1899, reprinted, Grand Rapids, Mich.: Eerdmans, 1953).
[3] *Ibid.*, 3.11.1.
[4] *Ibid.*, 3.11.7.

THE AUTHORSHIP OF THE GOSPEL OF JOHN

Of the historical origins of the gospel of John, unfortunately, nothing is known with certainty. The early traditions of the second century attribute it to the apostle John, son of Zebedee, who is reported to have lived to an advanced age in Ephesus.[5] Proponents of this authorship theory today claim that John's Greek reveals that he worked from or translated an Aramaic source.[6] In fact, however, a careful study of the Greek text of John shows that the language and vocabulary are paralleled in pagan usage of the first century A.D.[7] and that the Scriptural quotations are frequently based on the Greek translation of the Old Testament, the Septuagint,[8] thus implying that the author did not have a Semitic-language background. The Greek is smooth and literate, although it contains many expressions that sound Semitic, and its poetic style, especially in the prologue, may show Semitic influence. It is most likely, therefore, that John's gospel was written in a bilingual area, where both Greek and a Semitic language were spoken.

[5] The identification of the apostle John, the son of Zebedee, with the disciple who, according to the fourth gospel, was especially close to Jesus and the assumption that he is the disciple who wrote the fourth gospel are implied by Irenaeus in *Against Heresies* 3.1.1; moreover, in 5.33.4 he describes Papias, bishop of Hieropolis in Asia Minor in the second century, as one who was a "hearer of John"—apparently meaning John the son of Zebedee. But Papais himself distinguishes this John from another, John the Presbyter (or Elder), who is classed among "other of the Lord's disciples" (quoted in Eusebius, *Ecclesiastical History* 3.39.4). Probably Irenaeus confused these two men; John the Presbyter (see 2 John 1 and 3 John 1) is, then, the man who is identified with the Johannine literature from the second century on, but there is no sure tradition linking him or the gospel with Ephesus or Asia Minor.
[6] See C. F. Burney, *The Aramaic Origin of the Fourth Gospel* (Oxford: Clarendon, 1922). Burney attempts to show that Jesus taught in poetic form and that Aramaic poetry lies behind the Greek text of the gospel of John, in order to demonstrate the authenticity of the gospel as the words of Jesus.
[7] E. C. Colwell, *The Greek of the Fourth Gospel* (Chicago: University of Chicago Press, 1931).
[8] So G. D. Kilpatrick, "The Religious Background of the Fourth Gospel," in F. L. Cross, ed., *Studies in the Fourth Gospel* (London: A. R. Mowbray, 1957), p. 36. Also Barnabas Lindars, *New Testament Apologetic* (Philadelphia: Westminster, 1962), p. 269.

Syria is a possibility, since the Greek influence introduced in the fourth century B.C. had blended with the native Syrian culture by the second century A.D.[9]

Far more plausible than the theory that John was written by a single creative individual is the hypothesis that this gospel is the cumulative product of a distinctive Christian tradition that developed within an ongoing community. Studies of philosophers and the schools they founded in the Hellenistic period indicate that these movements were characterized by a strong sense of fellowship among the disciples, concern for the preservation and interpretation of a tradition, devotion to learning, and/or a deep commitment to the teacher or founder of the movement. The organization of a group might be loose or formal, but the activities consisted of instruction, study, and writing.[10] The itinerant teacher-preachers of the Stoic school are the closest analogue in this period to the wandering preachers sent out by Jesus, and the Cynic-Stoic movement flourished in Syria, which, as we have noted, is where John may well have been written.[11] Unlike the loosely organized Stoic movement, however, the community that lies behind John appears to have had a long and closely knit common life. Out of this esoteric study, worship, and contemplation came a variant form of the Jesus tradition that borrowed terminology from the wider Hellenistic world and employed it to reinterpret the language and concepts of the Jewish and earlier Christian communities. The result was a unique understanding of Jesus.

---

[9] See the further discussion in W. G. Kümmel, *Introduction to the New Testament*, 17th ed., trans. H. C. Kee (Nashville: Abingdon, 1975), pp. 188–247.

[10] On the schools in the Hellenistic-Roman world see R. A. Culpepper, *The Johannine School: An Evaluation of the Johannine School Hypothesis Based on an Investigation of the Nature of Ancient Schools* (Missoula, Mont.: Scholars Press, 1976) pp. 61–225; also Martin Hengel, *Judaism and Hellenism*, vol. 1 (Philadelphia: Fortress, 1974), pp. 65–83, where the impact of Greek education on Jewish culture is discussed.

[11] The features of charismatic itinerant preachers in the Cynic-Stoic tradition are described by Martin Hengel in his *Nachfolge und Charisma* [Discipleship and charisma] (Berlin: Töpelmann, 1968). See my discussion in *Community of the New Age* (Philadelphia: Westminster, 1977), pp. 87–91.

THE BACKGROUND OF JOHN'S PORTRAYAL OF JESUS

Although John shares with the synoptic gospels the accounts of Jesus' miracles as well as of his trial and crucifixion, these features and others are presented in a way that is noticeably different from the other gospels. The narrative accounts, for example, do not come to a conclusion in the expected sense. Jesus approaches John the Baptist (John 1:29), but there is no report of Jesus' having been baptized by John. Instead we have general statements about who Jesus is and why his disciples followed him (1:36–51). In the synoptics Jesus' action in cleansing the temple is the last straw that determines the Jerusalem leaders to seek his death (Mark 11:18), but in John the incident takes place at the outset of his public activity (2:13–22). The gospel account then shifts abruptly to a conversation with Nicodemus (John 3), which ends, again unexpectedly, with a discourse on God's love and eternal life. The text thus moves from narration to a consideration of cosmic significance.

This movement is fairly typical of John's gospel as a whole. John uses the history of Jesus not to convey information so much as to point beyond the outward events of Jesus' career to the eternal, spiritual meaning that faith can discern in them. This does not mean that John is primarily interested in presenting an allegory, where each person or event represents some abstract idea. Rather, his purpose is to create a kind of metahistory, in which the nature and history of God are disclosed through historical events. The presentation of Jesus' miracles in John's gospel highlights this tendency to move from public event to private significance for faith.

Jesus as Miracle Worker

Jesus' action in turning the water into wine at Cana is designated by John as "the first of his signs" (2:11); only after two extended narrative sections (Jesus' conversations first with Nicodemus and then with the Samaritan woman, in John 3 and 4) does John refer to the second sign: the healing of the official's son (4:54). In 20:30–31 John mentions the "many other signs" that Jesus did "in the presence of the disciples." On the basis of these references to signs, many commentators have assumed that John had access to a Signs Source, which he incorporated into his gospel.[12] There is no consensus, however, about what was included in the original Signs Source. Some think that it was merely a collection of miracles, while others contend that it contained narratives that reported what are not strictly miracles, such as Jesus' call of the disciples in 1:35–49.[13] Still others consider the Signs Source to have been a miniature gospel, which included a passion narrative.[14] No matter what the extent of the document may have been, the proponents of the Signs Source hypothesis assume that it presented Jesus as a Hellenistic-style "divine man"[15] of a type supposed to have been common in the Hellenistic world of the first century A.D. In fact, the charismatic miracle workers of the period —the so-called divine men—were variously represented, so that no single model can be presented for them, nor can any single set of inferences be drawn concerning their significance.[16] A more

[12] See, for example, Rudolf Bultmann, *Gospel of John: A Commentary* (Philadelphia: Westminster, 1971), pp. 113, 180, 203, 205, 211, 238, 289, 329, 393, 395, 401, 698, 705. The source has been reconstructed by D. M. Smith, *The Composition and Order of the Fourth Gospel* (New Haven, Conn.: Yale University Press, 1965), pp. 38–44. For a summary and critique of source theories, including Robert Fortna's (see note 14 below), see W. G. Kümmel, *Introduction to the New Testament*, pp. 200–17.

[13] Bultmann includes this passage with his Signs Source.

[14] Robert T. Fortna, *The Gospel of Signs: A Reconstruction of the Narrative Source Underlying the Fourth Gospel.* (Cambridge: Cambridge University Press, 1970), pp. 235–45, includes in his Signs Source a prologue and epilogue, the witness of John the Baptist, the call of the first disciples, seven signs, the Cleansing of the Temple (which Fortna thinks is placed just before the passion, as in the synoptics), the anointing, the entry into Jerusalem, the Last Supper, Jesus' arrest and hearings, and his crucifixion, burial, and resurrection. Only the teachings are omitted, which implies the existence of a kind of gospel that did not recount Jesus' teaching activity—in sharp contrast to Q, which consisted almost wholly of teachings material.

[15] See, for example, Bultmann, *Gospel of John: A Commentary*, pp. 101, 104, 106, 180, 188, 269.

[16] The term "divine man" is enjoying a vogue in biblical studies, but it is too imprecise to be serviceable, as has been shown by David L. Tiede, *The Charismatic Figure as Miracle Worker* (Missoula, Mont.: Scholars Press, 1972).

serious problem for the Signs Source, however, is that it is impossible to differentiate between the alleged source and the evangelist's adaptation of it.[17] Since some of the miracles in John resemble those in the synoptic tradition, both may have drawn on the same tradition, or John may have used one or more of the synoptics for his miracle stories.[18] But there is no unambiguous evidence in John that he or the source on which he drew was trying to put Jesus in competition with other miracle workers of that epoch, or conversely, that John was trying to combat such a notion by linking the stories of Jesus' miracles with that of his passion. The present state of the text of John moves for the most part so smoothly from narrative to discourse, and in both cases manifests so many common stylistic features, that there are no solid criteria for reconstructing either a Signs Source or a pre-Johannine picture of Jesus as miracle worker.[19] Since the isolation of John's sources is a highly subjective and inconclusive undertaking, we shall group together in our analysis much of the narrative in John, because it serves John's "sign" purpose, even when it is not presenting miracle accounts.

The fullest clue to the meaning of the signs is given, somewhat surprisingly, at the end of the narrative:

> Now Jesus did many other signs in the presence of the disciples, which are not written in this book; but these are written that you may believe that Jesus is the Christ, the Son of God, and that believing you may have life in his name. (20:30–31)

It is difficult to determine whether John intends for his recounting

---

[17] Smith, *The Composition and Order of the Fourth Gospel*, convincingly argues that the stylistic unity of the gospel as it stands is such as to show that whatever sources the evangelist had access to have been so thoroughly reworked as to render indecisive any appeal to them as a clue to interpretation (p. 114). He questions both the logic of converting an inconsistent and frequently awkward text into a unified and consistent version and the usefulness of an interpretation that is based on what the interpreter thinks the author/editor ought to have said (p. 241).

[18] So R. E. Brown, *The Gospel According to John I–XII* (Garden City, N.Y.: Doubleday, 1966), pp. xliv–xlvii.

[19] Barnabas Lindars, *Behind the Fourth Gospel* (London: SPCK, 1971), pp. 27–42,

of the signs to evoke faith among unbelievers or to enrich insight among those who already believe. The latter seems more probable, since throughout his gospel he shows that Jesus' miracles aroused hostility rather than faith among those who were not disposed to see in him the messenger and agent of God. The gospel, then, would be a book for the church, rather than an evangelistic appeal to the world. This impression is supported by the book as a whole, especially in the farewell chapters:

> I am praying for them; I am not praying for the world but for those whom thou hast given me. . . . (John 17:9)

Whether or not, with Rudolf Bultmann, we consider the call of the disciples to be part of the Signs Source, the narrative about the disciples points up for us several of John's favorite themes. One is the emphasis on the earthly origins of Jesus, as son of Joseph, whose home is in Nazareth (1:45). Another is the theme of Jesus as the fulfillment of the Scripture. But most striking is the prophecy of Jesus:

> Truly, truly, I say to you, you will see heaven opened, and the angels of God ascending and descending upon the Son of man. (1:51)

The scene recalls the experience of Jacob described in Genesis 28:12: In a dream Jacob saw a ladder reaching to heaven and heard the voice of God promising him the land and posterity under the blessing of Yahweh, the God of Abraham and Isaac. The title Son of Man recalls the promise given to Daniel in a dream that to "the saints of the Most High" God would give his Kingdom (Dan. 7:13–14, 27). Since Nathanael has just acclaimed Jesus "the Son of God, the King of Israel" (John 1:49), one cannot miss John's point here: Jesus is the one through whom God's Kingdom is to be established and the new people of God assembled to share in its rule. Only the *terminology* of apocalyptic expectation remains, however; nothing of the substance is to be found here—neither the urgency of the moment nor the shortness of time until the promise is fulfilled. Even the conflict with the demonic, which is so characteristic of the apocalyptic outlook, has all but vanished in John, except for a trace in the report that the devil put it into Judas' heart to betray Jesus (13:2). The real power that consigns men to the realm of darkness is their misguided will, not the power of Satan or demons:

> . . . men loved darkness rather than light, because their deeds were evil. For every one who does evil hates the light, and does not come to the light, lest his deeds should be exposed. (John 3:19–20)

The power that will achieve the divine purpose in history is God disclosing himself to men of faith. It is through word, sign, and symbol that that revelation takes place for John. The outward course of history with its principalities and powers, as in Acts 4 or Romans 13, is of no concern to him.

In the first miracle story, the Changing of Water into Wine at the Wedding in Cana (2:1–11), the symbolism of the narrative is apparent. The best wine coming at the end of the feast reminds the reader familiar with Jewish tradition of the eschatological meal when the new wine of the New Age will be available (Amos 9:13; Jer. 31:10–12; and in the apocalyptic literature, 1 En. 10:19 and 2 Bar. 29:5). In what purports to be a quotation from Jesus, the early second-century bishop Papias tells of the marvelous fruitfulness of the vines in the Kingdom of God:

> The days will come in which vines will grow, each having ten thousand branches, and in each branch ten thousand twigs, and in each twig ten thousand shoots, and in each one of the shoots ten thousand clusters, and on every one of the clusters ten thousand grapes, and every grape when pressed will give ten thousand measures of wine. And when any one of the saints shall lay hold of a cluster, another shall cry out, "I am a better cluster, take me; bless the Lord through me." (Quoted by Irenaeus, *Against Heresies* 5. 33. 3)

In contrast to Papias' expectation that the best comes last, John reports Jesus as reversing the expected order: He brings the best wine (= eschatological joy) now. One need not wait until the End of the Age; the goal of history is already present in Jesus.

The second sign (by our count, not John's) is the cleansing of the Temple (2:13–22). Its link with the signs is given in the story itself, in which Jesus' opponents ask him what *sign* he can give as authorization for his audacious assumption of the right to cleanse the Temple courts (2:18). But the overturning of tables and the expulsion of the money-changers—who, after all, were necessary to the continuance of proper offerings in the Temple— are not for John the important facts. The interest shifts in 2:18 from the cleansing to the destruction and rebuilding of the Temple, and then to the raising up of the body of Jesus. But even this is not an unequivocal reference to the resurrection of Jesus, since "his body" could as well be the church. And it is the establishment of a new people of God through whom the true worship of God will be carried out ("in spirit and truth," 4:23) that is a major theme in John. The eschatological community, like the one that the Dead Sea Scrolls claim was being formed at Qumran, was already taking shape in the postresurrection situation, according to John. The end of history was present in the life of faith as the new temple, the church, was being erected.

Another narrative that may be included among the signs (the third in our numbering system) is the recounting of the conversation between Jesus and Nicodemus (3:1–15), who appears in the latter part of the gospel as a secret follower of Jesus (19:39). Nicodemus recognizes the power of Jesus and attributes his authority to God, even though he thinks of Jesus as a rabbi (3:2) rather than as Messiah or prophet. The conversation moves along on the basis of three words with double meanings: again (= from above), wind (= spirit), and lifted up (= crucified and/ or exalted). Nicodemus assumes that to be born again means to begin life over again on the same basis (3:4); Jesus' meaning is that to be born from above is to enter into a new kind of life, which can be called (using the traditional eschatological terminology) the Kingdom of God (3:5). Nicodemus can make nothing of new life through "wind"; Jesus means, of course, the life given through the Spirit (3:8). The life is given through the lifting up of the Son of Man,[20] in an act analogous to the lifting up of the serpent of brass in the wilderness on the day of God's Judgment on faithless Israel (Num. 21:9). In the days of ancient Israel, a look in faith toward the snake on the pole brought recovery from the otherwise fatal bite of the serpents in the camp of Israel. Jesus is now saying that a look in faith toward the Son of Man lifted up (that is, on the cross) brings eternal life (3:14).

As we have remarked, the conversation shifts here abruptly to a discourse (by Jesus? by John?) on the gift of eternal life to those who recognize Jesus to be the Son of God (3:16–17). The Judgment is not something that has already fallen, as in the plague of serpents (Num. 21:6), nor is it something that will come in the last days, in accord with apocalyptic teaching; (Mal. 4:5–6); it is rather something that occurs in the moment when an individual makes the decision of faith in Jesus as the Son of God (3:18). The traditional view of the Day of Judgment at the End of the Age has been transformed into the present moment of decision.

Jesus' encounter with the woman at the well in Samaria (4:1–42)—a fascinating story in itself—is likewise filled with double and symbolic meanings. There is the implied contrast between the head of ancient Israel, Jacob, who gave the well at which succeeding generations could quench their thirst, and Jesus, whose gift of the Spirit is a source of eternal life, not merely the means of sustaining life on its old terms. Another contrast is presented concerning the true worship of God. The woman raises the ancient controversy between Jews and Samaritans as to the proper place for the worship of God: Jerusalem, where the Jewish temple was located, or Samaria, where the Samaritan temple once stood (4:20–22). Finally (4:25), the woman tries to demonstrate her piety by declaring her faith that the Messiah is coming, but Jesus' reply is that he for whom she is looking has already come (4:26). This series of exchanges is intended to confirm Jesus' claim that he is the one through whom true life may be gained and sustained, that he is the one who has established the true

20 For John's interpretation of this term, see pp. 242–43 below.

worship of God apart from any pridefully localized setting, that this Jew, whose thirst seemingly overcomes his Jewish reluctance to have dealings with Samaritans (4:9), is in fact the Messiah (4:26), the Savior of the world (4:42).

The fifth sign (the second by John's enumeration) is the Healing of the Official's Son (4:46–53). In one of the few Johannine passages with clear synoptic parallels (= Matt. 8:5–10 and Luke 7:2–10), the point of the story is not that Jesus' miracle of healing evoked faith, but that the official trusted Jesus' word before the miracle was performed. The details of the healing—that it occurred at the precise hour that Jesus had spoken (4:52–53)—confirmed the man's faith, but they were not the cause of his faith. John wants his reader to see beyond the son's recovery of physical health to the faith that, at the word of Jesus, true life becomes a reality (4:53).

Jesus' Healing of the Lame Man at the Pool of Beth-zatha (5:1–18) is for John far more than a work of mercy that happens to violate the Jewish Sabbath restriction. It is, in the first place, a vivid way of showing the inadequacy of the ordinary way of doing things. The man has waited in vain throughout a lifetime (5:5) to be healed, counting on the bubbling of the pool (caused perhaps by an intermittent spring) to restore his health. Even when Jesus asks him if he wants to be healed, his reply is that he wants someone to help him into the pool (5:7). But at the word of Jesus, responded to in faith, the man receives the gift of health. The second point is also the more important one: Jesus' opponents wrongly assume that to violate the Sabbath law is to break God's rule. But Jesus turns the argument around. He justifies his violation of the Sabbath regulation by identifying his work with God's work (5:18). He dismisses Sabbath desecration by what his opponents can only regard as a blasphemous claim: He identifies his work with God's. It is important to note that, for John, Jesus' oneness with the Father is not a matter of metaphysical substance, as it came to be formulated in the creeds of the church, but of identity of work, word, and will.

In the sequence of the seventh and eighth signs, Feeding of the Five Thousand (6:1–14) and Walking on the Water (6:16–21), John comes closest to following the synoptic order (Mark

6:32–44 and 6:45–51; also Matt. 14:13–33 and Luke 9:10–17, although Luke omitted all the Markan material, including the story of Jesus' Walking on the Water, from Mark 6:45 to 8:27). The details of the events vary from the synoptic accounts slightly, as though John were drawing on a variant of the tradition or perhaps recalling it from memory, with some embellishment of his own, such as the detail that a lad provided the fish and that the loaves were of barley. Most striking, however, is the response of the people, who first acclaim Jesus "the prophet" (= the eschatological prophet of Deut. 18:15–19), and then determine to make him king. Apparently the prospect of a king who can provide food without anyone working to produce it has irresistible appeal for the populace. Jesus rejects the offer of kingship on these terms, in a manner analogous to his struggle against Satan in the temptation stories of the synoptics.

John's only addition to the synoptic version of Jesus' Walking on the Water is the concluding detail: As soon as Jesus was aboard, the boat immediately reached its destination (6:21). This detail heightens the element of the miraculous in the story, but it is clearly intended here as a manifestation of Jesus' divine power in his lordship over nature.[21] Although his words addressed to the disciples, "It is I," are the same as in the synoptic accounts, there is no mistaking the special link between the "I am" phrase and its frequent recurrence elsewhere in John: John uses it in each case to disclose another facet of the revelation of God in Jesus.

In contrast to the story of Jesus' Walking on the Water, which simply reports an epiphany, the story of the Feeding of the Five Thousand sets forth an understanding of Jesus as the food that God supplies to feed his own people (6:25–58). The imagery builds on the Jewish tradition of the bread from heaven that sustained the life of Israel during its desert wanderings from Egypt to Palestine. Both the rabbis and Philo elaborated on this story and gave it an interpretation related to God's care of his people

---

[21] This type of pericope is designated by Martin Dibelius as an "epiphany story" in his *From Tradition to Gospel*, 3rd ed., trans. B. L. Woolf (New York: Scribner's, 1965), pp. 94–96.

in the End Time, when they would be restored in his Kingdom.[22] But for John, the bread from heaven has already come in the person of Jesus (6:41). John uses this image to refer not only to the spiritual strength and growth that come from living by faith in Jesus but also to the Eucharist. This is clear from the rather shocking words

> Truly, truly, I say to you, unless you eat the flesh of the Son of man and drink his blood, you have no life in you; he who eats my flesh and drinks my blood has eternal life, and I will raise him up at the last day. (6:53–54)

The shocking quality of these words is increased by John's use of a word for eating that is normally found only in connection with animals feeding. John's aim may have been to combat the notion that to partake of Christ is a purely spiritual experience. He may have wanted to stress the importance of participation in the Eucharist as well.[23] Whether "eating the flesh" is participation in the sacrament or a metaphor for meditation and devotion, the intended meaning is clear: To feed on Christ is to partake of eternal life, not merely to have life sustained as it was in the wilderness by the bread from heaven. John is telling his reader that Jesus is one whose meaning and power transcend the greatest redemptive events in Israel's history.

Jesus' Healing of the Man Born Blind (9:1–41) resembles the story of the Healing at the Pool in at least two ways: It occurs on a Sabbath day, and it raises the question of the link between Jesus' work and God's work (9:4, 14). Of all the sign narratives in John, this one has the highest degree of verisimilitude. The reader can sense the incredulity of the neighbors when the man receives his sight (9:8–10), the sinister motives of the Pharisees in questioning him (9:13–17), and the timidity of the parents in refusing to acknowledge anything more than that he

---

[22] Fully discussed in Peder Borgen, *Bread from Heaven* (Leiden: Brill, 1965).
[23] Bultmann is of the opinion that John wants to eliminate all references to the sacraments and to treat them as purely spiritual. See his *Theology of the New Testament*, vol. 2, trans. Kandrick Grobel (New York: Scribner's, 1955), pp. 54, 58–59. At the opposite extreme, Oscar Cullmann finds the sacraments pervasively present in John. See his *Early Christian Worship*, trans. A. S. Todd and J. B. Torrance (Naperville, Ill.: Allenson, 1953).

is their son and that he once was blind (9:20–23). They want to shift the responsibility to their son when they say, "Ask him; he is of age, he will speak for himself" (9:21). The Pharisees' interrogation of the man becomes an indictment of the interrogators, when they insist that a violator of the Sabbath law cannot be an agent of God, no matter how marvelous his healing powers (9:24).

The climax of the story comes in the words of Jesus:

> For judgment I came into this world, that those who do not see may see, and that those who see may become blind. (9:39)

The very fact that Jesus has come precipitates the Judgment. There is no question of waiting until a day in the future when men's deeds will be appraised, rewards and punishments meted out. The decisive moment is now, when men are confronted by Jesus' words and works. Those who know their own shortcomings, who acknowledge their need of God's revelation, are enabled to "see." On the other hand, those who pride themselves on their grasp of what they take to be the truth, are confirmed in their "blindness." The passage is a variation on the theme of Isaiah 6:10, in which God blinds those who refuse to repent at the word of God's messenger:

> Make the heart of this people fat,
>   and their ears heavy,
>   and shut their eyes;
> lest they see with their eyes,
>   and hear with their ears,
> and understand with their hearts,
>   and turn and be healed.

The story of Lazarus' Being Raised from the Dead (John 11) is generally regarded as the last of the sign narratives. It is not a *resurrection* account, since Lazarus is merely restored to the life of this age rather than to the life of the Age to Come. Jesus' power to restore life to a friend is, however, a sign of the resurrection; the act points to Jesus' ability to give eternal life, which is qualitatively different from the conditions of ordinary human life, to which Lazarus is brought back.

In the narrative Martha speaks for the orthodox Pharisaic

point of view that there will be a resurrection of the dead in the End Time (11:24). She and her sister, Mary, also have faith in the ability of Jesus to heal those who are sick, and she regrets that Jesus' delay in arriving prevented him from restoring Lazarus to health (9:21, 32). Jesus' intention is not to enable life to continue on its old basis, however, but to give a new kind of life that already shares in eternity in the midst of time (11:25–26). The grant of true life is not merely a future prospect but a present possibility.

The macabre details of the burial, the four-day period during which decay has set in, and the burial wrappings help to make John's point: Lazarus was really dead; Jesus revived him. John does not deny the reality of the resurrection at the Last Day; indeed, he refers to it repeatedly: 5:28–29; 6:35, 44, 54.[24] He continues to affirm the traditional beliefs in eschatological fulfillment in the End Time, including judgment and resurrection, but he sets over against this view the conviction that the important factor for the individual of faith is the decision for or against Jesus made in the present moment. In that moment the individual is judged and may be raised to new life. The Greek root *krisis* can mean either to judge or to make a decision. John capitalizes on both meanings at the same time. He reports Jesus as saying in 5:24,

> Truly, truly, I say to you, he who hears my word and believes him who sent me, has eternal life; he does not come into judgment, but has passed from death to life.

A person's decision (*krisis*) delivers him from the judgment (*krisis*).

Jesus as Gnostic Redeemer

The signs material in John does not help us to determine the precise religious background against which John is offering his inter-

---

[24] Bultmann considers these references to the future resurrection as incompatible with the basic outlook of John and therefore explains them as interpolations by a redactor who sought to make John's eschatology more orthodox. Cf. his *Theology of the New Testament*, vol. 2, p. 39, and *History and Eschatology* (Edinburgh: University of Edinburgh Press, 1957), p. 47, n. 1. There is no manuscript evidence that these passages are later additions. And,

pretation of Jesus. Especially perplexing is the motif of Jesus as one who comes "from above" (3:7, 13; 6:62). Bultmann, among others, claims that this feature of John is to be accounted for as John's adaptation of a pre-Christian myth of a heavenly redeemer, according to which an agent of God came down to liberate men from their entanglement in the material world.[25] Through this redeemer, man is able to return to his true and proper place, heaven. It is Bultmann's contention that the Logos hymn in John (1:1–18) is a Christianized version of this myth. Although some components of the redeemer myth are found in pre-Christian literature, such as 4 Ezra, in which the redeemer is hidden in heaven and preexistent, the surviving Gnostic texts in which the Gnostic redeemer appears come from the second century A.D. and later. Of Gnosticizing Jewish sources the best parallels with John are the second-century Odes of Solomon[26] and Mandaean writings, which were preserved by a Gnostic sect, originally Jewish, that still survives in southern Iraq and in Iran.[27] The speeches in the Odes of Solomon, in which the speaker predicates certain revelatory qualities of himself, closely resemble speeches in the gospel of John.

Detailed examination of the relevant texts, however, shows

---

more importantly, they demonstate that John was concerned with correcting an overemphasis on a futuristic eschatology, not with replacing it entirely by translating it without remainder into terms of a theology of present decision.
[25] Bultmann summarizes this myth in *Primitive Christianity in Its Contemporary Setting*, trans. R. H. Fuller (Cleveland: Meridian, 1957), pp. 163–69, and in *Theology of the New Testament*, vol. 1, pp. 166–68, and vol. 2, pp. 12–13.
[26] *The Odes of Solomon*, J. H. Charlesworth, with translation and notes (Oxford: Clarendon, 1973). See also his "Qumran, John and the Odes of Solomon," in *John and Qumran*, ed. J. H. Charlesworth (London: Geoffrey Chapman, 1972), pp. 107–36.
[27] There is a vast literature concerning this tiny sect, which still exists at the lower end of the Tigris-Euphrates valley. A Semitic-speaking group, the sect traces its origin to a migration from Palestine. John the Baptist is an important figure for the Mandaeans. They claim to possess special revelation, which is preserved within the sect in the form of sacred writings. Some of their documents have long been known, but through the indefatigable efforts of a learned British woman, Lady E. S. Drower, many of their documents have been translated and published. An account of the sect, including a compendium of its teachings, is given in Lady Drower's *The Mandaeans of Iraq and Iran: Their Cults, Customs, Magic, Legends, and Folklore* (Oxford: Oxford University Press, 1937).

that none of the links between John and these allegedly pre-Christian Gnostic sources can be maintained. Analysis of the Mandaean material has discredited the notion that John the Baptist fulfilled an incarnational-redemptive role for that sect,[28] and the Mandaean texts from Iran do not document the myth of the redeemer who is himself redeemed and offers it to the faithful, as Bultmann had conjectured from his "reconstructed" version of John.[29] The Odes of Solomon have been shown to share with John the light-dark imagery and the modified dualism that is found in the Qumran documents.[30] The source of that dualism is not Gnosticism, however, but Jewish apocalypticism and certain aspects of Jewish wisdom, as we shall observe shortly. There is some evidence that the self-presentation style of Jesus in the Johannine discourses ("I am") is similar to his revelatory claims made in some of the newly discovered Coptic Gnostic materials,[31] but the earliest of those documents is later than John's gospel. The Coptic material, in fact, may have drawn on John's discourses. Whether this is true or not, neither appears to be related to the alleged redeemer myth and both probably represent sectarian Jewish developments of the Wisdom tradition. It is to the Johannine discourses and their background that we now turn our attention.

JESUS AS REVEALER OF GOD

The series of revelatory discourses, most of which are readily identifiable by the phrase "I am," constitute the second major

[28] Kurt Rudolph, *Die Mandäer*, [The Mandaeans] vol. 1 (Göttingen: Vandenhoeck & Ruprecht, 1960), p. 69.

[29] See the critique of Bultmann in Carsten Colpe, *Die religionsgeschichtliche Schule: Darstellung und Kritik ihres Bildes vom gnostischen Erlösermythus* [The history-of-religions school: Sketch and critique of its image of the Gnostic redeemer myth] (Göttingen: Vandenhoeck & Ruprecht, 1961), pp. 186–89.

[30] J. H. Charlesworth, "A Critical Comparison of the Dualism in 1 QS 3:13—4:26 and the Dualism Contained in the Gospel of John," in *John and Qumran*, pp. 76–106.

[31] George MacRae, "The Ego-Proclamation in Gnostic Sources," in *The Trial of Jesus*, ed. Ernest Bammel (London: SCM, 1970), pp. 123–39.

cycle of material in John. In each case, the words "I am" are followed by two other terms: (1) a noun or noun phrase, in which some aspect of the redemptive function or the revelation that Christ brings is asserted; (2) a parallel phrase or sentence, in which either the function of Jesus as revealer is further defined or the response to the revelation is described. These elements can be seen clearly in the first of the revelatory sayings:

> I am the bread of life; he who comes to me shall not hunger, and he who believes in me shall never thirst. (6:35)

These words are presented in the setting of a controversy between Jesus and the crowd that followed him because they liked the idea of free meals. The issue turns very quickly to the question of the source of his authority (6:30). The contrast is explored between the manna given by God to the children of Israel in the Sinai desert and the bread that Jesus gave on the occasion of the miraculous feeding (6:1–12). In the Jewish tradition, the bread from heaven in the manna story was understood as a symbol for the Torah, the will of God embodied in the Law. By feeding on it, a person might learn how to live properly. As it is expressed in Deuteronomy:

> You shall walk in all the way which the Lord your God has commanded you, that you may live, and that it may go well with you, and that you may live long in the land which you shall possess. (5:33)

Obeying the Law guaranteed life, prosperity, and longevity. But the bread that Jesus offered promised a new kind of life—true obedience and life "for ever" (John 6:58).

There are two significant factors in the first of these revelatory speeches. The first is the form of the speech itself, which has its closest parallels in the speeches of the Mandaean writings, where the revealer addresses the community in the first person. The second is the direct description of Jesus as a revealer who has "come down from heaven" (6:38, 50, 58) and who is yet to ascend back to the Father (6:62). Although in the prologue John speaks only of the preexistence of the Logos, not of Jesus' preexistence, he asserts here that Jesus came from God and is going back to God. His departure "out of this world to the Father" is announced in 13:1 on the eve of the passion. In the postresurrection appearance of Jesus to Mary Magdalene (20:1–18), he tells her, "Do not try to hold me, for I have not yet ascended to the Father . . . I am ascending to my Father and your Father. . . ." Thus John follows through consistently on the picture of Jesus as the one who came from God and returns to God when his work is completed. This picture of Jesus has no parallel in the synoptic tradition. What image has provided the model for this understanding of Jesus? As an initial step in determining the probable background of this ascending-descending figure, we must examine other discourses in which the transcendent significance of Jesus is displayed.

In John 7:37 Jesus is represented as following up on the promise made in 6:35, "He who believes in me shall never thirst," which is in turn a development of the statement made to the Samaritan woman at Jacob's well:

> Every one who drinks of this water will thirst again, but whoever drinks of the water that I shall give him will never thirst; the water that I shall give him will become in him a spring of water welling up to eternal life. (4:13–14)

John brought together in 7:37–39 a whole series of allusions to Old Testament and later Jewish traditions. The feast day referred to is the Feast of Tabernacles, an autumn feast. When rain fell at that time of year, it gave promise of good winter rains and therefore of good crops in the following spring. But a symbolic meaning arose, according to which the concern was not for literal crops but for the pouring out of eschatological blessing in the End Time. John linked with this hope the experience reported in Exodus 13 and 14, which tell of God sustaining his people in the desert by causing water to flow from the rock at the command of Moses. This, too, was associated with the messianic age, as we can see from the Jewish interpretations of the passage and from Paul's comment in 1 Corinthians 10:1–3. The eschatological outpouring of the Spirit, which figures so prominently in the prophetic tradition (e.g., Isa. 61 and Joel 2:28–29), is seen here as already occurring through Jesus. Or, more accurately, it is described as about to occur when the Spirit comes, following Jesus' departure to be with the Father (John 16:5–11). To believe in Jesus is not only to share in the water of life that he provides but also to be a channel through which it is conveyed to others.

Although Jesus' declaration of his superiority to Abraham reaches a climax in the words "before Abraham was, I am" (8:58), the passage does not follow the pattern of the revelatory speeches. The ostensible question voiced by Jesus' opponents is one of lineage. But Jesus builds on their challenge to question whether they are the offspring of Abraham, the progenitor of the people of God, or of the devil, whose sons do the father's work (8:39–44). Jesus here dissociates himself from Israel, as may be inferred from his mentioning Abraham as "your father" rather than *our* father (8:56). The offspring of Abraham are supposed to enjoy "length of days" if they keep the words of Moses; Jesus promises eternal life to those who keep *his* word (8:51). Jesus' opponents react by stoning him (8:59). Their violent, hostile action is readily understandable, given the fact that Jesus is thought to be truly subversive of the foundations of Judaism: obedience to the Law of Moses and preservation of descent from Abraham. Add to this the seemingly blasphemous claim of eternal existence (8:58), and one can see why the religious leadership would seek to destroy Jesus.

Jesus places himself, as John here describes him, in the context of eternity rather than of chronological history. It is idle to speak of historical causes or antecedents when dealing with one who is portrayed as enjoying existence from before the founding of the ages. The history of Jesus is linked with the history of Abraham as fulfillment is linked with promise, since Abraham looked forward in faith to the day of Jesus' coming. But just as the Logos "was in the beginning," so Jesus "was" before Abraham. John has moved beyond the limits and categories of historical knowledge into theological assertions.

The metaphors of food and drink are replaced in John 10 by those of shepherd and flock. The first of these figures is somewhat strained:

> I am the door; if any one enters by me, he will be saved, and
> will go in and out and find pasture. (10:9)

Apparently what John intended to say here is that the only means
of access into the flock of God is through Jesus, though the detail
of moving in and out shows that the sheepfold is a place of
identity, not of refuge or withdrawal. We shall see later in this
chapter that the church is understood as an agent of mission, not
as an exclusivist conventicle concerned only with its own spiritual
welfare. The shepherd metaphor is all but self-explanatory; those
who follow Jesus constitute the true flock of God. John adds two
surprising elements to the Old Testament image of God's flock.
One is the fact that the shepherd must die in order to benefit the
sheep. The other is the merging of two flocks into one, although
any doubt about the meaning of that detail disappears when the
reader realizes that John is speaking of bringing together Jew and
Gentile ("other sheep") into the one fold. In short, the theme
of the reconstitution of the people of God is present in John 10
under an image different from the simple notion of Israel as the
flock and God as the shepherd.

Jesus anticipates his death and resurrection in the words of
John 10:17–18 about laying down life and taking it again. There
is no provision offered in the saying attributed to Jesus for historical development in the customary sense of the term. Everything is
predetermined in accord with the divine will: "This charge I have
received from my Father" (10:18). John has only secondary historical interest in the actual sequence of events leading up to the
crucifixion; he is primarily concerned with posing the issue of the
theological understanding of Jesus in order to show how, given
Jewish presuppositions, Jesus could be regarded as a subversive,
whereas, given Christian presuppositions, he could be seen as the
agent of God.

Again, John's transcending of historical concern is evident
in the revelatory speech (11:25–26) in which Jesus declares, "I
am the resurrection and the life." The characteristic response,
faith, is called for: To believe in Jesus is to receive life. The life
received is not historical existence under conditions of space and

time, but participation in a mode of spiritual existence in the midst of, but beyond the limitations of, ordinary life. Even death cannot bring it to an end: "Though he die, yet shall he live" (11:25). John sees this life not merely as something that Jesus gives but as what he *is*. Faith is therefore not belief in an idea or acceptance of certain spiritual values; it is a relationship of communion with and trust in a person. The way of knowing for John is accordingly not primarily by historical information about a life in the past, but by some kind of mystical participation with one who is thought to live in the present. This is dramatically stated in the promise attributed to Jesus in 14:2-3 that he is now preparing a place in his "Father's house" where he will take his own people to be with him. Mystical union of Jesus, the Father, and believers is also asserted in 17:11, 21, 23, and 26.

Precedent for the mystical aspiration to ascend to heaven and see God is evident in the *Merkebah*, or throne mysticism of Judaism.[32] Building on the accounts of Isaiah 6 and Ezekiel, especially Isa. 6 and Ezek. 1, whose commissioning was based on visions of God seated on his throne, a mystical movement developed in Judaism in Hellenistic times. It promised the faithful visions of the throne in the present, sustenance of their existence now, and transport to the divine presence when life ended. That theme pervades John, from the opening hymn, with its remarks about beholding God's glory (1:14) and seeing God (1:18), through the promises that Jesus will take his own to be with God (14:1-2; 17:24), to the postresurrection announcement of Jesus' ascent to God (20:17). This outlook was later adopted by Gnosticism, but the influence on Johannine thought seems to have come directly from the Jewish mystical sect. It is not surprising, therefore, that the final discourses in John are taken up with the theme of the union between Jesus and his community.

In contrast to the common mystical ways of knowing—that

---

[32] The basic studies of this movement are by Gershom G. Scholem: *Major Trends in Jewish Mysticism* (New York: Schocken, 1954) and *Jewish Gnosticism, Merkebah Mysticism and Talmudic Tradition* (New York: Jewish Theological Seminary of America, 1960). The apocryphal work, The Testament of Job, consists of retelling of the Job story from the standpoint of *Merkebah* mysticism.

is, through direct communion with God—John declares in 14:6 that Jesus is "the way, and the truth, and the life." He is the only means of access to knowledge of God. "No one comes to the Father, but by me." Jesus' claim to be the sole revealer of God is also found elsewhere in John, for example, in 10:8, where Jesus brands as thieves and robbers all who before him claimed to be revealers. Knowledge of God comes not through direct historical knowledge of the events of Jesus' life, but through God's indwelling Spirit, whom the Father will send after Jesus has left (14:16–17) and who will guide God's people into "all truth" (16:13).

The most overt mystical image used by John in the revelatory discourses is that of the vine (15:1–17). The life of the vine (= Jesus) flowing into the branches is what produces the fruit of obedience, which manifests itself in mutual love. There is little hint here of the Christian's responsibility toward the world. In fact, Jesus tells his followers in 15:19 that they should expect to be hated by the world. In the prayer of John 17, petitions in behalf of the world are explicitly excluded (17:9), although the unity of the people of God is a demonstration to the world that God sent Jesus into the world. The reader of John receives the impression that there is to be a sharp cleavage between the church and the world; the church's chief testimony in the world is to be communicated through the mutual love and the sense of unity that is to characterize the church's corporate life. Through their testimony, others will come to believe (17:20). But John envisions no scheme of world history, no cataclysmic change by which the rule of God will be established in the world. The Kingdom of God is for John that new sphere of life into which a person enters by faith and upon being baptized (3:5). God loves all the world (3:16) but does not intend to redeem it together with all its inhabitants. Rather, only the faithful are delivered, as by a new birth, from the present world with its limitations and its empty standards and values, and brought into a new order, eternal life. There will be suffering in the new life (15:18–21; 16:1–4; 17:13–18), but the faithful will be patient and obedient in the midst of difficulties, standing firm in the faith in spite of outward circumstances.

JESUS AS THE FULFILLMENT OF GOD'S PLAN

In spite of his emphasis on mystical union, John is not devoid of a sense of events moving toward the consummation of a plan. Referring to Jesus as the fulfillment of Scripture and redefining traditional messianic and redemptive categories, John shows that what happened to and through Jesus was the result of the outworking of God's purpose.

The Fulfillment of Scripture

John explicitly claims that Jesus actualizes what was promised in Scripture. There are at least twenty-five quotations from the Old Testament in John; six are quoted in such a way as to make clear that a claim of fulfillment is being made, and fourteen begin with a formula such as "Scripture is fulfilled," "Scripture says," "the word was fulfilled," "it is written," "Isaiah says." Five times the phrase "in order that it might be fulfilled" is used.

The Scriptures appear in John as the divine blueprint for the work of Jesus, especially in his passion (12:15; 12:40; 13:18; 15:25; 19:28; 19:36, 37) and in his special redemptive-revelatory role (1:51; 10:16; 6:45; 6:31). It is worth noting that much of the detail of the passion story is provided by, or at least conforms to the words of, the Psalms. In some cases there is exact correspondence between what is said in the Scriptures and what is reported as happening in the career of Jesus, as in 19:37 (= Zech. 12:10, "they look on him whom they have pierced"). In other cases the interpretation or fulfillment claim seems forced, as in John 10:34, in which Jesus, defending his use of the term Son of God, refers to Psalms 82:6. In Psalm 82 the whole point is that, though created in the image of God, man is mortal. Thus, it is scarcely a convincing passage in support of Jesus' alleged claim to divinity. Strangely, the Old Testament quotations in John are not appealed to in support of Jesus' messianic claims, with the possible exception of 12:13–15 (= Zech. 9:9). In at least one instance (7:42), John argues against the interpretation of Jesus' messiahship ac-

cording to the traditional messianic notion of the restored Davidic
kingly line (= Mic. 5:2). John's basic conviction is that perceptive reading of Scripture will show that the basic pattern of God's
purpose as laid down in Scripture is now moving toward completion. However, the freedom to achieve this purpose rests solely
with God, so traditional forms of expectation may be revised or
even rejected in the fulfillment that is already occurring through
Jesus.

Redefinition of Traditional Messianic
and Redemptive Categories

John's use of the messianic and redemptive categories drawn from
the Old Testament and Jewish tradition is both continuous and
discontinuous with Jewish ideas and hopes. Messiah was by no
means a fixed or even a well-defined concept in first-century Judaism, but John introduces four different conceptions or images of
messianic figures in his gospel—Prophet, Son of Man, Son of God,
and Savior of the World—all of them in polemical contexts. Thus
in 1:19–23, three questions are addressed to John the Baptist in
an effort to determine what his role is. He is asked if he is the
Christ (= Messiah), or Elijah, or the Prophet. Later in the same
chapter, Jesus is described as Lamb of God and as Son of Man. In
addition, Nathanael acclaims him Son of God and King of Israel,
both of which are synonyms for Messiah. Similarly, the question
initially raised by the woman at the well (4:29) is whether or not
Jesus is the Messiah. But at the end of the narrative he is acclaimed by the Samaritans, not Messiah, but "Savior of the world"
(4:42). The redefining of the traditional messianic categories is
implied by the tension between Martha's declaration that Jesus is
the Christ and her reluctance to have the tomb of Lazarus
opened, which shows that she does not understand the full implications of her own confession of faith.

The significance of John's use of these traditional messianic
categories is that, though in some sense Jesus is seen as their fulfillment, in another sense he does not fit any of them.

The title Messiah (= Anointed One) is a kingly designation, associated with David and his successors. Israel's basic pre-

supposition was that God was king (Ps. 5:2; 10:16; 93; 96; 97; 99; 103:19). Perhaps the clearest statement of this is in the familiar words of Psalm 24:7–10,

> Lift up your heads, O gates!
>   and be lifted up, O ancient doors!
>   that the King of glory may come in.
>
> Who is the King of glory?
>   The Lord, strong and mighty,
>   the Lord, mighty in battle!
>
> Lift up your heads, O gates!
>   and be lifted up, O ancient doors!
>   that the King of glory may come in!
>
> Who is this King of glory?
>   The Lord of hosts,
>   he is the King of glory!

Although God was king, he was understood to have granted royal authority to his vicegerent, David, as Psalm 110:1 affirms:

> The Lord says to my lord:
> "Sit at my right hand,
>   till I make your enemies your footstool."

In Psalm 2, the king is to be granted the justice of God in vindicating the oppressed, in defending those who have been mistreated. The Psalmist requested length of days and wide dominions in his behalf.

As the Davidic dynasty came to an end, however, with the captivity of the tribes of Judah in the sixth century B.C., the prophets began to project the hope of the messianic reign into the future, as can be seen in Isaiah 9:6–7 and especially in 11:1–10, in which the prophet depicts the Davidic royal house as a tree cut down and reduced to a stump. But from that stump he foresees a shoot or a branch coming forth. Unexpectedly, the hope of renewal of the kingship is revived through the descendant of David who appears like one from the dead; accordingly, the divine spirit will come upon him and grant him the understanding and wisdom to discharge his kingly duties with justice and with effective authority over his enemies. The consequence of this eschatological kingship will be to bring about the renewal of the whole creation, as symbolized by the cessation of hostility among the beasts of the field:

> The wolf shall dwell with the lamb,
>   and the leopard shall lie down with the kid.
>
>   . . .
>
> They shall not hurt nor destroy
>   in all my holy mountain;
> for the earth shall be full of the knowledge of the Lord
>   as the waters cover the sea.
>
> (Isa. 11:6, 9)

One of the specific details of this kind of expectation of the king was that he would be born in the home town of David, Israel's ideal king (Mic. 5:2). John, however, explicitly dissociates Jesus from the prophecy, asserting that Jesus' place of origin is Nazareth. It is possible that John knew nothing of the Christian tradition of Jesus' birth in Bethlehem (as it is seen in Luke and Matthew) or that if he knew it, he rejected it. While he unequivocally declares Jesus to be the Messiah (1:41), he emphasizes his purely human birth ("son of Joseph," 1:45) and the insignificance of his place of birth ("Can anything good come out of Nazareth?" 1:46). But John goes even further to show that Jesus is not to be identified with popular kingly hopes. In 6:15 Jesus escapes from a crowd eager to acclaim him king. Before Pilate, Jesus' replies concerning his role as king are ambiguous, but he directly repudiates kingship by any ordinary definition (18:36).

In Zechariah 4, especially 4:14, the prophet describes two messiahs: an anointed king and an anointed priest. Further documentation for the messianic diarchy is presented in the intertestamental writings,[33] such as the Testaments of the Twelve Patriarchs[34]

---

[33] By "intertestamental writings" is meant the Jewish works purported to have been written by biblical characters but actually written later than the second century B.C. They were not recognized by the Jewish community as authoritative. The writings are also called "Apocrypha" and "Pseudepigrapha."

[34] Some of the relevant texts are Testament of Judah 21:2; 25:1–2; Testament

and the Manual of Discipline[35] the latter, a document found at Qumran in which the structure and expectations of the community are outlined). The kingly and priestly functions are combined in Jesus, as John depicts him, since he is both the King of Israel (1:49) and the Lamb of God who takes away the sin of the world (1:29). But unlike the Jewish priest who offers the sacrifice, the Lamb is himself the sacrificial victim. The mingling of priestly and kingly imagery is surely characteristic of John's picture of Jesus, but he has modified the expectation in the light of the reality of Jesus, as faith understands him.

A second redemptive figure mentioned in John's gospel is Elijah. The Jewish understanding of Elijah was primarily built not on the account in 1 Kings 17–19, but on the prophecies of his return at the End of the Age in Malachi 3:1 and 4:5. In the (Wisdom of) Sirach 48:1–11, Elijah is extolled as one who was God's agent, who raised the dead, who "brought kings down to destruction" and anointed others "to exact retribution," and whose coming is expected to turn the hearts of the nation to its God. Significantly, Elijah's role is described by Malachi 3:3–4 as reforming the priesthood—that is, "purifying the sons of Levi" and making their worship acceptable to Yahweh. To associate the Messiah with Elijah, or to see Elijah as taking the place of the Messiah, is to lay stress on the purificatory, judgmental function of God's agent in the End Time. The synoptic tradition emphasizes the preparatory role of Elijah, who makes ready the Lord's way (Isa. 40 and Mal. 3), and therefore equates Elijah with John the Baptist. In John's gospel, however, John the Baptist rejects the title of Elijah (1:21). Although Jesus is not *identified* as Elijah in the gospel of John, it is perhaps implied that he *is* Elijah, by his being referred to as "the prophet," the term used of Elijah at times in the rabbinic sources.

---

of Issachar 5:7; Testament of Levi 8:14; Testament of Dan 5:4, 7; Testament of Naphtali 8:2.

[35] There are two messianic figures in the Manual of Discipline (1 QS 9:10–11), and a king and an anointed priest in the Annex to the Manual (1 QSa 2:11–22). See the essay on this theme by K. G. Kuhn, "The Two Messiahs of Aaron and Israel," in Krister Stendahl, ed., *The Scrolls and the New Testament* (New York: Harper & Row, 1957), pp. 54–64.

According to John 1:21, John the Baptist also rejects the title of the eschatological "prophet" of Deuteronomy 18. But it is linked to Jesus by the populace after the Feeding of the Five Thousand (6:14) and by those who heard Jesus' announcement about the Spirit being poured out (7:37–40). And the fact that the title prophet is followed by the question of Jesus' being Messiah (7:41) shows that both titles carry significance in John's gospel as redemptive roles. That impression is confirmed by the fact that Jesus' detractors exclude the possibility that he could be a prophet since he comes from Galilee (7:52). Once more, then, John is showing that Jesus both fulfills the categories of Jewish redemptive expectation and transforms them. John summarizes his own point of view well in the words of Philip:

> We have found him of whom Moses in the law and also the prophets wrote, Jesus of Nazareth, the son of Joseph. (1:45)

Other titles are used for Jesus, such as "the Holy One of God" in 6:69, which is presented as the confession of faith in Jesus by the disciples. But the climax of all the confessions is attributed to the one disciple whose doubt has become proverbial: Thomas. After seeing for himself the reality of the resurrection of Jesus and the corporeality of Jesus' body, Thomas exclaims, "My Lord and my God!" (20:28). In both the Greek-speaking and the Aramaic-speaking branches of the early church (Phil. 2:10–11 and 1 Cor. 16:22, respectively), Jesus was from the beginning acclaimed Lord. It is widely recognized that the earliest Christian confession was "Jesus is Lord."[36] The fact that the Septuagint translated the holy name of God, YHWH (or Yahweh), as *kurios* (= lord), combined with the fact that the church designated Jesus as Lord, paved the way for interpreting the Old Testament through Christian eyes, and many of the attributes and functions of God were assigned by Christian faith to Jesus.

Probably the most important christological title in John's gospel is Son of Man. In Daniel 7 the Son of Man is a corporate

---

[36] So, for example, Oscar Cullmann, *The Earliest Christian Confessions*, trans. J. K. S. Reid (London; Lutterworth, 1949).

figure—representing the faithful remnant of the Jews in the Maccabean period—who appears on the clouds of heaven at the end of the age to establish God's Kingdom. The Son of Man moves, therefore, from heaven to earth, where God's rule is established. In John, however, the Son of Man has already come to earth (1:51) and will complete his work when he returns to heaven (6:58, 62). In 2 Esdras 13:3, 26, the man who comes with the clouds of heaven (as does the Son of Man in Dan. 7:13) is explicitly said to be the agent of redemption "whom the Most High has been keeping for many ages." That is to say, he is a preexistent being, just as Jesus is represented in John. Unlike the figure in Daniel and 2 Esdras, however, Jesus' final action is declared by John to be his return to the Father (6:61; 20:17). Indeed, for John the Kingdom of God has to do with "heavenly things" (3:12). It was disclosed by one who came from heaven and will be entered only by those who are "born from above" (3:3). What moved John to use this apocalyptic title, Son of Man, in a manner that has so little to do with traditional Jewish apocalyptic expectations? The answer lies in the wisdom tradition of Hellenistic Judaism.

Jesus as Wisdom Incarnate

In the late biblical tradition, as well as in Jewish writings of the Hellenistic period, there is another figure in addition to the Son of Man who is depicted as preexistent: Wisdom (Prov. 8:22–23; Sir. 24:9; Wisd. of Sol. 6:22). Wisdom not only preexists but has a role in the creation of the world (Prov. 8:23–31), since she serves as God's companion in the bringing of the world into existence (Wisd. of Sol. 8:4–6; Sir. 1). As R. E. Brown has shown, Wisdom is portrayed in this literature as the effulgence of divine glory (Wisd. of Sol. 7:25, 26), as the illuminator of mankind (Wisd. of Sol. 7:10, 29), as descended from heaven (Prov. 8:31; Sir. 24:8; Wisd. of Sol. 9:10), as returning to God (1 En. 42:2), as having the chief role in instructing mankind concerning heavenly things (Job 11:6–7; Wisd. of Sol. 9:16–18), as taking the initiative to engage hearers of her message (Prov. 1:20–21; 8:1–4; Wisd. of Sol. 6:16), and as experiencing rejection (Prov.

1:24–25; Bar. 3:12; 1 En. 42:2).[37] All these features and functions are also discernible in John's picture of Jesus. However, instead of identifying Jesus with the feminine figure Wisdom (= *Sopia*, in Greek), John links Jesus with the masculine figure Logos (= Word).

For John, the Logos is the divine purpose for the creation and the redemption of the world. It is not an expedient that God came up with when matters went out of control. The Logos is eternally with God (1:1) and partakes of the divine nature, although it is not simply to be equated with God. The Logos is essential to God's purpose but is not identical with God. John's point is that it is in no way alien to the nature of God to create the world and then to redeem it (1:3). This divine purpose, shining like a light among men, has always been disclosing itself, although opposition has sought to extinguish it (1:4–5, 9). The Logos was present and active in the world, but it was not recognized for what it was (1:10), neither by the created order nor by its own people (1:11). Possibly John shifts at this point from describing the Logos as impersonal to depicting the Logos as manifest in human form in Jesus of Nazareth, in which case the translation would be "He came . . . his own people received him not." In 1:14, John states explicitly that the Logos is manifest in human form. The revelation of God that the Logos brings is accessible to all who are willing to receive it, not just to those who by descent or by racial origin consider themselves to have some special claim on God (1:12–13).

This possibility of universal recognition of God's purpose for man and the world has been given a new basis in the advent into the world of the Logos in a human form, the Word become flesh (1:14), through whom the glorious purpose and nature of God are disclosed for the faithful. The Jews assumed that the full revelation of God was available through the Law of Moses, but John declares that the full knowledge of God's gracious purpose and the final disclosure of his truth have been granted by God through Jesus Christ (1:17). The incarnation, therefore, is the crucial moment in the whole of history. God's purpose has always

---

[37] Brown, *The Gospel According to John I–XII*, pp. cxxii–cxxv.

been present and operative, though in a partly hidden way, but now it is fully revealed, at least for the faithful, who "have beheld his glory, glory as of the only Son from the Father" (1:14).

Martin Hengel has drawn attention to a development in Jewish understanding of the Law during the Hellenistic period that resembles John's representation of the Logos. Although the influence was probably not conscious, the equating of Law with Wisdom (Bar. 4:1; Sir. 24: esp. 23) led to the view that Law is cosmic in its meaning, absolute in its demands. Like the Stoics, devotees of the law sought to live their lives in conformity to it. It came to be regarded as coexistent with God and the object of devotion and even love, as is evident in Ps. 119:47–48, 97, 113, 159, 163, and 167. Its existence as an eternal paradigm is reminiscent of the Platonic concept of the ideal world. This view of revelation as timeless contrasts with the traditional view of God's self-disclosure as historical, as set forth in the biblical narratives and as summarized in passages such as Deuteronomy 26:5–9, Joshua 24, Psalms 78, and Sirach 44–50. Although the Law originates with God, it has a distinct ontological status of its own, whereby it serves as "the mediator of creation and revelation between God and the world."[38] What distinguishes this view of Law from John's view of Logos, however, is that only the Logos "becomes flesh." The Law, though personified at times, is never identified with an historical person, as the Logos is with Jesus.

In John, the concept of incarnate Wisdom has been further enriched by its association with three great figures of Israel's past: Jacob, Abraham, and Moses. The stage is set for this transformation of the Jewish tradition in John 1:51, where the imagery of

---

[38] Hengel, *Judaism and Hellenism*, vol. 1, pp. 169–75. R. G. Hamerton-Kelly, *Pre-Existence, Wisdom, and Son of Man* (Cambridge: Cambridge University Press, 1973), also emphasizes the Jewish Wisdom myth as the primary historical precedent for the development of the Johannine Logos–Son of Man figure (pp. 206–09). See, as well, James M. Reese, *Hellenistic Influence on the Book of Wisdom and Its Consequences* (Rome: Pontifical Biblical Institute, 1970), who graphically demonstrates the verbal similarities between the portrayal of divine Wisdom in the Jewish tradition and the Hellenistic veneration of Isis as the stabilizer of the cosmos and the guardian of the human race, who also speaks in "I am" language, resembling Johannine discourses (pp. 45–49).

angels ascending and descending on the progenitor and epony-mous hero of Israel in Jacob's dream (Gen. 28:12) is linked with Jesus, who is identified as the Son of Man. In Genesis 28:13, Abraham is mentioned as the one with whom God first entered into the covenant relationship; in John 9:51–58, Jesus claims that Abraham as a prophet foresaw and rejoiced in his coming, and that he existed before Abraham. But the most extensive set of comparisons and contrasts with a figure out of ancient Israel is with Moses.

In 1:17 John contrasts the revelation that came through Moses (the Law) with that given through Jesus (grace and truth). According to John, the coming of Jesus was foretold in Moses and the prophets (1:45). Moses' act of deliverance of his people from the deadly serpents has its analogue in Jesus' cruci-fixion and exaltation (3:14). Rejection of Jesus is tantamount to rejection of Moses, whose writings tell about Jesus. Jesus' provi-sion of bread in the desert (John 6) surpasses the provision of manna through Moses (6:32). Jesus' acts of healing are contrasted with the legal demands of Moses (7:22–23). Ironically, as John sees it, rejection of Jesus is based on an appeal to the teachings of Moses (9:28–29). In addition to these explicit links, Jesus is pre-sented in John as the fulfillment of the roles of prophet (6:14) and King of Israel (1:49), assigned in Jewish tradition to Moses.

John's understanding of Jesus as king and prophet converge in John 6, which is an adaptation of the synoptic account of Jesus' Feeding the Five Thousand (cf. Mark 6:32–44), developed on the basis of the Old Testament miracle of the manna in the desert (Exod. 16:11–35; Num. 11:7–9; Ps. 78:23–25). John's ac-count represents an interpretive expansion of the biblical text along the lines of Jewish Midrash, which is known from both rabbinic and Qumran sources of the period.[39] In Deuteronomy 33:5, and in rabbinic and other Jewish exegetical texts building on this passage, Moses is depicted as king in Israel.[40] His role as

[39] This insight has been developed fully by Borgen in *Bread from Heaven.*
[40] The biblical, rabbinic, philonic, and Hellenistic Jewish literature on the theme of Moses' dual role as prophet and king has been illuminatingly treated by Wayne Meeks in *The Prophet-King: Moses Traditions and the Johannine Christology* (Leiden: Brill, 1967), esp. pp. 186–95.

prophet is linked with his performance of "signs and wonders" in Deuteronomy 34:10–11:

> And there has not arisen a prophet since in Israel like Moses, whom the Lord knew face to face, none like him for all the signs and the wonders which the Lord sent him to do.

The attribution of signs and wonders to Moses is found in the Wisdom of Solomon 10:16 as well. The Johannine portrayal of Jesus builds upon this picture of Moses. In John 6:14–15, Jesus is acclaimed as prophet and king as a consequence of a miracle, which parallels but transcends the biblical account of God's deliverance of his people (Moses' miracle sustains life; Jesus' bestows eternal life—6:5). Jesus, referred to in 6:14 as the "prophet who is to come," is thus seen as fulfilling the promise made through Moses (Deut. 18:18) of an eschatological prophet.[41] John's comprehensive title for this eschatological redeemer is Son of Man (6:27, 53, 62).

JOHN'S UNDERSTANDING OF HISTORY

John's gospel is a theological interpretation of Jesus with belief in the incarnation at its core. This does not imply, however, that John had no interest in historical information. In fact, it is because the idea of incarnation is so central to his thought that John uses the gospel form and recounts the facts of Jesus' earthly, human life. Not only does he adapt the synoptic tradition to serve his own ends, but he supplies additional valuable historical information of his own. Throughout his gospel, John's purpose is to instruct his community about its resources and responsibilities and to articulate its role in the wider world.

---

[41] In the Qumran Community Rule (1 QS 9:11) and in 4 Q Testamonia, the collection of messianic texts, there is a clear reference to the eschatological prophet.

John and the Synoptics

The relationship of John to the synoptic tradition is complex. On a number of points John actually supplements or even corrects the synoptic accounts. For example, John records the importance of John the Baptist, both for the launching of Jesus' ministry and for the tensions that arose after Jesus' death between his followers and John's.[42] John 1:35–42 shows that Jesus took over the nucleus of his followers from the disciples of John the Baptist. The parallel between Jesus' activity and John's, including baptisms performed by both, is only thinly disguised behind the rather ambiguous or even contradictory language of 3:22–26 and 4:1–3. It is plausible to assume that there was a period of direct competition between Jesus and John, and that Jesus accordingly withdrew from public activity (4:3) until John's imprisonment (3:24) made it clear that there would be no further rivalry between the two men. Their respective disciples seem to have perpetuated the conflict, however, as is apparent from the anti-Baptist polemic inserted into the Logos hymn. If we omit verses 6, 7, 8, and 15 from John 1, the prologue moves along smoothly and is symmetrically structured:

> God's Logos: verses 1, 2, 3
>
> Logos and Light: verses 4, 5, 9
>
> Logos and World: verses 10, 11, 12
>
> Logos and God: verses 14b, 16, 17
>
> Logos as Revelation: verses 14a, 18

It seems clear that John was writing his gospel at a time when a claim was being made that the Baptist came before Jesus and therefore should be considered superior to him. The interpolated verses are intended to show not only that John is subordinate in his role, but that Jesus originated before him: "He who comes after me ranks before me, for he was before me" (John 1:15).

---

[42] On the probable connection between Jesus and the John the Baptist, see C. H. Kraeling, *John the Baptist* (New York: Scribner's, 1951), and Maurice Goguel, *Life of Jesus*, trans. Olive Wyon (New York: Macmillan, 1946), pp. 264–79.

The argument is based on John's claim that the Logos is pre-existent. Thus, John combined a historical fact about Jesus—his situation of dependence on and then tension with John the Baptist—with a fact about the history of the church—the hostility between the followers of the Baptist and those of Jesus. We see concretely how John understands history: as a dialectic between what happened in the past and the meaning of those events in the life of the church in his own time.

Another historical point already noted is John's stress on the humble birth of Jesus in Nazareth. He gives no hint of belief in the virgin birth. Instead, he states directly that Joseph is the father of Jesus (1:45; 6:42). John took for granted Jesus' Galilean origins (7:40–42), as did the Jewish opponents of the early church who attempted to discredit Jesus because he was not born in Bethlehem according to the traditional Jewish messianic expectation. For John, however, birth in Nazareth was quite in keeping with Jesus' nature: The true and full humanity of Jesus as it was evident in the ordinariness of his birth and the insignificance of his birth-place was an essential element in his role as the Word made flesh (= human).

A third area in which John may be more accurate than the synoptics is the chronology of the passion story, which combines historical tradition and symbolic meaning. In the synoptic accounts, the Last Supper is a Passover meal, and Jesus dies in the closing hours of the Passover, on the eve of the Sabbath, which would have begun at sundown on Friday. In John, however, Passover and the Sabbath coincide, so that Jesus takes his last meal with his followers the night before the Passover, and he dies on Friday at the very hour the faithful Jews are slaughtering the lambs in preparation for the Passover, which will begin with the Sabbath at sundown. John is most explicit in declaring that Jesus' final meal was before the Passover, not on the feast itself (13:1; 18:29; 18:39; 19:31). In addition to preserving a more accurate historical recollection (in Luke, there is an apparent conflict between 22:8, which describes the Last Supper as a Passover meal, and 22:15, which implies that Jesus will not live to eat the Passover), John heightens the symbolic meaning of Jesus as the Passover lamb by setting his death outside the city at the moment the lambs are being killed in the Temple enclosure.

Elsewhere, John alters the probable historical facts, or at least the sequence of events, in order to bring out more forcefully the theological meaning he sees in them. The contrast between John as the one who baptizes with water and Jesus as the one who baptizes with the Spirit is intensified by omitting the report that Jesus was baptized at all. We should expect it to take place in 1:31, but only the coming of the Spirit upon Jesus is described.

In the synoptic accounts, one of the factors that brings the resentment of the Jewish leaders against Jesus to a head is his unauthorized action in cleansing the Temple courts (Mark 11:15–17 = Matt. 21:12–13 and Luke 19:45–46). Although some scholars think that this incident may have actually occurred earlier than Jesus' final week in Jerusalem,[43] it was a turning point in the minds of the Jewish authorities; afterward, his execution was inevitable. But in John's narrative (2:13–22), as noted earlier, both the cleansing of the Temple and the discussion of its destruction occur at the beginning of Jesus' ministry. The function that they serve is not to provide a climax to the hostility of official Judaism toward Jesus, but to point out at the outset (1) that Jesus intends nothing less than the complete transformation of the worship of God, and (2) that his death and resurrection will be the actions of God by which the true worship (= temple) will be established. Once more John moves from reporting the event (Jesus' announcement of the new temple) to describing the situation of the early church (to which the meaning of that event was disclosed "when . . . he was raised from the dead").

According to the synoptic accounts, Jesus spent nearly the whole of his ministry in Galilee and other adjacent northern regions, but according to John, he was active primarily in Jerusalem and vicinity, although the geography and sequence of his movements to and from Jerusalem are not always easy to follow. John's preference for Jerusalem as the setting for Jesus' ministry may be an actual historical recollection, but it is more likely intended to serve a polemical purpose, since Jesus' conflict with the Jewish

[43] For example, Goguel, *Life of Jesus*, p. 418, who thinks Jesus withdrew to Perea after predicting the Temple's destruction.

leaders and challenge to the Jewish institutions seems to serve a clearer symbolic function in Jerusalem, the central focus of Judaism.

Because John is depicting a human life as the vehicle of divine revelation, he is concerned for action as well as word, for sequence as well as significance. Accordingly, his gospel is a real narrative, not merely a collection of sayings, as is the apocryphal Gospel of Thomas (see below, pp. 274–80). The course of the story moves from the beginnings in the baptism by the Spirit through the public career of teaching and healing and controversy to the cross and resurrection. As such, it is in a general way similar to the other gospel narratives. But the differences from the synoptics are more evident. From the very outset of Jesus' ministry, according to John, the hour of his death is predetermined. Nothing can happen to him apart from this divinely ordained plan. The theme is merely announced without explanation in 2:4: "My hour has not yet come." But it is made clear in 7:6 and, especially, 7:30 and 8:20 that no one can seize Jesus until the designated hour. The climax of this series of sayings comes in 12:23, on the eve of the passion, when Jesus announces that the hour has arrived for him to be "glorified," which in 12:32 is interpreted to mean the hour of his being lifted up in death. There is at this point in John's account a vestige of the struggle in Gethsemane, when Jesus is facing the prospect of death and prays for the "cup" of suffering to pass from him (cf. Mark 14:32–42 and parallels). But in John the question is no more than a rhetorical one: "And what shall I say, 'Father, save me from this hour'? No, for this purpose I have come to this hour" (12:27). John is asserting that the force at work in Jesus' fate is not one of inevitable apocalyptic struggle and suffering, as is the case in Mark's view, but the calm unfolding of the predetermined course of events in accordance with the divinely established schedule.

Jesus' Significance for the Johannine Community

At the same time that John wants to place Jesus at the point of intersection of the historically concrete and the timeless, he seeks also to interpret Jesus in such a way as to demonstrate his meaning for John's own community and its situation in life. The very emphasis that John gives to the corporeality of Jesus—"the Word made flesh" (1:14), Jesus as weary and thirsty (4:6–7), "put your hand . . . in my side (20:27)—is aimed in part at the need of his community to combat the heretical notion that Jesus was a purely spiritual being. Or it may have had as its target an incipient Gnosticism that denied the goodness of the created world. But in either case, its historical setting is the Johannine community, not the larger historical setting in the time of Jesus.

We can infer from John that there were serious problems confronting his community as a result of outside opposition, especially from the Jewish leadership, who resented the Christians' attempt to make their own both Scripture and the covenant relationship with God. The community opened its membership to non-Jews, as is indicated by the tradition's recalling the words of Jesus to the Samaritan woman about the impossibility of locating the true place of worship in Jerusalem or elsewhere (4:21–23), and the inclusion of "other sheep" (10:16) in the flock of God. In all probability the hostility between the synagogue and the Johannine church mounted to the point where the Christians demanded public confession of Jesus and the Jews excluded from the synagogue those who made such a witness. This tension is reflected in such passages as 9:22; 12:42; and 16:2. The conclusion of the story of the Healing of the Man Born Blind (9:8–41) illustrates vividly the mutual antipathy that must have been a feature of the situation of John's community.[44]

Both the hostility from without and the mystical bent within seem to have led John's community to turn in upon itself in sectarian fashion. Wayne Meeks has noted that the inconclusiveness of the dialogues, the use of double-meaning words, and the statements in riddles, as well as the evident misunderstandings of Jesus and his words on the part of the disciples and others, are evidences of a theory of knowledge that supported this sectarianism.[45] Truth is not transmitted by direct communication

[44] J. L. Martyn, *History and Theology in the Fourth Gospel* (New York: Harper & Row, 1968), pp. 18–27.
[45] W. A. Meeks, "The Man from Heaven in Johannine Sectarianism," *Journal of Biblical Literature* 91 (1972): 52–65.

based on public information but is arrived at by meditation, reflection, dialogue, and above all by spiritual revelation within the community itself. He has characterized the gospel of John as "a book for insiders . . . to provide reinforcement for the community's social identity. . . . It provided a symbolic universe which gave religious legitimacy, a theodicy, to the group's actual isolation from the larger society."[46]

The Johannine school engaged in adapting and reappropriating the Jesus tradition in the way that it thought would best serve its own needs. This is evident in the editing process that was apparently not yet completed when the gospel of John assumed its present form.[47] Many scholars have noted the rough transitions in John and even some apparent contradictions. For example, did Jesus perform baptisms (John 3:22) or did he not (4:2)? Attempts have been made to account for these irregularities on the ground that John was using sources that he did not fully assimilate. More plausible is the proposal that this gospel is the product of an interpretive school, like the later first- and second-century rabbinical schools (see n. 16, p. 178). In some cases the tensions in the text reflect issues under discussion within the community and points of controversy with opponents. In other cases the abrupt shifts seem to be purely literary.

Evidence of awkward editorial connections can be seen, for example, in 4:54 and 5:1. At the end of chapter 4 Jesus is in Galilee, having recently come back from Jerusalem (4:43). But in 5:1 he is back in Jerusalem, even though in 6:1 he is suddenly in Galilee once more and crossing the sea. The transition from 4:54 to 6:1 would be smooth, but from 4:54 to 5:1 it is inexplicably abrupt; thus chapter 5 seems to be out of place. Equally rough transitions can be seen between 7:52 and 8:12[48] and between 8:59 and 9:1. Additionally, although 14:25–31 reads like a farewell to the disciples and ends in the instruction, "Rise, let us go hence," there are three long discourse chapters to be uttered by

[46] *Ibid.,* 49.
[47] See Smith, *The Composition and Order of the Fourth Gospel,* p. 239, and Kümmel, *Introduction to the New Testament,* p. 216.
[48] It is almost universally accepted that 7:53–8:11, the story of the adulterous woman, does not belong in the text of John. It does not appear in any of the oldest manuscripts of John, and in some manuscripts it is found in Luke, after 21:38.

Jesus before he actually sets out for the garden (of Gethsemane, although the name is not mentioned in John 18:1; see Mark 14:32). Some commentators try to get around this difficulty by designating these discourses as having been "spoken on the way to the garden," which hardly seems convincing.

A clear case of textual inconsistency caused by controversy can be seen in 3:25 and 4:1. In both cases, it looks as if there were disputes between Jesus (together with his followers) and the disciples of John the Baptist. The implied question in 3:26 ("What are you [John] going to do about it?") concerns Jesus' success in finding candidates for baptism, not a dispute with an unspecified Jew. The apparently contradictory statements mentioned earlier about Jesus' baptizing are also part of this controversy. What seems to have happened is this: (1) The conflict with the Baptist's followers has been toned down, and (2) the presumably undignified act of performing a baptism has been attributed to Jesus' disciples, rather than to him personally.

A special, unmistakable case of editing that was not completed can be seen in John 21, which by style and vocabulary has long been recognized as an appendix. John 20:30–31 forms an appropriate conclusion to the rest of the gospel, whereas John 21 is rather lame as an end to the book. All the manuscripts of John include this chapter, however, so it must be as old as the gospel in its present literary form, even though it is not integrated into the gospel in form, content, or style, and probably represents a later development than the material John assembled and synthesized more completely for the main part of his gospel.

The passage of time and the heightening of hostility did not bring discouragement to the Johannine community. The members' perception of God and themselves freed them from anxiety about conflicts in the present life: God had guaranteed to preserve them from both the world and the Evil One (17:6–19). They were to be apprehensive about neither death (12:24) nor the delay in the Parousia, which they continued to believe would occur "in a little while" (12:35–36). The Last Day, with resurrection and judgment, would come in its own time (5:28–29). Meanwhile, they were conscious of the preparations even now in progress that would usher them into the presence of God (14:3).

John's Concern for the Church in the World

John replaced the concern for the End of the Age, which is dominant in the synoptic tradition, with a concern for the church's fulfillment of its mission in the world. Jesus is reported to have prayed not for deliverance of Christians from the world but for their preservation in the midst of the world. Christians are to see to it that the flock is fed and cared for, as the epilogue of John (chapter 21) phrases it ("Feed my sheep," 21:17). With the disappearance of the sense of an imminent parousia, it is anticipated that the witness of the church will continue from generation to generation: "Blessed are those who have not seen and yet believe" (20:29). The bounds of the church are to be extended beyond Judaism ("I have other sheep, that are not of this fold; I must bring them also," 10:16).

The work of the church in the world is primarily that of standing faithful to Jesus' command to obey his commandment of love:

> By this all men will know that you are my disciples, if you have love for one another. (13:35)

His followers are to be set apart in the truth (17:17), although they are not to withdraw from the world. Rather, they will experience joy in the midst of the world's hostility toward them (17:13). The unity of their community will be the chief witness to the oneness of Jesus with God (17:11). There is no suggestion of a mission to convert the world totally, and no call to become the instrument through which God will defeat the evil powers. The history of the world will not be altered by their work; it is their own personal history and the history of those who come to have faith that will be transformed through Jesus.

THE RELATIONSHIP OF THEOLOGY AND HISTORY IN JOHN'S GOSPEL

For John it is essential that Jesus be portrayed as a historical person, truly human, with human birth, parentage, needs, and even limitations. At the same time, Jesus is more than human, according to John, and at many points can also transcend human limitations, as he does in performing the many signs John attributes to him. In some ways, as we have seen, John seeks to supplement or even to correct the historical tradition preserved in the synoptic gospels. But the narrative framework of John is not an end in itself, through which John seeks to present a primarily historical account of Jesus. John's gospel is rather a theological essay in the form of a gospel. The historical dimensions of his account are of use to him, but his main concern is his theological understanding of Jesus as the Word of God becoming human (1:14).

John does believe that the intention of God to reveal himself to man took place in the historical reality of Jesus, but he has no interest in the course of history as such. He has no scheme of the ages, such as we have found in Mark and Luke and, to a lesser extent, Q. It is the history of the self that is John's primary focus. The awesome prospect of death, resurrection, and judgment does not lie in the unpredictable future for John; these events occur again and again in every moment when the claim of Jesus calls the individual to a decision for or against the will of God.[49] John does not deny that there will be a resurrection or a judgment in the future, but the anxiety is removed from these future events by the belief that the decisive factor is the decision of faith that is made in every present moment. Using the form of historical narrative and locating the goal of history in the moment of decision, John succeeds in presenting his theology as history.

SUGGESTIONS FOR FURTHER READING

The two most important studies in the background of John's thoughts are by C. H. Dodd: *The Interpretation of the Fourth*

---

[49] See Bultmann, *Theology of the New Testament*, vol. 2, pp. 38–40, and *History and Eschatology*, pp. 47–55, where this theme is elaborated.

*Gospel** (Cambridge: Cambridge University Press, 1953), and *Historical Tradition in the Fourth Gospel** (Cambridge: Cambridge University Press, 1963). The most original theological interpretation of John is offered by Rudolf Bultmann, *Theology of the New Testament,** vol. 2 (New York: Scribner's, 1955). Three fine commentaries on John are C. K. Barrett, *The Gospel According to St. John* (New York: Seabury, 1956), R. H. Lightfoot, *St. John's Gospel: A Commentary** (Oxford: Oxford University Press, 1956), and most recently the learned but readable two-volume commentary by R. E. Brown in the Anchor Bible, *The Gospel According to St. John* (Garden City, N.Y.: Doubleday, 1966 [vol. 1], 1970 [vol. 2]).

Special studies of particular aspects of Johannine thought are Peder Borgen, *Bread from Heaven* (Leiden: Brill, 1966), in which the influence of Jewish Passover interpretations on John's story of the Feeding of the Five Thousand are traced, J. L. Martyn, *History and Theology in the Fourth Gospel* (New York: Harper & Row, 1968), D. M. Smith, Jr., *The Composition and Order of the Fourth Gospel* (New Haven, Conn.: Yale University, 1965), in which Bultmann's theories about the sources of John are expounded and criticized; C. K. Barrett, *The Gospel of John and Judaism* (Philadelphia: Fortress, 1975); and *John and Qumran,* ed. J. H. Charlesworth (London: Geoffrey Chapman, 1972).

* *Available in a paperback edition.*

8 The Gospels in the History of the Early Church

It is not possible that the gospels can be either more or fewer than they are. For, since there are four zones of the world in which we live, and four principal winds, while the church is scattered throughout the world, and the "pillar and ground"[1] of the church is the Gospel and the Spirit of Life; it is fitting that she should have four pillars, breathing out immortality on every side, and vivifying men afresh.[2]

Thus wrote Irenaeus in the second century in an effort to justify the church's use of four different gospels.

THE ATTITUDE OF THE EARLY CHURCH TOWARD THE GOSPELS

That Irenaeus had to strain so hard shows that the existence of

---

[1] Quoted from 1 Timothy 3:15.
[2] Irenaeus, *Against Heresies* 3.11.8, in *The Ante-Nicene Fathers*, vol. 1, trans. Alexander Roberts and James Donaldson (New York: 1899; reprinted, Grand Rapids, Mich.: Eerdmans, 1953).

these diverse documents was an embarrassment to the church.[3] The problem was not so much that the divergences among the four gospels raised questions for the church or its critics, but that elements in the church tended to seize upon one or the other of the gospels to the exclusion of the rest. Irenaeus noted that each of four different heretical groups of his day had selected one of the gospels to justify its position. Those who considered Christianity a special form of Judaism, and accordingly laid heavy stress on the Law, chose Matthew.[4] The second-century church leader Marcion, who denied that the God and Father of Jesus was the creator and who sought to rid Christianity of all its Jewish elements, settled on the gospel of Luke, although he had to expurgate it in order to render it non-Jewish. Another heretical group, called by their opponents the "Docetists"—the "Seemists," who denied the true humanity of Jesus Christ by claiming he only "seemed" to have a body—used the gospel of Mark as the basis for their distinction between the heavenly Christ and the earthly Jesus, who was no more than a phantasm.[5] The gospel of John was the favorite of Valentinus, one of the early Gnostics, whose elaboration on and speculative additions to the Christian faith are documented in the Gospel of Truth.[6] As we have noted,[7] the kinship between the mystical approach to truth represented by the gospel of John and Gnosticism of the second

[3] See the essay by Oscar Cullmann, "The Plurality of the Gospels as a Problem in Antiquity," in his *The Early Church*, trans. A. J. B. Higgins and Stanley Godman (London: SCM Press, 1956), pp. 39–58.

[4] These were the Ebionites, though Irenaeus' statement is not accurate since they actually had their own gospel or gospels. Of the gospel of the Ebionites mentioned by Epiphanius in his *Panarion* (sec. 29), Philip Vielhauer, writing in Hennecke-Schneemelcher, *New Testament Apocrypha*, vol. 1, trans. R. McL. Wilson (Philadelphia: Westminster, 1966), p. 153, states that it "must have been an abridged and falsified Gospel of Matthew . . . which he [Epiphanius] incorrectly entitles the 'Gospel of the Hebrews' and the 'Hebrew Gospel.'"

[5] Denial of the reality of Jesus' humanity developed early in the church, as the warning against this notion in 1 John 4:2 suggests. The term "Docetist" is derived from the Greek word *dokéō*, "to seem."

[6] An English translation of *The Gospel of Truth* has been published by Kendrick Grobel (Nashville: Abingdon, 1960). A summary is available as Appendix 2 of Hennecke-Schneemelcher, *New Testament Apocrypha*, vol. 1, pp. 523–31.

[7] Chapter 7 on the gospel of John, pp. 228–30.

century A.D. is so close that scholars have conjectured that John and the Gnostics employed, in different ways, certain Jewish concepts (e.g., preexistent Wisdom) and Gentile religious forms (e.g., the self-revealing speeches of Isis). These have influenced both the prologue and the "I am" speeches of his gospel.

The point that Irenaeus was making in the quote with which this chapter began is not that there is anything wrong with the gospels separately, but that the only guarantee that they will be interpreted in accordance with true catholic faith is to hold them all together so that the faith may be grasped in its fullness. His defense of the four-part arrangement of the gospel literature excludes by implication other documents that claimed to be of equal authority, such as the noncanonical gospels, but does not address itself to the problem of the differences among the four gospel accounts.

It might seem appropriate to account for this diversity on the ground that each of the four gospels represented a local tradition that originated in a different center of the primitive church. Such a theory has been developed: Mark is assigned to Rome, John to Ephesus, Matthew to Antioch, and Luke to Rome, their respective places of writing.[8] But Matthew and Luke used Mark, and perhaps John did too.[9] Thus the notion that any one gospel is a product of purely local origin and therefore reflects local theological or historical preferences cannot be sustained.

Indeed, there is some evidence that all four gospels may have originated in Syria, which might account for the fact that it was there in the late second century that the first known attempt was made to resolve the problem of the multiplicity of the gospels by weaving them together into a single consecutive narrative, called the Diatessaron, that is, "through the four" (see pp. 281–91).

[8] Thus B. H. Streeter in *The Four Gospels* (New York: Macmillan, 1925). On the provenance of Mark and Matthew, see pp. 485–527; of Luke, pp 531–40; of John, pp. 431–61. Streeter assigns M, the Matthean source, to Jerusalem and L, the Lukan source, to Caesarea in Palestine.

[9] The much-debated question of John's dependence on Mark is decided negatively by C. H. Dodd in *Historical Tradition in the Fourth Gospel* (Cambridge: Cambridge University Press, 1963), esp. pp. 423–32. For a positive view of the relationship, see C. K. Barrett, *Commentary on John* (London: SPCK, 1956), pp. 34–45.

Mark and Luke have traditionally been assigned to Rome, but on the dubious grounds that they were supposed to have been written by men who were, respectively, the companions of Peter and Paul, both of whom met martyrdom in Rome. Actually, Syria is a more likely place of origin for Mark[10] as well as for John,[11] and an eastern Mediterranean origin is also possible for Luke.[12] That Matthew was written in Antioch or at least in Syria has long been maintained.[13] The likelihood of the theory that all four gospels were written in Syria might suggest that the gospel tradition was first preserved and then propagated in the churches of Syria because of a special understanding of the meaning of Jesus that flourished there.

It may well be that the type of theological outlook represented by Mark and Q, for example, flourished in the Syrian church, where, in spite of the Semitic-language culture that stretched back into antiquity, Greek was widely spoken and understood. This could account, on the one hand, for the preservation there of an oral tradition in Aramaic (a Semitic dialect closely related to Syriac) and, on the other hand, for its early translation and recording in Greek, which from the time of Alexander the Great had been the language of culture and international relations. The authority of these gospels was established by associating each of them with one of the apostles; each was purportedly authored by either an apostle (Matthew and John) or an apostle's companion (Mark and Luke). That critical analysis of the gospels discredits these claims for apostolic authorship makes no difference in the matter of their authority as testimonies of faith: It was as books bearing the weight of apostolic origin that they found their way out into the wider church, and as such they were received.

By the end of the second century, the four—and only these

---

[10] See W. G. Kümmel, *Introduction to the New Testament*, 17th ed., trans. H. C. Kee (Nashville: Abingdon, 1975), p. 98.

[11] *Ibid.*, p. 175.

[12] *Ibid.*, pp. 105–06, where all suggested sites are regarded as no more than conjecture.

[13] So B. W. Bacon in his *Studies in Matthew* (New York: Holt, Rinehart and Winston, 1930), pp. 24–36. See also the discussion of the provenance of Matthew in Kümmel, *Introduction to the New Testament*, pp. 119–20.

four—were widely recognized as canonical,[14] or authoritative, and this recognition is attested in the main areas of the empire: by Irenaeus in Gaul, by Tertullian in North Africa, by Clement of Alexandria in Egypt, and by an ancient document preserved in what is known as the Muratorian Canon, which originated in Rome.[15] Discoveries of other gospels dating back to the second century, including the gospel of Thomas discovered in a Coptic version in Egypt in 1945, have not seriously called into question the wisdom of the church in choosing the four canonical gospels and no others as authoritative. Although there may be a few authentic sayings of Jesus preserved in noncanonical gospels and sayings collections,[16] none of the other gospels or collections has been able to establish a wide claim for canonicity. Even these supposedly authentic sayings are judged so only by reference to the material contained in the four familiar, canonical gospels. The chief concern of the church seems to have been to preserve the authority of the four gospels by demonstrating their apostolic origin rather than to raise questions about divergences between the accounts. Specifically, the church was more embarrassed by having to show why four authoritative gospels were necessary than by having to explain how the discrepancies among them were to be accounted for.

Before the question of the canonicity of the gospels was more or less settled—that is, before the first half of the second century—the sayings of Jesus and stories about him that had al-

[14] On the development of the concept of canon, see Kümmel, *Introduction to the New Testament*, pp. 475–501. For the specifics of the acceptance of the gospels as canonical, see pp. 340–47 and Hennecke-Schneemelcher, *New Testament Apocrypha*, vol. 1, pp. 21–60, where translations are given of the ancient sources and lists from which the development of the canon can be traced. See also Hans von Campenhausen, *The Formation of the Christian Bible* (Philadelphia: Fortress, 1971).

[15] A brief description and a translation of the Muratorian Canon are given in Hennecke-Schneemelcher, *New Testament Apocrypha*, vol. 1, pp. 42–45. Unfortunately, the first part of the canon, in which Matthew and Luke were certainly described, is now lost.

[16] This claim is made in behalf of a "very small residue of sayings in the case of which content, form and attestation justify the opinion that they stand on a level with the sayings of our Lord (themselves historically of very differing value) contained in our four Gospels" (Joachim Jeremias, "Isolated Sayings of the Lord," in Hennecke-Schneemelcher, *ibid.*, p. 87).

ready been incorporated into the gospels were still being circulated orally. As a result, different variations of these gospel traditions were preserved in the memories of Christians and, accordingly, found their way into the church leaders writings[17]—including both New Testament writings and others that were omitted from the canon but prized by the early church. The persistence of a free process of transmitting the gospel tradition helps to account for the wide range of variations found in the most ancient manuscripts of the gospels, the earliest of which are fragmentary and date from the second century, and the most important of which are from the fourth century.[18] The variants now found among the ancient manuscripts, as well as those variants that seem to have developed while the gospel tradition was transmitted orally and then were written down during the second century, are of a relatively minor nature and do not introduce additional information or modify substantially the historical evidence available from the canonical gospels.[19]

The early church clearly regarded our four canonical gospels as the basic source for knowledge about Jesus. And, in spite of variants in the manuscripts of the gospels, a remarkably reliable text of these gospels can be reconstructed. But, can we obtain additional information from the noncanonical sources?

[17] This phenomenon has been noted by Helmut Köster in *Synoptische Überlieferungen bei den apostolischen Vätern* [Synoptic traditions in the apostolic fathers] (Berlin: Akademie Verlag, 1957). See also the discussion by R. M. Grant, "Scripture and Tradition in Ignatius of Antioch," in his *After the New Testament* (Philadelphia: Fortress, 1967), pp. 37–54.

[18] A concise discussion of the causes of error in the transmission of the text of the New Testament is provided by B. M. Metzger, *The Text of the New Testament* (Oxford: Oxford University Press, 1964), pp. 186–206. Although Metzger takes into account unconscious (p. 193) and conscious (p. 197) harmonization of the various gospel accounts, he does not seem to allow for another important factor that contributed to the rise of textual variants: the continuing influence of oral tradition after the gospels were available in written form. Presumably, copyists introduced into the text that they were copying variants that they recalled and preferred to the version in their master copy, preferring the authority of living memory to that of the written record, even though producing written records was the source of their own livelihood.

[19] The question of alterations of the text of the gospels has been treated by C. S. C. Williams, *Alterations of the Words of Jesus as Quoted in the Literature of the Second Century* (Cambridge, Mass.: Harvard University Press, 1952).

FILLING THE GAPS IN KNOWLEDGE OF JESUS

The Infancy Gospels

Pious curiosity about the circumstances of Jesus' birth and child-hood beyond the limited information available in the canonical gospels aroused pious imaginations to fill in the gaps. Legendary stories arose. By the second half of the second century, they had been brought together in a form resembling the canonical gospels. These works were concerned, however, only with the background, birth, and childhood of Jesus. Of these infancy gospels, two have survived: the Protevangelium of James and the gospel of Thomas (not to be confused with a document bearing the same name but consisting entirely of hidden sayings of Jesus[20]).

The Protevangelium of James. In this infancy gospel, the miraculous stories depicting the circumstances of Jesus' birth in the canonical gospels of Matthew and Luke were expanded and some miraculous details were projected backward into the life of Mary and her family. At times the very words of the canonical gospel accounts are used, but they are applied to Jesus' supposed ancestors. For example, the report of the annunciation to Anna that she is to have a child (= Mary) uses the exact words of Luke 2 and builds on the tradition of the birth of Samuel, just as the author of the infancy story in Luke did:[21]

> And *behold an angel of the Lord came to her* and said: "Anna, Anna, the Lord has heard your prayer. You shall conceive and bear, and your offspring shall be spoken of in the whole world." And Anna said: "As the Lord my God lives, if I bear a child, whether male or female, I will *bring it as a gift to the Lord my God*, and it shall *serve him all the days of its life.* (Prot. of James 4:1)[22]

[20] See below, pp. 274–80.
[21] The Lukan and Matthean infancy stories were themselves influenced by the legends that arose from pious speculation about Jesus' birth. Such speculation produced accounts of miracles attending his birth and of his miraculous powers even as a child that are similar to stories about Buddha, Osiris, and other *Wunderkinder*.
[22] From the translation by Oscar Cullmann in Hennecke-Schneemelcher, *New Testament Apocrypha*, vol. 1, p. 376.

It is obvious that this passage is based on the canonical Greek gospels and the Old Testament and therefore is not earlier than the canonical infancy stories; nor was it written in Hebrew or Aramaic, as has sometimes been supposed by scholars wanting to claim that very old tradition lies behind the Protevangelium. It is instead composed of phrases taken from 1 Samuel 1 and 2 and from Luke 1 and 2, in sections dealing with the miraculous circumstances surrounding Hannah, Elizabeth, and Mary at the births of Samuel, John the Baptist, and Jesus, respectively. Not only phrases but the basic ideas of the birth and childhood accounts were taken over from the older Greek gospels. In addition, the author included some fantastic tales. For example, there is the story that Mary, sent by her parents to serve in the Temple and fed there by the angels (Prot. of James 8:1), was assigned the task of weaving the veil of the Temple, which was torn at the moment of Jesus' death (10:1–2). Another passage reports that as Joseph was out looking for a midwife in Bethlehem, the stars stood still and all earthly activity, human and animal, came momentarily to a halt. Not surprisingly, the account weaves together elements from both the Lukan and Matthean versions, a procedure that, as we shall see later in this chapter, was to be widely adopted, with far-reaching consequences for the church's understanding of Jesus.

The Infancy Gospel of Thomas. In this second infancy gospel, which seems to have been written only slightly later than the Protevangelium of James, the miraculous element was further expanded and the incredibility of the stories increased. Jesus is portrayed as a powerful wonder-worker, whom people are well-advised not to trifle with. Rebuked for fashioning clay sparrows on the Sabbath, he clapped his hands and made them fly away (Inf. Thos. 2:1–5). When taunted, he caused his opponents to wither or die, although on occasion he did a kind deed for a playmate:

> Now after some days Jesus was playing in the upper story of a house, and one of the children who were playing with him fell down from the house and died. And when the other children saw it they fled, and Jesus remained alone. And the parents of

him that was dead came and accused him of having thrown him down. And Jesus replied, "I did not throw him down." But they continued to revile him. Then Jesus leaped down from the roof and stood by the body of the child, and cried with a loud voice: "Zenon"—for that was his name—"Arise and tell me, did I throw you down?" And he arose at once and said: "No. Lord, you did not throw me down, but raised me up." And when they saw it they were amazed. And the parents of the child glorified God for the miracle that had happened and worshipped Jesus.[23] (Inf. Thos. 9:1–3)

Jesus performed the miracle, however, not as an act of compassion of the sort familiar from the synoptic accounts, but as a peevish way of vindicating himself in the face of the false accusation that he was responsible for the child's death.

Somewhat more worthy motives appear in other miracle stories, such as the one in which Jesus heals a man's foot that has been split by an ax (10:1–3). Among the more charming stories are those of Jesus bringing water home to his mother in the fold of his garment after the pitcher had broken (11:1–2) and of his helping his father finish a furniture-making assignment by stretching a board that had mistakenly been cut too short (13:1–2). Elsewhere (19:1–3), an entire pericope is taken over, with only slight changes, from the Lukan account (2:41–52) of Jesus among the teachers in the Jerusalem Temple.

The conclusion to be reached from an examination of the infancy gospels is clear: They contain no independent historical information. This inference is confirmed when we consider the differences between the portrayal of Jesus in the canonical gospels and in the noncanonical narratives. The latter make no attempt to show how the miracles of Jesus were performed in the interests of his serving others, and, significantly, the miracles are not interpreted as signs of the inbreaking of the Kingdom of God. In the infancy gospels the miracles are portrayed precisely as forms of Jesus' public authorization—something the Jesus of the synoptic

[23] From the translation by Cullmann in Hennecke-Schneemelcher, *ibid.*, pp. 395–96.

tradition refuses (Mark 8:11–12). The overwhelming impression the reader receives from the canonical gospels—namely, that all of Jesus' teachings and actions are made to serve the interests of the coming reign of God—is totally missing from these second-century documents. Instead, Jesus is portrayed as a precocious prig, revolting and ruthless in the exploitation of his supernatural powers. Such a picture simply cannot be brought into congruity with the image of Jesus that comes through the canonical accounts. The fact that the writers of these infancy narratives heaped miracle on miracle, with no awareness that they might strain the credulity of their readers, indicates that the modern questions of historical accuracy and credibility simply did not figure in literature of this type. The major aim was to heighten the aura of supernatural mystery around the figure of Jesus[24] and thus to make of him an even more noteworthy figure than he would be on the basis of the gospel accounts alone, replete with miracles though they are too. By the very effort to make the story of Jesus more spectacular, the writers removed him even further from the sphere of ordinary humanity than did, for example, the author of Mark, who sought to place Jesus the man in a scheme of apocalyptic history.

The Acts of Pilate

Another narrative that was supplied by pious imagination to fill the gap in historical knowledge of Jesus is the Acts of Pilate, purportedly translated by a certain Ananias, who identifies himself merely as an official of the guard and a faithful Christian. "Ananias" claims that he took his translation from Hebrew documents that originated with Nicodemus, the secret disciple of Jesus, who, with Joseph of Arimathea, claimed Jesus' body and buried it. He dates his translation during the reign of Emperor Theodosius II, or about A.D. 425, but of course the document translated goes back, according to "Ananias," to the time of Jesus. The work is, however, demonstrably dependent on the canonical Greek

---

[24] One aspect of the tendency in the Infancy Gospel of Thomas to heighten the supernatural qualities of Jesus—attributing to him occult knowledge—is discussed later in this chapter in connection with the Gnostic gospels.

gospels, especially on John and to a lesser extent on Matthew, and cannot therefore be regarded as an independent source. According to one theory, it originated as a Christian reaction to pagan documents purporting to be Pilate's records concerning Jesus, in which Jesus is portrayed in a bitterly hostile light.[25] These spurious official "annals" were used at the beginning of the fourth century A.D. to obtain popular support for the persecution of Christians ordered by Emperor Galerius, and primary-school teachers required their pupils to commit them to memory.[26] But in spite of ferocious efforts to coerce Christians into participating in the sacrifices connected with the cult of the emperor—including forcing them to taste the sacrificial offerings—popular feeling turned against Galerius' nephew and protégé, Daia, during his reign as Emperor Maximinus Galerius Valerius (A.D. 308–14) for his excessively harsh attempts to suppress Christianity.[27]

More likely than the theory that Christians developed their own Acts of Pilate in response to those promulgated by Maximinus, however, is the supposition that Justin Martyr's references to reports of Jesus' hearing before Pilate as well as Pilate's confirmation of Jesus' miracles of healing the sick and raising the dead were a part of a document called the Acts of Pontius Pilate[28] that was already in existence in Justin Martyr's day (A.D. 100?–165?). Although the gospel of Nicodemus, which contains our

---

[25] Mentioned in Eusebius, *Ecclesiastical History* 1.9.3. Kirsopp Lake, in notes to the Loeb edition (Cambridge, Mass.: Harvard University Press, 1957) remarks that the Acts of Pilate were "introduced in the time of the great persecution under Maximin" (i.e., Maximinus Daia, who bore the title of Caesar in the East from A.D. 305 to 312).

[26] Eusebius, *Ecclesiastical History* 9.5.1. The Acts of Pilate, with their anti-Christian polemic, were to be "exhibited openly for everyone to see in every place, both town and country, and . . . the primary teachers should give them to the children, instead of lessons, for study and commital to memory" (from the translation by H. J. Lawlor and J. E. L. Oulton, *The Ecclesiastical History and the Martyrs of Palestine* [London: Macmillan, 1927–28; reprinted, 1954]).

[27] A full account is given in Eusebius, *Concerning the Palestine Martyrs* 9.2–3 (from the translation by Lawlor and Oulton). Even the pagan populace was revolted by Maximinus' cruelty (9.9–12).

[28] Confirmation of the trial is given in Justin's *First Apology*, chapter 35; corroboration of the miracles is implied in chapter 48 (in *Fathers of the Church*, vol. 6, New York: Christian Heritage, 1949).

oldest version of the Acts of Pilate, was written in the early fifth century, it probably incorporates much older material, going back to the first half of the second century.[29] Working primarily from Matthew, as we can infer from details in the passion story (Pilate washing his hands) and the resurrection appearances (in Galilee), the author has introduced miraculous details (the soldiers' standards bow of themselves when Jesus enters the judgment hall) and has gone even farther than Matthew to exonerate Pilate of blame for Jesus' death. The work reads like a Hellenistic romance, therefore, and only in those passages where the author is most heavily dependent on Matthew can we consider seriously the possibility of a basis in the early Jesus tradition. The heightening of both the miraculous features and the anti-Jewish elements renders the document of value only for understanding the history of the church in the third and fourth centuries. As a primary historical source, the Acts of Pilate are valueless.

The Gnostic Gospels

Another attempt to fill in the gaps in knowledge of Jesus was undertaken by those who were persuaded—or at least sought to persuade their readers—that the reason Jesus was not more fully known by his contemporaries in general was that he had disclosed fuller knowledge of himself to his inner circle of followers only after his resurrection. This idea was not new in the second century; rather, it developed from at least two factors that were present in the synoptic tradition in the first century. The first of these is the claim, so basic to Mark, that only Jesus' most intimate followers understood the hidden meaning of his words and actions. Mark believed that they had been given special insight so that they could discern in Jesus' teaching and activity the inbreaking of the End of the Age, which was soon to take place. What they possessed was not special information but revealed insight, which enabled them to recognize the true meaning of

---

[29] So Felix Scheidweiler, "The Gospel of Nicodemus, Acts of Pilate, Descent into Hell," in Hennecke-Schneemelcher, *New Testament Apocrypha*, vol. 1, pp. 444–49, on whose analysis the argument set forth here depends.

Jesus. While others found him threatening, offensive to, or even subversive of the established religious and political values and institutions, his disciples saw in him the inbreaking Kingdom of God.

Second, in the canonical gospels Jesus does make private disclosures to his inner group of followers both during his public ministry—in the transfiguration scene, for example—and after the resurrection. One postresurrection appearance is promised in Mark 14:28, and another in 16:7, in which the young man who appears at the empty tomb says to the distraught women, "Go, tell his disciples and Peter that he is going before you to Galilee; there you will see him, as he told you." Some of the ancient manuscripts—although none of the most ancient and reliable ones—include a description of this appearance, given in the King James Version and other versions as Mark 16:9–19.

Matthew inserted at this point in his gospel (28:8–20) a report of Jesus' appearance to the disciples in Galilee after the resurrection, when he greeted them and then commissioned them to carry out their mission to the world, promising to be present with them until the Consummation of the Age. The fact that Mark hints at and Matthew recounts a postresurrection appearance in Galilee, whereas the postresurrection appearances in Luke 24 and John 20 take place in Jerusalem or its vicinity, may reflect a tradition preserved by the primitive church in Galilee. The question of the location of the appearances does not concern us here;[30] what is important is the implication of these gospel records that the full meaning of Jesus was not grasped by the disciples until after they had seen him risen from the dead. In Luke especially, the disciples are depicted as "foolish men, and slow of heart to believe" (Luke 24:25). On confronting the risen Lord, their minds were "opened . . . to understand" not only the Scriptures as such but also the intention of God through Jesus (Luke 24:45).

The knowledge imparted in each of these briefing sessions is not secret. What Jesus discloses is as much a part of the church's public tradition as what he taught in the Capernaum synagogue or on the Mount. Nevertheless, the precedent was established for

---

[30] For those interested in the topic, see R. H. Lightfoot, *Locality and Doctrine in the Gospels* (New York: Harper & Row, 1938).

an esoteric knowledge of Jesus and for private sessions in which the risen Lord disclosed hidden truth to his own.

This pattern of postresurrection disclosures, which made possible a fuller grasp of the significance of Jesus, was developed further in the second century in so-called gospels that had no interest in the earthly ministry of Jesus but concentrated solely on his secret revelations, granted to the faithful after his crucifixion and resurrection. Indeed, neither the cross nor the resurrection figures in most of the accounts. The esoteric revelation is the paramount concern.

Although we cannot trace the stages in the development of Gnosticism, the interest in hidden knowledge evident in the second-century expansion and modification of the gospel tradition is related to the emergence of that movement. In our study of the gospel of John we considered the antecedents of Gnosticism as seen in the Jewish concepts of personified Wisdom and the ascent of the soul to union with God. But by the time the apocryphal gospels now under consideration began to appear, Christianity had itself been deeply influenced by Gnostic thinking; there was a movement within the church to transform Jesus into a heavenly redeemer who brought secret knowledge (*gnosis*) to earth so that men could be freed from their enslavement in the world of matter and thus be able to ascend to the world of spirit.

One important step in the Gnostic direction was taken by certain Christians who became persuaded that the bodily urges, especially the sexual drive, were evil. A man of true faith would be able to overcome the sexual urge, they maintained, by abstaining from marriage or sexual intercourse. Those who shared this view became known as *Encratites* (from the Greek, meaning "those who exercise self-control"). The asceticism of the Encratites also forbade drinking wine or eating meat. Their negative estimate of the body, and of the material creation, was an important factor in the developing Gnosticism of the period, although one cannot be sure if the Encratites took over this view from an existing movement or if this was their contribution to incipient Gnosticism. Several of the apocryphal gospels show the influence of Encratitism, and accordingly they were adopted by the Gnostics as their own.

So numerous are the gospels that show the influence of

Encratitism and Gnosticism that only representatives of the various types can be given here.

The Infancy Gospel of Thomas. The development of the occult-knowledge tradition is seen in the Infancy Gospel of Thomas, in which Jesus sets his teacher straight on the hidden meaning of the letters of the alphabet:

> When Joseph saw the understanding of the child and his age, that he was growing to maturity, he resolved again that he should not remain ignorant of letters; and he took him and handed him over to another teacher. And the teacher said to Joseph: "First I will teach him Greek, and then Hebrew." For the teacher knew the child's knowledge and was afraid of him. Nevertheless he wrote the alphabet and practiced it with him for a long time; but he gave no answer. Then Jesus said to him: "If you are indeed a teacher, and if you know the letters well, tell me the meaning of the Alpha, and I will tell you that of Beta." And the teacher was annoyed and struck him on the head. And the child was hurt and cursed him, and he immediately fainted and fell to the ground on his face. And the child returned to Joseph's house. But Joseph was grieved and commanded his mother: "Do not let him go outside the door, for all those who provoke him die."[31] (Inf. Thos. 14:1–3)

Apart from the despicable behavior attributed to the boy Jesus in this story, interest centers on the implication that he possesses certain occult knowledge of the letters of the alphabet. This claim that Jesus possessed esoteric information paved the way for the Gnostic gospels.

The Apocryphon of John. One of the oldest[32] of the Gnostic gospels is the Apocryphon of John, in which the circumstances of the revelation to the disciples are described vividly:

---

[31] From the translation by Cullmann in Hennecke-Schneemelcher, *New Testament Apocrypha*, vol. 1, p. 397.

[32] Dated to the middle of the second century by H. C. Puech, "Gnostic Gospels and Related Documents," in Hennecke-Schneemelcher, *New Testament Apocrypha*, vol. 1, p. 330, although it is not clear how Irenaeus' version of the Apocryphon of John, from which Irenaeus quotes in *Against Heresies* (1.29), corresponds to the versions of the Apocryphon of John found in Berlin Papyrus 8502 and Nag Hammadi Codices 1, 3, and 8. See Puech, pp. 314–31.

It happened one day when John, the brother of James (these are the sons of Zebedee) went up to the temple [Acts 3], there a Pharisee named A[.]manaias approached him and said to him, "Where is your master whom you followed?" He said to him, "He has returned to the place from which he came." The Pharisee said to him, "This Nazarene deceived you with deception [. . .] and hardened your hearts and estranged you from the tradition of your fathers."

When I [John] heard this, I went away from the temple to the mountain, to a desert place, and with great grief in my heart I said, "How then was the Saviour appointed? And why was he sent into the world by his Father who sent him? And who is his Father? And what is the nature of that Aeon to which we shall go? He told us, 'This Aeon received the type of that imperishable Aeon,' but he did not reveal to us what its nature is."

As I had these thoughts the heavens were opened and the whole creation shone with a light [not of earth] and the universe was shaken. I was afraid and fell down, and behold a child appeared to me; but I saw the form of an old man in whom was light. When I looked upon him I did not comprehend this wonder. If it is a unity . . . with many forms because of the light? Then its forms [appear] through their [. . .]. If it is a unity, how would it have three aspects?

He said to me, "John, why do you doubt? When I [. . .]you? For it is not foreign to you. Do not be of little faith; I am the one who is with you always. I am [the Father], I am the Mother, I [am the Son]. I am [the Father] eternally Existent, the unmixable [for there is no one] who mixed himself with him. Now I have come to reveal to you that which is, that which has been, and that which will be, so that you may know the things which are seen and the things not seen and to reveal to you about the Perfect Man. Now lift up your face and come and hear and learn what I shall tell you today, so that you yourself may reveal it to spirits of the same sort, who are of the unwavering race of the Perfect Man and are able to understand."[33]

In what follows, "John" is told about the Aeons, the immeasurable Light, the ineffable Thought, the indefinable Spirit,

---

[33] R. M. Grant, ed., *Gnosticism: A Sourcebook of Heretical Writings from the Early Christian Period* (New York: Harper & Row, 1961), pp. 69–70.

and the process of creation. The number and names of the angels and the archons are given. In all the maze of detail, however, Christ appears as the sole revealer of the hidden truth. He has no personal features, no activity, no ministry, and nothing corresponding to the teaching given in the canonical gospels. There is in the Apocryphon of John nothing that contributes to knowledge of Jesus in history. In fact, the Apocryphon is not interested in the story of Jesus at all, but portrays him solely as the mediator of secret knowledge about the nature of God and the universe.

The gospel of Thomas. Another gospel originated about the middle of the second century, which stands much closer in content to the synoptic gospels: the gospel of Thomas. Until thirty years ago this gospel was known only by name, through references to it by the fathers of the early church in their lists of heretical books, but about 1945 a virtually complete text was found among the codices from Nag Hammadi in Upper Egypt in a translation in Coptic, a late form of Egyptian used chiefly by Christians in Egypt. The editors of the text have divided it into 114 sayings, or *logia*, which, apart from a brief introductory word and the repetition of the title at the end, comprise the entire text of the gospel. The introduction runs as follows:

> These are the secret words which the Living Jesus spoke and Didymos Judas Thomas wrote.[34]

The designation of Jesus as "the Living Jesus" implies that he is regarded as risen from the dead, an implication that is almost certainly confirmed by the first logion, which follows immediately:

> And He said: Whoever finds the interpretation of these words will not taste death.

The representation of Thomas as the special custodian of the hidden teaching of Jesus is paralleled in the description of him that is given in the Acts of Thomas, a work of the early third century,[35]

---

[34] All quotations from the gospel of Thomas are from the so-called Brill text, trans. and ed. Antoine Guillaumont, H. C. Puech, and others (New York: Harper & Row, 1959).

[35] See A. F. J. Klijn, *The Acts of Thomas: Introduction, Text, Commentary* (New York: Humanities Press, 1962). The third-century dating is suggested on p. 26.

in which he is depicted as a fellow initiate in the hidden word of Christ[36] and the receiver of his hidden mysteries.[37] It is not likely, therefore, that one would look to the gospel of Thomas as a source of historical knowledge about Jesus, since, by definition, the sayings included are those of the risen Christ, not the earthly Jesus.

The situation is more complex, however, because the gospel of Thomas contains logia that stand very close to those attributed to Jesus in the canonical tradition. Some scholars have even suggested that the gospel of Thomas may contain older forms of Jesus' sayings than those known from the synoptics.[38] Since the early years of this century, scholars have known of the existence of collections of Jesus' sayings that closely resemble those preserved in the synoptic gospels. The first such group, known as Oxyrhynchus Papyri from the place of their discovery in Egypt, was published by G. P. Grenfell and A. S. Hunt in 1903.[39] They were subsequently studied by H. G. Evelyn-White[40] and later by Joachim Jeremias.[41]

The fact that Thomas is mentioned in the preface to the

---

[36] In chapter 39 the colt of an ass addresses Thomas in a manner reminiscent of Balaam's ass (Num. 22), but instead of offering reproof, the colt acclaims Thomas: "Twin of the Messiah, and apostle of the Most High, and sharer in the hidden word of the Life-giver, and receiver of the secret-mysteries of the Son of God" (Klijn, *ibid.*, p. 85).

[37] The enumeration of the mysteries—up to twenty-four—is given in the Gnostic document Pistis Sophia, also from the early third century, which claims to be a report of Jesus' secret teaching during an eleven-year period after his resurrection. See H. C. Puech in Hennecke-Schneemelcher, *New Testament Apocrypha*, vol. 1, pp. 250–53. The text of Pistis Sophia is given in W. O. Till's revision of Carl Schmidt, *Koptisch-gnostiche Schriften* [Coptic-Gnostic writings), 2nd ed. (Berlin: Akademie Verlag, 1954).

[38] So, for example, C. H. Hunzinger, "Aussersynoptisches Traditionsgut im Thomas-Evangelium" [Extracanonical traditional material in the gospel of Thomas], *Theologische Literaturzeitung* [Journal of theological literature] 85 (1960): cols. 843–46, esp. secs. 2a and 2b. Ernst Haenchen, *Die Botschaft des Thomas-Evangelium* [The message of the gospel of Thomas] (Berlin: Topelmann, 1961), pp. 67–68, is highly dubious about the possibility of finding new, genuine sayings of Jesus in the gospel of Thomas.

[39] *Oxyrhynchus Papyri*, vol. 4 (London: Egypt Exploration Fund, 1903), pp. 1–22; also in Grenfell and Hunt, *New Sayings of Jesus and Fragment of a Lost Gospel from Oxyrhynchus* (London: H. Frowde, 1904).

[40] *The Sayings of Jesus from Oxyrhynchus* (Cambridge: Cambridge University Press, 1920).

[41] *Unknown Sayings of Jesus*, 2nd ed., trans. R. H. Fuller (London: SPCK, 1964).

first logion of the Oxyrhynchus sayings (known to scholars as Papyrus Oxy. 654) had raised the possibility that this fragmentary collection was part of the gospel of Thomas, but it is now clear that three of these papyri—Oxy. 654, 1, and 655—are parts of what was originally one work, which is preserved in the Coptic version of the gospel of Thomas. J. A. Fitzmyer has reconstructed the Greek text behind the Coptic version and has published a detailed comparison of it with the sayings from the Oxyrhynchus Papyri.[42] What he has rendered highly probable is that the Coptic gospel of Thomas is a version of a Greek original. What cannot be demonstrated persuasively is that the Greek gospel of Thomas contains material that is independent of or older than that preserved in the synoptics.[43]

Some of the logia do little more than reproduce what is found in the synoptics, and without significant change, as the following logia (31–35), with synoptic parallels in the margin, reveal.

Matt. 13:57;	Jesus said: No prophet is acceptable in his vil-
Mark 6:4	lage, no physician heals those who know him.
Luke 4:24	Jesus said: A city
Matt. 5:14	⎱ being built on a high mountain cannot fall nor
(7:24–25)	⎰ can it be
Matt. 10:27;	⎱ hidden. Jesus said: what thou shalt hear in
Luke 12:3	⎰ thine ear and
Mark 4:21;	⎱ in the other ear, that preach on the housetops;
Luke 8:16	⎰ for no one
Matt. 5:15;	⎱ lights a lamp and puts it under a bushel, nor
Luke 11:33	⎰ does he put it in a hidden place, but he sets it
	on a lampstand so that all who come in and go
	out may see its light.[44]

---

[42] J. A. Fitzmyer, "The Oxyrhynchus *Logoi* of Jesus and the Coptic Gospel According to Thomas," *Theological Studies* 20 (1959):505–60.

[43] *Contra* Hunzinger (see n. 38, p. 275).

[44] This saying is dependent on Luke 8:16 rather than on the more original parallel in Matthew 5:15, as Jeremias has shown (*The Parables of Jesus*, 6th ed., trans. S. H. Hooke [New York: Scribner's, 1963], pp. 26–27). Luke's version presupposes a house with a lighted vestibule, whereas Matthew faithfully portrays a one-room Palestinian house in which a single light can be seen throughout.

| Matt. 15:14;
Luke 6:39 | }Jesus said: If a blind man leads a blind man,
both of them fall into a pit. Jesus said: It is
not possible for me |
| Mark 3:27;
Matt. 12:29 | }to enter the house of the strong man and take
him by force unless he bind his hands; then he
will ransack his house. |

Other logia, such as logion 44, alter the synoptic tradition substantively:

> Jesus said: Whoever blasphemes against the Father, it shall be forgiven him, and whoever blasphemes against the Son, it shall be forgiven him; but whoever blasphemes against the Holy Ghost, it shall not be forgiven him, either on earth or in heaven.

Logion 44 is obviously a development from Mark 3:28–29, which reads:

> Truly, I say to you, all sins will be forgiven the sons of men, and whatever blasphemies they utter; but whoever blasphemes against the Holy Spirit never has forgiveness, but is guilty of an eternal sin.

What has happened is that the reference to grossly insulting remarks about other men (= "sons of men") has been transformed into a reference to Jesus as Son (of Man), while a third term, "the Father," has been prefixed to the saying. The result is a statement strongly influenced by the doctrine of the Trinity, a teaching that is found only in the latest stratum of the synoptic tradition (for example, in Matthew's epilogue, 28:19, where the Trinitarian baptismal formula is given).

Similarly, the idea of becoming like a child in order to enter the Kingdom is retained in the gospel of Thomas (logia 22 and 46) on the basis of Mark 10:15, but the force has been fundamentally altered.[45] The distinction would not be clear if we were limited in our evidence to logion 45:

---

[45] See H. C. Kee, " 'Becoming a Child' in the Gospel of Thomas," *Journal of Biblical Literature* 82 (1963): 307–14.

> Jesus said: From Adam until John the Baptist there is among
> those who are born of women none higher than John the Bap-
> tist, so that his eyes will not be broken. But I have said to you
> that whoever among you becomes as a child shall know the
> Kingdom, and he shall become higher than John.

Except for the curious expression about the eyes not being broken,
the logion sounds like a combination of Jesus' word concerning
John (Matt. 11:11 = Luke 7:28) with the saying from Mark
10:15 about becoming like a child in order to enter the Kingdom.
But logion 22 shows that far more is involved:

> Jesus saw children who were being suckled. He said to his dis-
> ciples: These children who are being suckled are like those who
> enter the Kingdom. They said to him: Shall we then, being
> children, enter the Kingdom? Jesus said to them: When you
> make the two one, and when you make the inner as the outer
> and the outer as the inner and the above as the below, and
> when you make the male and the female into a single one, so
> that the male will not be male and the female not be female,
> when you make eyes in the place of an eye, and a hand in the
> place of a hand, and a foot in the place of a foot, and an image
> in the place of an image, then shall you enter the Kingdom.

The meaning of this string of curious contrasts has been investi-
gated by A. F. J. Klijn, who has shown that to become a "single
one" means to return to the androgynous state of Adam before
he was divided into male and female, when Eve was fashioned
from his side.[46] But the other image in the gospel of Thomas for
regaining the asexual condition is to "become as a child."[47] What
was in the earlier Jesus tradition a metaphor of acceptant sim-
plicity or childlike trust has become in the gospel of Thomas a
Gnosticizing appeal to divest oneself of sexuality in order to return
to the primordial state of innocence. Far from representing an

[46] "The 'Single One' in the Gospel of Thomas," *Journal of Biblical Literature*
81 (1962): 271–78.
[47] Kee, " 'Becoming a Child' in the Gospel of Thomas." My interpretation is
challenged in Helmut Köster and J. M. Robinson, *Trajectories Through Early
Christianity* (Philadelphia: Fortress, 1971), p. 174.

older form of the synoptic tradition, the gospel of Thomas represents the gospel material at a later stage of its development, when
it has been adapted to serve the interests of Encratitic or even
Gnostic groups.

There are, however, simpler and therefore possibly older
versions of the parables in the gospel of Thomas. For example,
logion 57 reads like an earlier form of the Parable of the Weeds
found in Matthew 13:24–30:

> Jesus said, The Kingdom of the Father is like a man who had
> [good] seed. His enemy came by night, he sowed a weed among
> the good seed. The man did not permit them [the workers] to
> pull up the weed. He said to them: Lest perhaps you go to pull
> up the weed and pull up the wheat with it. For on the day of
> harvest the weeds will appear, they [will] pull them and burn
> them.

There are fewer details in Thomas than in Matthew, and there
is no hint of the allegorical interpretation that Matthew introduces in 13:36–43.[48] This may well be one of the instances where
the gospel of Thomas preserves a more primitive form of the
gospel tradition, although even here we can see the influence of
the gospel writer's theology when he uses the phrase "Kingdom
of the Father" rather than the simple Matthean "kingdom of
heaven" (= God).

The Parable of the Supper, which occurs in Q (Matt. 22:2–
10 = Luke 14:16–24), may also appear in an older form in
Thomas, logion 64. But the conclusion, with its warning that
"Tradesmen and merchants [shall] not [enter] the places [*topos*]
of my Father," shows beyond question that the parable serves a
Gnostic viewpoint,[49] since *topos* is for Gnostics a technical term
for the place of redemption.[50]

---

[48] So Jeremias, *The Parables of Jesus*, p. 224.
[49] Cf. logion 4: "Jesus said: The man old in days will not hesitate to ask a
little child of seven days about the place (*topos*) of Life, and he will live."
[50] In the Acts of Thomas (chapters 6 and 7) a hymn to the church (probably
based on a Jewish hymn to Wisdom; see Klijn's commentary, *The Acts of
Thomas*, p. 164) describes the Celestial Female, whose hands "proclaim the
place of life" (lines 19–20), which is interpreted in the next line to mean
heaven.

Even if we assume that in some places Thomas preserves older forms of the sayings of Jesus, these instances do not materially change our understanding of the message of Jesus, nor do they tell us anything about the context of meaning and action in which Jesus first proclaimed his message or in which the first-century church came to understand that message. Rather, the sayings are used in a way that serves the interests of a Gnostic viewpoint, which has no concern for the historical but is intended instead to help deliver men from their involvement in the material world. As such, the gospel of Thomas has no important contribution to make to our understanding of Jesus in history. Its concern is to show how through Jesus man may escape from history.

ATTEMPTS TO IMPOSE UNITY ON THE GOSPEL TRADITION

Although various parts of the church in specific areas of the Roman Empire seem to have preferred one of the canonical gospels above the others, there was an inclination on the part of some Christians in the second century to choose one gospel and eliminate the others. In the first half of the second century, Marcion, a native of Pontus on the Black Sea, was apparently active in the church at Edessa, an important center of Syriac-speaking Christianity. In A.D. 138 he left the church to form his own group, for whom he prepared his own canon, which included a single gospel, generally thought to have been a drastically edited version of the gospel of Luke.[51] Whether he began with Luke as his basis or worked from the mass of gospel tradition including Luke,[52] he removed any elements from the story of Jesus that he regarded as

---

[51] This opinion about Marcion's single gospel was held by Adolf von Harnack in *Geschichte der altchristlichen Literatur* [The history of early Christian literature], vol. 1, part 1 (Leipzig: J. C. Hinrichs, 1893–1904), p. 195, and is simply assumed by Kümmel, *Introduction to the New Testament*, p. 486.
[52] This is the theory about Marcion's "gospel" advanced in F. C. Burkitt's treatment of Marcion in *Cambridge Ancient History*, vol. 12 (Cambridge: Cambridge University Press, 1939), pp. 452–54.

Jewish perversions of the true gospel.[53] Although Marcion's brilliance and effectiveness as a leader gave him a large following in his own day, his chief enduring contribution seems to be that he moved the catholic church to form its own canon, including the four gospels,[54] as a way of combating his own anti-Judaic canon. The impact that he had on the church at Edessa, even though he was regarded as a heretic, is evidenced by the fact that Marcion is mentioned in the official history of the church at Edessa in the Edessene Chronicle.[55]

It was another prominent man connected with the second-century church in Edessa and, like Marcion, considered a heretic, whose handling of the problem of the plurality of the gospels had the most enduring influence on the church's understanding of the story of Jesus. That man was Tatian. He called himself an Assyrian, and he probably was a native of Adiabene, a district that lay east of the Tigris and had long been a buffer zone between the eastern edge of the Roman Empire and the territory of the Parthians, although it was included as a Roman province of Assyria after Trajan's defeat of the Parthians in A.D. 116.[56] By at least the middle of the second century, the Greek gospels had been translated for the use of the church in northern Syria and Mesopotamia into Syriac, which in spoken form closely resembled the Aramaic of Syria and Palestine, though it was radically different in script. It was these Syriac gospels that Tatian later wove together into his harmony of the gospels, the Diatessaron.

The Diatessaron

The discovery of a fragment of the Diatessaron in Greek at Dura-Europos[57] revived the supposition that Tatian originally composed

---

[53] *Ibid.*, p. 453.
[54] So John Knox, *Marcion and the New Testament* (Chicago: University of Chicago Press, 1942).
[55] So Paul Kahle, *The Cairo Genizah* (Oxford: Oxford University Press, 1947), p. 279. Marcion is not included, however, in Adolf von Harnack's list of the three most important figures at Edessa in his *The Mission and Expansion of Christianity in the First Three Centuries*, rev. ed., vol. 2, trans. and ed. James Moffatt (New York: Putnam's, 1908), pp. 292–300.
[56] Kahle, *The Cairo Genizah*, p. 283.
[57] A brief account of this discovery, with a translation of the fragment, is given by B. M. Metzger in *The Text of the New Testament*, pp. 90–91. Earlier, F.

his harmony in that language. It is widely agreed, however, that he did the work in his native Syriac. Until rather recently, no copies of the work in that language were known to have survived. And the Commentary of Ephraem on the Diatessaron, written in Syriac in the fourth century, had also disappeared, except for a few fragments.[58] In the past few decades, however, the original text of Ephraem's Commentary, and through it, of the Diatessaron itself, has become available in the Syriac original. The Armenian version, which had long served as one of the important sources for reconstructing the text of the Diatessaron, is now known to diverge from the Syriac original. The major English translations currently available, however, are still based on yet another version (Arabic) of Tatian's influential harmony of the gospels.[59] The original, almost certainly written in Syriac, was composed in all likelihood after Tatian returned to Mesopotamia at the end of his extended stay in Rome.[60]

Very little is known of Tatian's life. Irenaeus reports that he was a pupil of Justin Martyr in Rome, but that he erred in denying, as did the Gnostics, both the salvation of Adam and the sanctity of marriage.[61] He was also the teacher of Clement of Alexandria, presumably after the martyrdom of Justin, who was largely responsible for Tatian's conversion to Christianity. Tatian's mastery of Greek and knowledge of Greek philosophy are well attested in his *Oration to the Greeks*, which is the only one of his writings that has been preserved. His espousal of the Encratite

---

C. Burkitt had suggested (in *Cambridge Ancient History*, vol. 12, p. 494) that Tatian's original Diatessaron was in Latin; his chief argument apparently was that the oldest manuscripts of the Diatessaron are Latin versions, for example the Codex Fuldensis, prepared in the middle of the sixth century by Victor of Capua and based on an earlier harmony, which he correctly associated with Tatian. The codex found its way to Fulda, in Germany, apparently by way of England, whence it was taken back to the continent by Boniface or one of his fellow Saxon missionaries in the eighth century.

[58] Details can be found in Metzger, *The Text of the New Testament*, p. 91, esp. n. 1.

[59] H. W. Hogg in *The Ante-Nicene Fathers*, vol. 9 (New York: Christian Literature, 1896), pp. 35–138. Also the translation by J. H. Hill, *The Earliest Life of Christ* (Edinburgh: T. & T. Clark, 1894).

[60] So Kahle, *The Cairo Genizah*, pp. 293–95.

[61] Irenaeus, *Against Heresies* 1.28.1.

position led to his being discredited and probably to the destruction of his writings. Indeed, Theodoret, Bishop of Cyrrhus on the Euphrates, in A.D. 423 set about systematically destroying all the copies of Tatian's Diatessaron that he could find.[62] He boasted:

> He [Tatian] composed the so-called Diatessaron by cutting out the genealogies and whatever goes to prove the Lord to have been born of the seed of David according to the flesh. And this work was in use not only among his own party but even amongst those who follow the tradition of the Apostles, who used it somewhat innocently as a compendium of the Gospels, without recognizing the craftiness of its composition. I myself found more than 200 copies in reverential use in the churches of my diocese, all of which I removed, replacing them by the Gospels of the Four Evangelists.[63]

It is impossible at a distance of 1800 years to determine the motive Tatian had in weaving together the four gospel records. Even from such learned opponents of Christianity as Celsus, a Platonist of the late second century who denounced the incarnation as absurd and whose detailed attacks on the credibility of the gospels were the most serious intellectual challenge the church had then encountered, there is no evidence that the differences among the accounts raised for Tatian any serious questions about the trustworthiness of the records. We must constantly remind ourselves that devotion to fact is a relatively modern dimension of human thought and that precise analysis of historical sources is largely a development of the post-Enlightenment period in the West. Celsus did scoff at certain aspects of the gospel narrative because he found the miraculous claims incredible. He preferred the Jewish account of Jesus' birth—as the illegitimate child of an adulterous village woman[64]—to the gospel report of the virgin birth. The story of the descent of the Holy Spirit in bodily form struck Celsus as especially preposterous. But, significantly, Origen,

[62] See Metzger, *The Text of the New Testament*, p. 89.
[63] From the translation of Theodoret's *On Heresies* by Rendel Harris in his *Diatessaron of Tatian* (London: Clay & Sons, 1890), p. 13.
[64] So Origen *Contra Celsum* 1.28 (from the edition by Henry Chadwick [Cambridge: Cambridge University Press, 1965]).

the learned leader of the Christian School in Alexandria (c. 185–254), who devoted a full-scale book to answering Celsus, did not respond with a rational explanation of the miracles, nor was he willing to set them aside as not integral to the gospel record. Rather, he showed that the reader of every myth-filled history must exercise his own judgment "as to what statements he will give assent to [that is, as historically accurate], and what he will accept figuratively, seeking to discover the meaning of the authors of such inventions."[65] Origen's quite sophisticated method of handling the miracle accounts—as mythical or figurative[66]—anticipated the method of analyzing the gospels that developed 1600 years later in the work of David Friedrich Strauss. But neither Origen nor Celsus seems to have been troubled by divergent accounts in the various gospels.

Tatian's aim was to include the whole of the four gospels, with three notable exceptions: (1) The genealogies from Matthew and Luke are missing, as are the story of the woman taken in adultery and the preamble to Luke (Luke 1:1–4); (2) pericopes found only in Mark, such as the Parable of the Seed Growing of Itself (Mark 4:26–29), are included, but connective phrases are omitted; and (3) where Mark has a fuller account of a miracle performed by Jesus, as in the Healing of the Woman with the Hemorrhage (Mark 5:21–43, esp. 29–34), Tatian has included all the Markan detail.

The Diatessaron shows a preference for John, whose Passovers provide the chronological structure for the entire narrative. Otherwise, the order of events comes closer to following Matthew's sequence than that of any other gospel. But Tatian felt free to shift positions radically when it served his aims. For example, the Johannine account of the cleansing of the Temple, which comes at the beginning of the gospel (John 2), is blended with the synoptic account and is placed at the time of Jesus' last journey to Jerusalem. Similarly, the story of Jesus' dialogue with Nicodemus, which comes early in John (John 3), is assigned in the Diatessaron to the section dealing with the controversies be-

[65] *Ibid.*, 1.40–41.
[66] *Ibid.*, 1.42.

tween Jesus and the Pharisees, that is, with material found in Matthew 21. Because the lengthy Johannine discourses must be positioned prior to the passion narrative, the incident of cleansing the Temple is found in the Diatessaron slightly past the halfway point, although it comes toward the end of each of the synoptic accounts (Mark 11; Matt. 21; Luke 19). The story of Jesus' washing the disciples' feet (John 13) is merged with Jesus' promise of a Kingdom to his disciples (Luke 22:27–30). Tatian skillfully linked it with both the preceding and subsequent narratives by placing it just after the Markan saying about preparing for the Passover (Mark 14:12), which then leads directly into the meal which is eaten "before the Passover" (John 13:1). Similarly, in 44:10–33, John 13:20 ("He that receives me receives him that sent me") blends smoothly with Luke 22:27 ("Which is greater, he that reclines or he that serves? I am in the midst of you as he that serves").

Tatian's work does not add to our store of information about Jesus, since his procedure limited him largely to the four canonical gospels as sources, although there is some evidence that he had access to other gospels or to oral tradition as well.[67] But what makes his work of such great importance for the study of the gospels is that he set the pattern for the vast majority of subsequent readers of the gospels by his program of harmonization. Only when we look at the interwoven text of the Diatessaron with marginal references to the individual gospel sources do we realize how much thinking about Jesus has been shaped by the unconscious blending of the different, or even disparate, accounts.

The following extended excerpt from the Diatessaron (from an English translation of the Arabic version)[68] shows with what care Tatian went about his task. The references to the gospel material, which are given in the margin, reveal Tatian's great skill at blending his four sources into a single flowing account.

Matt. 3:13	Then cometh Jesus from Galilee to the Jordan unto John, to be baptized of him.

[67] See J. H. Charlesworth, "Tatian's Dependence upon Apocryphal Traditions," *Heythrop Journal* 15 (1974): 5–17.
[68] From Hill's translation in *The Earliest Life of Christ.*

Luke 3:23	And Jesus was about thirty years of age, and was supposed to be the son of Joseph.
John 1:29	Now John saw Jesus coming unto him, and saith, This is the Lamb of God, which taketh
John 1:30	away the sin of the world. This is he of whom I said, After me shall come a man, which is preferred before me, for he is
John 1:31	before me. And I knew him not; but that he may be made manifest to Israel, for this
Matt. 3:14	cause am I come baptizing in water. Now John was forbidding him, saying, I have need to be baptized of thee, and comest
Matt. 3:15	thou to me? Jesus answered him, and said, Suffer *it* now: thus it becometh us to fulfill all righteousness. Then he suffered him.
Luke 3:21	And when all the people were baptized,
Matt. 3:16	Jesus also was baptized; and he went up straightway from the water: and the heaven
Luke 3:22	was opened unto him. And the Holy Spirit descended upon him in the form of a dove's
Matt. 3:17	body: and lo, a voice from heaven, saying, This is my beloved Son, in whom I am well
John 1:32	pleased. And John bore witness, saying, Furthermore I saw the Spirit descending as a dove out of heaven; and it abode upon
John 1:33	him. And I knew him not; but he that sent me to baptize in water, he said unto me, Upon whomsoever thou shalt see the Spirit descending and abiding, this is he
John 1:34	that baptizeth in the Holy Spirit. And I have seen, and have borne witness, that this is the Son of God.
Matt. 21:12	And when Jesus had entered Jerusalem,
John 2:14	he went up into the temple of God; and he
Matt. 21:12	found there oxen, sheep, and doves. And
John 2:14	when he saw them that sold and bought,
John 2:15	and the money changers sitting, he made for himself a scourge of cords, and cast all of them out of the temple, the sheep also, and the oxen, and the money changers, whose money he poured out, and overthrew

Matt. 21:12	the tables, and the seats of them that sold
Matt. 21:13	the doves; and he was teaching and saying unto them, Is it not written, My house is a house of prayer for all nations: but ye have
John 2:16	made it a den of robbers? And to them that sold the doves, he said, Take these things hence; and make not my Father's
Mark 11:16	house a house of merchandise. And he suffered not that any man should carry
John 2:17	vessels through the temple. And his disciples remembered the scripture, The zeal
John 2:18	of thine house hath eaten me up. The Jews answered and said unto him, What sign shewest thou unto us, that thou
John 2:19	shouldest do this? Jesus answered, and said unto them, Destroy this temple, and in
John 2:20	three days I will raise it up. The Jews said unto him, In forty and six years was this temple built, and wilt thou raise it up
John 2:21	in three days? But he spake unto them of the temple of his body: that when they destroyed it, he would raise it up in three
John 2:22	days. And when he rose again from the dead, his disciples remembered that he had said this; and they believed the scriptures,
Mark 12:41	and the saying that Jesus spake. And Jesus sat down over against the treasury, and observed how the multitudes cast their offerings into the treasury: and many that
Mark 12:42	were rich cast in much. And there came a poor widow, and she cast in two mites.
Luke 21:3	And Jesus called his disciples, and said unto them, Verily I say unto you, This poor widow cast in more than *they* all into the
Mark 12:44	treasury: for all these did cast in of the superfluity of their substance into the ark of the offering of God; but she of her want did cast all that she possessed.
Luke 19:28	And when he had said these things, Jesus went forth slowly to proceed to Jerusalem.

Luke 19:29	And when he was arrived at Bethphage and Bethany, near the mount that is called the
Matt. 21:1	mount of Olives, Jesus sent two of his
Matt. 21:2	disciples, saying unto them, Go into the
Mark 11:2	village that is over against you, and when
Matt. 21:2	ye are entered into it, ye shall find an ass
Luke 19:30	tied, and a colt with her, whereon no man
Matt. 21:2	ever yet sat: loose it, and bring *them* unto
Luke 19:31	me. And if anyone say unto you, Why do
Matt. 21:3	ye loose them? say thus unto him, We seek them for the Lord; and straightway send
Matt. 21:4	them both hither. All this is come to pass, that it might be fulfilled which was spoken through the prophet, saying,
Matt. 21:5	Tell ye the daughter of Sion,
	Behold, thy King cometh unto thee
	Meek, and sitting upon an ass,
	And upon a colt the foal of an ass.
John 12:16	This understood not his disciples at that time: but after Jesus was glorified, his disciples remembered that these things had been written of him, and that they did these things unto him.
Matt. 21:6; Luke 19:32	} And the disciples went, and found even
Matt. 21:6	as he had said unto them, and they did as
Luke 19:33	Jesus had commanded them. And when they had loosed them, the owners thereof
Luke 19:34	said unto them, Why loose ye them? They said unto them, We seek them for our Lord;
Mark 11:6	and they let them go.
Matt. 21:7	And they brought the ass and the colt, and put their garments upon the colt, and
Matt. 21:8	Jesus rode thereon. And the most part of the multitude spread their garments before him on the ground; and others cut branches from the trees, and spread them in the way.
Luke 19:37	And when he drew near his descent of the mount of Olives, all the disciples began to rejoice and praise God with a loud voice for all the mighty works which they had seen;

Matt. 21:9	saying, Glory in the highest: glory to the son of David: blessed is he that cometh in the
Mark 11:10	name of the Lord: and blessed is the kingdom
Luke 19:38	which cometh, *even* our father David's: peace in heaven, and glory in the highest.
John 12:12	And a great multitude that had come to the feast, when they had heard that Jesus
John 12:13	was coming to Jerusalem, took the branches of the palm trees, and went forth to meet him, and cried out, saying, Praise: blessed is he that cometh in the name of the Lord,
Luke 19:30	even the King of Israel. And some of the Pharisees from the multitudes said unto him,
Luke 19:40	Master, rebuke thy disciples. He saith unto them, Verily I say unto you, If these held their peace, the stones would cry out.

It is evident that Tatian went about his task with enormous literary dexterity and with profound respect for the gospel tradition itself. Even though Theodoret saw a sinister motive in Tatian's failure to include the genealogies—as if for Docetic reasons he were denying the true humanity of Jesus—there are only occasional evidences that Tatian altered his canonical sources out of theological prejudice, as in the modification of Matthew 11:19 to avoid depicting Jesus as a drinker of wine.[69] Irenaeus may well be correct in labeling Tatian an Encratite and attributing to him Gnostic notions, but there is no trace of Gnosticism in the Diatessaron. One must infer either that he arranged his harmony before he became heretical in his views or that his devotion to the text of Scripture led him to incorporate it unchanged in content even though its message was not compatible with his own theological outlook. However, if he was an Encratite at the time he prepared the Diatessaron, it is striking that the tradition was not adapted to serve Gnostic aims as it was in the contemporaneous Gnostic gospel of Thomas, which seems to have originated in the nearby church of Syria.

[69] So Charlesworth, "Tatian's Dependence upon Apocryphal Traditions."

The influence of Tatian's work was of two kinds: direct and indirect. The direct influence is seen in the gospel harmonies preserved in the church in many languages and over a wide geographical range. The popularity of the Diatessaron is further attested by the fact that commentaries on it were translated into other languages, among them the Armenian version of Ephraem's commentary. There are two Arabic versions of the Diatessaron, one of which includes the genealogies Tatian omitted.[70] The presence or absence of the genealogies does not seem to have affected the use made of the harmony in the church. It functioned as the vehicle of a unified representation of Jesus, which simply never raised questions about differences among the interests of the evangelists. The sequence of events in the Diatessaron came to be regarded as not merely useful but canonical. The implications of any discrepancies that might appear from the study of the individual gospels were forgotten in favor of the harmonious whole.

The basic Tatianic pattern was influential for centuries: it was adopted by Victor of Capua, whose harmony either provided the norm for or employed the same norm as the subsequent harmonies developed in Western Europe. The structure of Dutch, Italian, French, German, and English harmonies can thus be traced back to Tatian.[71] In the East, a Coptic harmony preserved by a heretical group known as the Manicheans can be shown to rest on the structure and even the Syriac text of the Diatessaron.[72] Although the general pattern of the Diatessaron may lie behind the Heliand, an Old Saxon epic poem apparently written to give the Christian faith competitive appeal with the pagan Teutonic heroes, the case is weak for the notion that one can reconstruct the text of Tatian from this medieval poetic work.[73]

As for its indirect effect, Tatian's work set the pattern from

[70] Kahle, *The Cario Genizah*, pp. 297–301.
[71] So B. M. Metzger, *Chapters in the History of New Testament Textual Criticism* (Grand Rapids, Mich.: Eerdmans, 1963), pp. 99–100.
[72] Kahle, *The Cairo Genizah*, p. 295.
[73] See Willy Krogman, "Heliand, Tatian, und Thomasevangelium," [Heliand Tatian, and the Gospel of Thomas], *Zeitschrift für die neutestamentliche Wissenschaft* [Journal for New Testament Study] 51 (1960): 255–68, *contra* Gilles Quispel, "Some Remarks on the Gospel of Thomas," *New Testament Studies* 5 (1959): 276–90.

the second century on for regarding the harmonized gospel accounts as historically trustworthy in both sequence and content. Popular passion plays and nativity pageants—both ancient and modern—wove together quite disparate elements from the divergent records, and both writers and audiences ignored the implications of the fact that there were differences. From Augustine to Calvin, however, profound thinkers in the church were aware of the difficulties raised by differences among the gospel accounts, but they regarded these divergences either as capable of reconciliation or as indications of special interests on the part of the individual evangelists.[74] In the case of Calvin, the priority on questions of order of events was usually decided in favor of Mathew's sequence. But since all parts of Scripture were thought to have equal authority, the order of events did not really matter. Though one writer might find more meaning in one sequence than another, every pericope was a part of Holy Scripture, and all were equally to be believed. Readers might have personal preferences among the gospels—mystics for John and moralists for Matthew—but if they had doubts about seeming discrepancies, their doubts reflected on their faith, not on the gospel record.

There were available no critical tools by which the student of Scripture could differentiate the aim of one writer from another. The question of the historical credibility of any given narrative could be decided only by the predilection of individual readers, since there were no norms of critical historiography by which to evaluate historical texts. Even those ancient historical and religious texts that were known to early Christians and might have been studied on a comparative basis for critical analysis of the New Testament were not so utilized, since the gospels were understood by Christians to be sacred books and therefore beyond comparison with pagan writings. All but rare minds such as Origen accepted the gospels as factual in all their miraculous and supernatural detail. Any historical questions raised were quickly decided by appeal to authoritative accounts of Jesus written down by, or on the authority of, the apostles. This view of the authority of the gospels as equal and unassailable continued unchallenged

---

[74] See H. K. McArthur, *The Quest Through the Centuries* (Philadelphia: Fortress, 1966). On Augustine, see pp. 49–55; on Calvin, see pp. 97–99.

until the supernatural factor in general was examined critically in relation to the concept of natural order, and until the notion of the gospels as miraculous narratives was set aside under the impact of emerging critical study of mythology and history in the late eighteenth century.

It was not until more than a century later, however, that the critical tools were developed that made possible a detailed historical analysis of the history of the gospel tradition. Recent manuscript discoveries make possible study of the fate of the gospel tradition in the early church beyond the time when it was recorded in the form of the canonical gospels. But does the emergence of new critical methods and newly found sources enable us to settle with finality our questions about the place of Jesus in history?

SUGGESTIONS FOR FURTHER READING

On the origins of Gnosticism, see Rudolf Bultmann, *Primitive Christianity in Its Contemporary Setting** (Cleveland: World, 1956), R. M. Grant, *Gnosticism and Early Christianity,** rev. ed. (New York: Harper & Row, 1961). The basic Gnostic documents have been edited by H. C. Puech, *The Gospel According to Thomas* (New York: Harper & Row, 1959), and by Kendrick Grobel, *The Gospel of Truth* (Nashville: Abingdon, 1960). The apocryphal Christian writings have long been available in M. R. James, *The Apocryphal New Testament* (Oxford: Oxford University Press, 1924), but are now available in a more complete edition with superb introductory essays in Hennecke-Schneemelcher, *New Testament Apocrypha*, vol. 1, trans. R. McL. Wilson (Philadelphia: Westminster, 1966).

Essays on the Diatessaron and its influence are included in B. M. Metzger, *Chapters in the History of New Testament Textual Criticism* (Grand Rapids, Mich.: Eerdmans, 1963), and in Paul Kahle, *The Cairo Genizah* (Oxford: Oxford University Press, 1947).

* Available in a paperback edition.

Conclusion:
Positive and Negative Results of the Search for Jesus in History

The most gratifying product of research is the achievement of spectacular new findings; equally important, however—though often painful for the researcher—is the identification and acknowledgment of inappropriate methods and unattainable goals. This is as true of research in the field of Jesus in history as of research in any other field.

DISCOVERING INAPPROPRIATE METHODS
AND UNATTAINABLE GOALS

As this book demonstrates, it is inappropriate to seek to reconstruct the life of Jesus, tracing the development of his thought and his sense of mission, either by harmonizing the divergent gospel accounts or by choosing one gospel as a basic biographical framework and treating the others as supplements. Friedrich Daniel Ernst Schleiermacher (1768–1834) tried the second procedure using John; Heinrich Julius Holtzmann using Mark; and Albert Schweitzer using Matthew. All three men produced works that are remarkable in their own way but wholly unsatisfactory as reconstructions of the life of Jesus or of the pattern of his ministry. Attempts at this kind of inclusive reconstruction fail because the evangelists arranged the gospel material in sequences determined by their individual dogmatic aims rather than by historical recollection or biographical interest. Since the sequence of events in Mark—demonstrably the oldest of the gospels—unfolds as much by a dogma of apocalyptic determination of history as by actual historical recollection, it would be methodologically unsound to adopt it or any of the later gospels as a genuinely historical base for reconstructing the career of Jesus.

Some scholars, recognizing that they cannot achieve historical certainty either by selecting one gospel as normative or by harmonizing the differences among the four, have turned to a reductionist approach: They extract from the gospel tradition certain elements that they believe can be proved authentic through the application of a formula. Sometimes the formula is one of multiple attestation, resting on the assumption that an event or a saying reported in more than one strand of the tradition—in Mark and Q, for example—is likely to be authentic. This formula can be useful in evaluating the gospel tradition, but only when it is employed in conjunction with methods other than a purely literary separation of strands of tradition. Mark and Q both include material that in its present form reflects the situation of the early church rather than facts about Jesus, so the mere fact of dual attestation proves nothing about the actual course of Jesus' life. The degree of probability that we are dealing with authentic material is increased, however, by employing the form-critical method as a way of distinguishing earlier from later strata of the Jesus tradition.

Another formula of authenticity proposes a *via negativa*: Whatever in the tradition can be explained as originating in the early church or as taken over by the tradition from Judaism may not be regarded as authentic.[1] This criterion is weak, because it

---

[1] Ernst Käsemann, "The Problem of the Historical Jesus," in his *Essays on New Testament Themes* (Naperville, Ill.: Allenson, 1964), p. 44. See the discussion of criteria of authenticity of the sayings of Jesus in Norman Perrin, *The New Testament: An Introduction* (New York: Harcourt Brace Jovanovich, 1974), pp. 281–82.

presupposes a more complete discontinuity between Jesus and Judaism on the one hand and between Jesus and the early church on the other hand than may actually have been the case.[2] Since the tradition portrays Jesus as a critic speaking to Judaism from within, it would be surprising if his teaching did not take over from Judaism a great deal relatively unchanged. Similarly, although it must be acknowledged that the impact of the cross and the growth of the resurrection faith transformed Jesus' followers' understanding of him, it is not necessary to assume that the early church simultaneously transformed all facets of the message attributed to him or its recollection of events in his public activity. One would expect, on the contrary, considerable carryover from the message and ministry of Jesus to that of the early church. The changes that occurred were generally modifications, not always innovations.

Another kind of formula that has been advanced depends on the establishment of a formal thought structure that might serve as a distinctive clue to the authentic words of Jesus. J. M. Robinson claims, for example, that "the message of Jesus consists basically in a pronouncement to the present in view of the imminent eschatological future."[3] He goes on to explain, however, that the temporal distinction between present and future is not the primary factor, so that "eschatological" is not used in its ordinary sense to point to the future events that will bring to a close the present age and open up the Age to Come. Rather, the term is used in a nontemporal sense to refer to an event or utterance in which individuals find a meaning so profound and pervasive in its implications that they see their lives in a new light and they discover new opportunities for fulfillment. "Eschatological" is thus a way of speaking of a person's present stance toward his or her own future, rather than of the future of the world. It is in this sense that Robinson uses the term when he says that "the eschatological message of Jesus is directed to an eschatological under-

---

[2] For appreciative comment on Käsemann's criterion, and for development of other possible criteria, see Norman Perrin, *Rediscovering the Teaching of Jesus* (New York: Harper & Row, 1967), pp. 39–43.

[3] For example, J. M. Robinson, "The Formal Structure of Jesus' Message," in William Klassen and M. F. Snyder, eds., *Current Issues in New Testament Interpretation* (New York: Harper & Row, 1962), p. 97.

standing of existence in the present,"[4] with the result that "the temporal distinction [between this age and the Age to Come] is replaced by the material contrast" between man's condition apart from faith and under faith.[5]

It is true that the contrast between present difficulty and future deliverance is a characteristic of the teaching of Jesus throughout the gospel tradition, but both the terms used (for example, the coming of the Son of Man "in the glory of his Father with the holy angels," Mark 8:38) and the syntax of Jesus' sentences ("Blessed are you that weep now, for you shall laugh," Luke 6:21) point unambiguously to an event in the chronological future of the world when, as we are told by Jesus' total eschatological message, the whole order of life will be transformed by God's direct action. Not all of Jesus' eschatological sayings refer to the present, as is true of Luke's (more original) version of the Lord's Prayer: "Father, hallowed be thy name. Thy kingdom come" (11:2). On the other hand, some sayings of Jesus are eschatological only implicitly and contain no direct mention of the future, as when he declares, "If it is by the finger of God that I cast out demons, then the kingdom of God has come upon you" (Luke 11:20). Robinson's formula is therefore inappropriate on two counts: (1) Not all the sayings of Jesus that are eschatological in intent contain direct references to present and future; and (2) whether explicit or implicit, the eschatological element is always focused on the chronological future, when the promised fulfillment will occur and the creation will be renewed. Furthermore, it is precisely in gospel sayings such as John 5:24, in which the temporal distinction (between this age and the age to come) has been replaced by a material contrast (between life apart from faith and life in faith), that we can be certain we are dealing with formulations of the early church and not with authentic sayings of Jesus. At times the formal structure of contrast between present and future proves to be a mark of Jesus' teaching, but it is only one criterion among several and is not reliable when used apart from other critical methods.

---

[4] *Ibid.*, pp. 98–99. Here Robinson subtly shifts the meaning of "eschatology" from a pronouncement about the future to an understanding of existence in the present—thereby assuming what he seeks to prove.
[5] *Ibid.*, p. 103.

POSITIVE RESULTS

Martin Kähler was correct in asserting that it is the biblical picture of Jesus as the Christ that has had the transforming impact on lives down through the history of the church. And Paul Tillich was justified in taking over this aspect of his teacher's theological view of the church's understanding of Jesus. However, this position ultimately deprives the church of the richness of interpretive diversity that is a proper part of its heritage: Failing to take with full theological seriousness the diverse pictures of Jesus represented in the biblical tradition, the theologian must either settle for a monochrome portrait, painted by conscious or unconscious harmonization of the tradition, or adopt one perspective—usually that of the Pauline kerygma—and force the gospel tradition to conform to that view of Jesus.

On the other hand, when modern serious students of the gospels take into account the range of understandings of Jesus that critical study has shown to exist within the Jesus tradition as preserved in the New Testament and elsewhere, in early Christian literature, the real diversity of interpretive structures for "Jesus in history" becomes evident. Understanding Jesus at various stages in the development of the gospel tradition provides insight into interpretations of him that have not been taken up by the mainstream of the church or that have been obscured by subsequent developments in christological formulations. Form criticism, together with other modes of critical analysis, can bring to light ways in which earlier understandings of Jesus were reformulated as a result of special interests already at work in the church before the tradition became fixed in the form of the canonical gospels.

Form-critical study of the gospel tradition makes possible differentiation between older and later forms of the Jesus tradition. Although the older forms stand closer to the event of Jesus than do the later ones, there is no guarantee that what is old is also authentic. Nevertheless, critics can extrapolate backward along the lines that they can trace in the development of the tradition and arrive at some general features that seem to have originated with Jesus of Nazareth. In some cases this process will be aided by converging lines of tradition. In other instances the distinctiveness of what is attributed to Jesus from what is known to have been taught by Judaism or by the early church will provide additional evidence. The fact that the church did not pick up on certain themes that remain embedded in the tradition serves as a clue that these undeveloped strands of the tradition are not the creation of the church's faith but may go back to Jesus. In that case they would have a right to consideration as more nearly authentic than those that the church exploited or modified for its own theological ends. For example, the coming Son of Man words, which do not accord well with either Markan or Pauline theology, are widely thought to be authentic. And growing knowledge of the Jewish world of Jesus' day sheds new light on certain elements of the gospel tradition and heightens the probability of the authenticity of certain puzzling or little understood features of the gospels. An instance of this is the correlation between the terminology of Jesus' exorcisms and the eschatological expectations at Qumran.[6]

But what are the specific historical results from the critical assessment of the gospel tradition? Admittedly, we are dealing with probabilities, and the results are subject to modification in light of new insights. But a consistent picture does emerge:

Jesus appeared on the Palestinian scene as an itinerant teacher, probably self-taught, so that there was deep resentment of his authoritative manner among the official religious leadership of Palestine. He held his central mission to be the announcement of the imminent coming of God's Kingdom, and he regarded his extraordinary powers of healing and exorcism as evidence that the powers of the Kingdom were already breaking into the present situation. He sought to call together a band of followers who by repentance would prepare themselves for the impending event, and he therefore offered a severe critique of Israel and new criteria for acceptance within the membership of the covenant community. He interpreted the Law in a radical way that challenged the

---

[6] See my discussion of exorcism terminology in "The Terminology of St. Mark's Exorcism Stories," *New Testament Studies* 14 (1968): 232–46.

authority of its official interpreters.[7] The impetus for the redefinition of the people of God is likely to have come as a consequence of his associations with John the Baptist, although he parted company with John, probably on the issue of Jesus' conviction that the Kingdom was open to sinners and religious outcasts who truly repented. At the same time, Jesus refused to join with the insurrectionist movements of his time, which sought to establish God's rule by their own initiative. Ironically, it was through the false charge that he was a revolutionary that he was put to death by the Romans—a charge brought by the religious leaders whose authority his pronouncements seemed to threaten. His method of teaching was characterized as to content by eschatological pronouncement, and as to form by parable and reinterpretation of the Law and of religious institutions. It is likely that he came to realize that the path he had set out on would lead to death, though we have no way of knowing when he came to this conclusion or whether he sought to force the issue. His metaphorical references to the "baptism" and the "cup" in Mark 10, and to the impossibility of drinking the cup until the coming of the Kingdom of God (Mark 14:25), suggest that he expected both death and ultimate vindication. But this is not to say he predicted his passion and resurrection, as the gospel tradition later reported. The tradition faithfully points to the genuineness of his anxiety in the face of death, even though it was starting to swallow up his humanity in various types of divine-man conceptions, and even though the whole of the tradition was placed in a new framework of meaning by the resurrection faith.

What we are dealing with in the gospel tradition is not objective historical evidence that has become overlaid with the claims of Christian faith, but with evidence that in its entirety stems from the witness of faith at various stages of development. Critical analysis of the tradition enables us to differentiate between earlier and later stages of the faith and provides us our best

---

[7] On the theme of Jesus and the Law, see Herbert Braun, *Spätjüdisch-häretischer und frühchristlicher Radikalismus*, Part 2: *Die Synoptiker* (Tübingen: J. C. B. Mohr, 1957).

—indeed, almost our only—clues to the personal life that evoked that faith. Such study enables us to achieve a modest but significant goal: to discern how diverse were the ways in which the tradition about Jesus was appropriated in the period from the history of Jesus in his own time to the history of Jesus in the church and the modern world.

SUGGESTIONS FOR FURTHER READING

In addition to the studies of the historical Jesus question mentioned earlier, the following are valuable: Hugh Anderson, *Jesus and Christian Origins* (New York: Oxford University Press, 1964), Günther Bornkamm, *Jesus of Nazareth** (New York: Harper & Row, 1961), Ernst Käsemann, *Essays on New Testament Themes** (Naperville, Ill.: Allenson, 1964), Gustaf Aulen, *Jesus in Contemporary Historical Research* (Philadelphia: Fortress, 1976), and Geza Vermes, *Jesus the Jew* (London: Collins, 1973).

* *Available in a paperback edition.*

Appendix:
A Classification System
for the Synoptic Tradition

The nomenclature for classification of the gospel tradition used by Rudolf Bultmann and Martin Dibelius has raised unintended and unnecessary difficulties for at least two reasons: (1) The terminology derives from classical literature and conveys little meaning to the modern reader; and (2) the terms, or the translations of them, imply certain historical judgments that are inappropriate in a formal classificatory system. Examples of the first type are "Apophthegms" and "Chriae"; examples of tendentious terms are "Tales" and "Myths." Perhaps some readers will find that the classification proposed here is subject to similar criticisms, but the terms employed are standard English. And they are used without prejudice to historicity.

More important, perhaps, is the fact that in literary analysis a sharp distinction is not possible between form and function. Some detractors of form-critical method have sought to show that the classification systems are not purely formal, as though that were a fatal flaw. But the use of form-critical method in the present work lays stress on a factor to which Bultmann and Dibelius gave little more than lip service: the social and cultural functions of the tradition. The twin questions to be asked are,

"What was the tradition as the evangelist or his sources found it?" and then "What function has it been made to serve as reflected in the adaptation of the tradition?"

In the following classificatory scheme no attempt is made to include all the synoptic material under one of the groupings; rather, a sufficiently wide range of material is provided to suggest the main categories and to illustrate them. In a few cases, examples are offered from noncanonical sources, such as the Oxyrynchus Papyri and the Gnostic gospel of Thomas.

SAYINGS TRADITION

1. *Aphorisms*

    Mark 4:9
    Thos. 24
    Matt. 13:43
    Luke 14:35b
    Mark 4:25 = Matt. 25:29 and Luke 19:26
    Mark 9:35
    Mark 10:43 = Luke 22:26; Matt. 20:26
    Mark 10:15 = Luke 18:1; Matt. 18:3; cf. John 3:5; Thos. 37, 46
    Matt. 10:39 = Luke 17:33; Matt. 16:25; Mark 8:35; Luke 9:24 (John 12:25)
    Matt. 10:33 = Luke 12:9; Mark 8:38; Luke 9:26
    Matt. 10:26 = Luke 12:2; Mark 4:22; Luke 8:17 (1 Cor. 4:5?); Thos. 5; Oxy. 654
    Luke 17:20–21
    Luke 13:30 = Mark 10:31; Matt. 19:30; 20:16

2. *Parables*

    Mark 4:1–8
    Mark 4:30–32
    Matt. 13:33
    Mark 4:26–29
    Matt. 13:47–48
    Matt. 18:12–13 = Luke 15:3–6
    Matt. 18:23–33
    Luke 10:29–37; 12:16–20; 14:15–23 = Matt. 22:1–10; Thos. 64

3. *Sayings Clusters*

    a. Topical groupings

        Matt. 5:13 = Luke 14:34–35 (Salt)

        Matt. 5:14–16 = Luke 11:33; Mark 4:21 (Light)

        Matt. 5:17–20 (Law)

        Mark 13:33–37 (Watchfulness)

        Mark 2:18–20 (Fasting)

        Mark 2:21–22 (Old and New)

        Matt. 10:26–31 = Luke 12:2–7 (Freedom from Fear)

        Matt. 10:37–38 = Luke 14:26–27 (Discipleship)

        Matt. 11:7–19 = Luke 7:24–35 and 16:16 (John the Baptist)

        Matt. 5:33–37 (Oaths)

        Matt. 5:38–42 (cf. Luke 6:29–30) (Retaliation)

        Luke 6:27–28, 32–36 = Matt. 5:43–48 (Love of Enemies)

        Matt. 6:25–34; Luke 12:22–31 (Anxiety)

        Matt. 7:1–5; Luke 6:37–38, 41–42 (Judging)

        Matt. 19:1–12 = Mark 10:1–12 (cf. Matt. 5:32) (Marriage and Divorce)

        Mark 4:10–12; 4:21–25 (Hidden and Revealed)

        Mark 6:8–11 = Matt. 10:9–14; Luke 10:4–11 (Advice to Disciples)

    b. Formal groupings

        Matt. 5:3–12 = Luke 6:20–23 (Beatitudes)

        Luke 6:24–26 (Woes)

(The parables of the Kingdom in Mark 4 (= Matt. 13) and the woes against the Pharisees in Mark 12:38–40 (= Matt. 23:1–36) exhibit a definite formal pattern and were probably preserved in the tradition in cluster form.)

NARRATIVE TRADITION

The terminology used for classifying the narrative tradition deserves some explanation:

Anecdote is used in the usual sense of a brief narrative, usually biographical, that reveals some unusual feature of the person described. The stories are short and lack biographical or chronological links with what is otherwise known of the person who is the subject of the anecdote.

Aphoristic narratives are brief accounts that culminate in a proverbial or pithy saying. The stories were probably not created as a vehicle for the saying, but they point up an issue to which the saying is a response.

Wonder stories are told to demonstrate the extraordinary powers of Jesus. They are often longer and provide more vivid detail than aphoristic narratives or anecdotes, including development of the situation along dramatic lines. On grounds other than form, the wonder stories of the synoptic tradition show the influence of the non-Christian miracle-story tradition, for example in the inclusion of thaumaturgic detail in the narratives of healing or exorcism (Mark 5:41; 7:34).

Legends are narratives that imply that a supernatural aura surrounds the central figure. The specific aim of a legend may be biographical or cultic. If biographical, it serves to amplify, illuminate, or enrich the christological significance of Jesus for the church, often closely correlating detail of the narrative with Old Testament predictions. If the aim is cultic, the narrative provides the background and therefore the authorization for the place of Jesus in the worship life of the Christian community. Thus Baptism, the Eucharist, and the christological interpretation of Scripture are all grounded in the ministry of Jesus by means of the cultic legends.

The *passion narrative* is included here as a separate category of narrative, although with considerable reservation. There is good reason to question the older notion that the passion story received a more nearly fixed form earlier than did the rest of the gospel tradition and that it served as the nucleus around which the rest of the tradition was later arranged. The passion story itself does not appear to have been as unified as was once supposed by form critics, since Luke and Matthew felt free to introduce new material and to alter the substance of Mark's account. Mark's understanding of history and his community's interpretation of Scripture led him to modify the tradition about Jesus' trial and death to an extent that cannot now be determined with certainty but that must have been very great. Furthermore, some scholars think that Luke had an independent passion narrative that he accommodated at some points to Mark's. John certainly had an independent tradition for his passion story. But in at least one "gospel"—Q—there seems to have been no passion account at all. The probability is that as the passion kerygma became dominant in the church's thinking, the passion narrative was developed and expanded, partly on the basis of tradition units and partly on the basis of Christian reading of the Old Testament.

1. *Anecdotes*
    Mark 1:23–26 = Luke 4:33–35
    Mark 1:29–31
    Mark 2:1–4, 11–12
    Mark 1:16–20 (cf. Luke 5:1–11)
    Mark 1:40–44
    Luke 7:18–23 = Matt. 11:2–6
    Luke 19:1–10

2. *Aphoristic Narratives*
    Mark 2:23–28
    Mark 3:1–5
    Mark 10:17–22
    Mark 10:13–16

3. *Wonder Stories*
    Mark 5:1–20
    Mark 5:21–43
    Mark 9:14–27
    Mark 10:46–52
    Luke 7:11–17

4. *Legends*
    a. Biographical legends
        Matt. 1:18–25 (Birth of Jesus)
        Luke 2:1–20 (Birth of Jesus)
        Luke 2:21–40 (Presentation in the Temple)
        Mark 1:12–13; Matt. 4:1–11 (Temptation)
        Mark 6:45–32 (Walking on the Water)
        Mark 9:2–8 (Transfiguration)
        Mark 10:35–45 (Baptism of Suffering)
        Mark 14:12–16 (Preparation for the Passover)
        Mark 14:32–42 (cf. Luke 22:43–44) (Prayer in Gethsemane)

Matt. 27:62–66 (Guard at the Tomb)

Matt. 28:2–4, 11–15 (Wonders Accompanying the Resurrection)

Luke 4:16–30 (Sermon and Rejection in Nazareth)

Luke 5:1–11 (Miraculous Catch of Fish)

b. Cult legends

Mark 1:9–11 (cf. Matt. 3:14–15) (Baptism of Jesus)

Mark 6:30–44; Mark 8:1–10; John 6:1–13 (Eucharist)

Mark 14:22–25 (Lord's Supper)

Luke 24:13–35 (Christ's Presence in Word and Sacrament)

5. *Passion Narrative*

Mark 14:1—16:8 (= Matt. 26:1—28:10)

Luke 21:1—24:11

John 18:1—20:29

Index of Subjects

Index of Authors Cited

310